Intergovernmental Fiscal Relations

in the United States

Studies of Government Finance

TITLES PUBLISHED

Federal Fiscal Policy in the Postwar Recessions, by Wilfred Lewis, Jr.

Federal Tax Treatment of State and Local Securities, by David J. Ott and Allan H. Meltzer.

Federal Tax Treatment of Income from Oil and Gas, by Stephen L. McDonald.

Federal Tax Treatment of the Family, by Harold M. Groves.

The Role of Direct and Indirect Taxes in the Federal Revenue System, John F. Due, Editor. A Report of the National Bureau of Economic Research and the Brookings Institution (Princeton University Press).

The Individual Income Tax, by Richard Goode.

Federal Tax Treatment of Foreign Income, by Lawrence B. Krause and Kenneth W. Dam.

Measuring Benefits of Government Investments, Robert Dorfman, Editor.

Federal Budget Policy, by David J. Ott and Attiat F. Ott.

Financing State and Local Governments, by James A. Maxwell.

Essays in Fiscal Federalism, Richard A. Musgrave, Editor.

Economics of the Property Tax, by Dick Netzer.

A Capital Budget Statement for the U.S. Government, by Maynard S. Comiez.

Foreign Tax Policies and Economic Growth, E. Gordon Keith, Editor. A Report of the National Bureau of Economic Research and the Brookings Institution (Columbia University Press).

Defense Purchases and Regional Growth, by Roger E. Bolton.

Federal Budget Projections, by Gerhard Colm and Peter Wagner. A Report of the National Planning Association and the Brookings Institution.

Corporate Dividend Policy, by John A. Brittain.

Federal Estate and Gift Taxes, by Carl S. Shoup.

Federal Tax Policy, by Joseph A. Pechman.

Economic Behavior of the Affluent, by Robin Barlow, Harvey E. Brazer, and James N. Morgan.

Intergovernmental Fiscal Relations in the United States, by George F. Break.

Intergovernmental

Fiscal Relations

in the United States

GEORGE F. BREAK

A background paper prepared for a conference of
experts held November 18-19, 1965, together
with a summary of the conference discussion

Studies of Government Finance

THE BROOKINGS INSTITUTION

WASHINGTON, D.C.

THE BROOKINGS INSTITUTION
1775 Massachusetts Avenue, N. W., Washington, D. C.

Published January 1967
Second printing January 1968
Third printing June 1968
Fourth printing April 1969
Fifth printing July 1970

ISBN   0-8157-1073-9 (paper)
ISBN   0-8157-1074-7 (cloth)
Library of Congress Catalogue Card Number 66-28890

THE BROOKINGS INSTITUTION is an independent organization devoted to nonpartisan research, education, and publication in economics, government, foreign policy, and the social sciences generally. Its principal purposes are to aid in the development of sound public policies and to promote public understanding of issues of national importance.

The Institution was founded December 8, 1927, to merge the activities of the Institute for Government Research, founded in 1916, the Institute of Economics, founded in 1922, and the Robert Brookings Graduate School of Economics and Government, founded in 1924.

The general administration of the Institution is the responsibility of a self-perpetuating Board of Trustees. The trustees are likewise charged with maintaining the independence of the staff and fostering the most favorable conditions for creative research and education. The immediate direction of the policies, program, and staff of the Institution is vested in the President, assisted by the division directors and an advisory council, chosen from the professional staff of the Institution.

In publishing a study, the Institution presents it as a competent treatment of a subject worthy of public consideration. The interpretations and conclusions in such publications are those of the author or authors and do not purport to represent the views of the other staff members, officers, or trustees of the Brookings Institution.

Foreword

INCREASES IN EXPENDITURES are placing great strains on the financial resources of state and local governments. The demand for services continues unabated, but state and local financial resources are not flexible enough to meet the needs. One of the major problems is the lack of coordination in fiscal matters among federal, state, and local governments. It is now clear that both state and local governments will need assistance from the national government if they are to perform their traditional roles in our federal system.

The purpose of this volume is to present the major problems of intergovernmental finance in the United States and to suggest alternative solutions. The manuscript, which was prepared by George F. Break of the University of California at Berkeley, was used as a background paper for the discussion at an experts' conference held at the Brookings Institution on November 18 and 19, 1965, attended by thirty economists, political scientists, and government officials.

The author wishes to acknowledge the valuable assistance of the reading committee, which consisted of John F. Due of the University of Illinois, Harold M. Groves of the University of Wisconsin, and Allen D. Manvel of the Bureau of the Census. Many helpful comments were also contributed by Luther Gulick of the Institute for Public Administration, by Selma J. Mushkin of the Council of State Governments, and by Earl R. Rolph of the University of California at Berkeley. Jane Lecht edited the manuscript and prepared the index.

vii

This study is part of a special program of research and education on taxation and public expenditures, supervised by the National Committee on Government Finance and financed by a special grant from the Ford Foundation.

The views expressed in this study are those of the author and do not purport to represent the views of the National Committee on Government Finance or its Advisory Committee, or the staff members, officers, or trustees of the Brookings Institution, or the Ford Foundation.

Robert D. Calkins
President

September 1966
Washington, D. C.

Studies of Government Finance

Studies of Government Finance is a special program of research and education in taxation and government expenditures at the federal, state, and local levels. These studies are under the supervision of the National Committee on Government Finance appointed by the trustees of the Brookings Institution, and are supported by a special grant from the Ford Foundation.

MEMBERS OF THE ADVISORY COMMITTEE

Contents

Text Tables

Figure

Appendix Tables

CHAPTER I

Introduction

OF THE IMPOSING ARRAY OF FISCAL PROBLEMS facing the United States in recent years, some have been entirely new and some simply intensified versions of old difficulties. While federal officials have worried alternately about inflation and the drag on the economy imposed by rapidly rising federal tax revenues, state and local governments have struggled, frequently with only indifferent success, to provide the wide variety of services their citizens are increasingly demanding. All too often in the governmental sector, the money is not where the needs are; or if it is there, the means for mobilizing it are far from obvious. As a result there are many deficiencies, and the costs are heavy, widespread, and often not recognized for what they are.

The price of inadequate education, for example, is paid not only by those who lack the opportunity to develop their talents fully but by the public which loses the important capital resources represented by these talents. Comfortably housed suburbanites, who spend much of their time on congested highways breathing unclean air and worrying about the rising tide of crime and violence, often overlook the fact that their withdrawal to the suburbs has contributed to these problems. By extending the metropolitan area, they have added to the freeways and the smog and also helped to impoverish the central city of whose difficulties they tend to take a chill

1

and distant view. Individuals with more and more leisure time find less and less opportunity to enjoy it because of growing river pollution and crowded public parks—situations intensified by their penuriousness as taxpayers as well as by official timidity and general public shortsightedness.

The failure of local governments to cope adequately with mushrooming communities and, above all, the strange reluctance of the taxpayer to protect his own welfare have resulted in urgent public needs which are only gradually being recognized as their critical points approach. This uncomfortable situation raises serious questions about the continued vitality of federalism in the United States. We live in an age of impatience, and if state and local governments make only halting progress toward the nation's basic goals, they may find themselves coming increasingly under the influence or control of Washington. The present study focuses on these issues, exploring ways in which current fiscal problems can be solved under a strong and flexible federal system of government.

Fiscal Trends in the U.S. Federal System

There is no need to dwell on the rapidity with which government purchases of goods and services have risen during this century. In 1900, for example, the output of all three levels of government was 6 percent of Gross National Product; in 1964 it was over 20 percent. During a period of such rapid growth one would expect to observe numerous changes in the structure of American governments. That there have been some major ones will be clear from the discussion in the rest of this section. What is even more impressive, however, is the number of stable relationships that have persisted over fairly long periods of time. The federal fiscal system, it would appear, has been able to adapt itself to changing economic conditions without losing its basic characteristics. Whether it can continue to do so is the major issue to be considered in later chapters.

Relative Shares of Direct General Expenditures

In any comparison of the roles of the three levels of government as sources of expenditure, it is important that the terms of reference be clearly defined. If all public expenditures (omitting those made to other governments or by insurance trust funds) are considered,

TABLE I-1. Shares of the Three Levels of Government in Direct General Public Expenditures, Selected Years, 1902–64

(Percentage distribution)

Year	Defense and Civil				Civil Only			
	Federal	State	Local	Total	Federal	State	Local	Total
1902	34	8	58	100	17	10	73	100
1913	30	9	61	100	18	11	71	100
1922	40	11	49	100	18	15	67	100
1927	31	12	57	100	15	15	70	100
1938	44	16	40	100	36	19	45	100
1948	62	13	25	100	23	26	51	100
1954	67	11	22	100	26	24	50	100
1964	58	15	27	100	23	27	50	100

Source: Frederick C. Mosher and Orville F. Poland, *The Costs of American Governments: Facts, Trends, Myths* (Dodd, Mead & Co., 1964), pp. 44–45, and U.S. Bureau of the Census, *Governmental Finances in 1963–64* (1965), p. 25. In this and other tables, the data on governmental finances relate to fiscal years. Most of the economic data, including Gross National Product figures, are on a calendar-year basis.

the results will show a dramatic shift in the direction of centralization. In 1902 local governments made 58 percent of all direct general expenditures; in 1964 the federal government had exactly that share (Table I-1).[1] If, on the other hand, defense and war-related expenditures are excluded, the picture is quite different. Then, as Table I-1 shows, local governments in 1964 were about twice as important as either of the other two levels. Moreover, these relative federal-state-local shares of ¼-¼-½ have remained remarkably stable during the postwar period. Compared to 1902 or 1927, however, this new pattern represents a definite shift in civil government expenditures from the local to the federal and state levels.

As would be expected, this shift has not been the same for each major type of spending. In Table I-1, 1927 is the most recent year that was relatively unmarked by severe unemployment or the effects of hot and cold wars. Since 1927 education, highway, and public welfare expenditures have been shifted mainly from local to state governments, while spending for health and natural resources has been moved from the local to the federal level. Table I-2 shows the nature of these changes. It should be stressed that these patterns are based on the expenditures actually made by each level of govern-

[1] Inclusion of insurance trust fund expenditures in the totals would accentuate the trend but not by much, the local share being 55 percent in 1902 and the federal share being 61 percent in 1964.

TABLE I-2. General Civil Expenditures by the Three Levels of Government, 1927 and 1964[a]

(Percentage shares)

Level of Government	Type of Expenditure									
	Education		Highways		Public Welfare		Health and Hospitals		Natural Resources	
	1927	1964	1927	1964	1927	1964	1927	1964	1927	1964
Federal	0	4	1	1	6	2	18	31	31	53
State	10	21	28	66	25	48	39	35	26	20
Local	90	75	71	32	69	51	43	35	43	28
Total	100	100	100	100	100	100	100	100	100	100

Source: Mosher and Poland, op. cit., pp. 46–47, and Governmental Finances in 1963–64, p. 25.
[a] Federal expenditures for veterans have been allocated to the relevant categories. Local parks and recreation are included in natural resources. Figures are rounded and may not add to totals.

ment whether they were financed by it or by some other level. The next step, therefore, is to consider what has happened to the intergovernmental sharing of program costs during the present century.

Intergovernmental Aid

Since 1902 both federal and state expenditures representing payments to other levels of government have grown more rapidly than GNP, though not in any regular fashion (Table I-3). Both expanded rapidly during the Great Depression, receded during World War II, and then remained stable over much of the postwar period. Federal aid, for example, remained close to 1 percent of GNP between 1948 and 1958, rose to 1.4 percent between 1959 and 1963, and increased again in 1964 to 1.7 percent. Since 1950 state payments to local governments have remained within a range of 1.7 to 2.1 percent of GNP, though they have tended to remain near the top of that range more consistently in recent years than earlier.

When the budgetary significance of intergovernmental aid is considered, the proportions are also stable. Local governments have received funds for 25 to 27 percent of their total expenditures from higher levels of government since the mid-1930's; state governments received 15 to 16 percent between 1948 and 1957 and then 21 to 23 percent in the early 1960's (Table I-4). Looked at from

TABLE I-3. Federal and State Intergovernmental Expenditures as a Percentage of Gross National Product, Selected Years, 1902–64

Year	Federal	State
1902	0.1	1.0
1922	0.3	0.9
1927	0.3	1.3
1934	3.7	5.0
1940	2.1	3.9
1942	1.1	2.2
1948	0.9	1.6
1957	0.9	1.8
1959	1.4	1.8
1964	1.7	2.1

Source: Mosher and Poland, *op. cit.*, p. 162, and *Governmental Finances in 1963–64* pp. 19, 23.

the point of view of the giver, state aid has shown the greater stability. While federal payments to state and local governments, as a percentage of federal expenditures, have receded during wartime and expanded thereafter, state aid has remained close to 35 percent of state general expenditures throughout the postwar period (Table III-9).

TABLE I-4. Intergovernmental Revenue as a Percentage of the Recipient's Expenditures,[a] Selected Years, 1902–64

Year	State Receipts from Federal Government as Percentage of State Expenditures	Local Receipts from Federal and State Governments as Percentage of Local Expenditures
1902	1.6	5.8
1922	7.4	7.1
1932	8.0	12.8
1934	27.5	24.9
1940	14.5	25.4
1942	16.6	25.4
1948	16.2	26.6
1957	16.0	25.0
1958	18.3	24.9
1960	22.7	26.1
1964	21.2	27.0

Source: Mosher and Poland, *op. cit.*, p. 162, and *Governmental Finances in 1963–64*, pp. 22, 23, and 53.
[a] Insurance Trust Funds excluded.

Since the Great Depression, state governments have functioned as grant intermediaries. In 1922 and 1932 only 8 percent of their spending was financed by the federal government and 23 to 29 percent represented aid to local governments. By 1934, 27.5 percent of their spending was federal money, and nearly 40 percent of their budgets was for state aid. Though neither of these levels was reached again, states in the early 1960's were receiving aid equal to 22 percent of their expenditures and granting aid to local governments constituting 35 percent of their total spending. The nature of these transactions is discussed in Chapter III.

State and Local Tax Systems

While the flow of financial aid from Washington has been increasing, state and local governments have not been idle in expanding old taxes or in enacting new ones. As a result, state-local tax revenues have more than kept pace with the growth of the economy, rising from 4 percent of GNP in 1902, to 5 percent in 1942 and 1948, and to nearly 8 percent in 1964. As Table I-5 shows, however, the increase has not been a steady one, nor did it match the federal increase up to the end of World War II. Since then federal tax receipts have little more than kept pace with GNP (except during the Korean War), but state-local taxes have increased their ratio by over one-half. Also worth noting in Table I-5 is the ap-

TABLE I-5. General Tax Revenues[a] as a Percentage of GNP by Level of Government, Selected Years, 1902–64

Year	Federal	State and Local	State	Local	Total
1902	2.4	4.0	0.7	3.3	6.4
1927	3.5	6.4	1.7	4.7	9.8
1932	3.1	10.5	3.2	7.3	13.6
1940	4.8	7.8	3.3	4.5	12.6
1942	7.7	5.4	2.5	2.9	13.1
1946	17.2	4.7	2.3	2.4	22.0
1948	14.6	5.1	2.6	2.5	19.7
1952	17.2	5.5	2.8	2.7	22.8
1958	15.3	6.9	3.4	3.5	22.1
1964	15.0	7.9	4.0	3.9	22.9

Sources: Mosher and Poland, op. cit., p. 165, and Governmental Finances in 1963–64, p. 22.
[a] As defined by the Census Bureau. Excludes revenues of the insurance trust funds.

proximate equality of state and local tax collections as a ratio of GNP during the postwar period (in contrast to the one-third to two-thirds share of the two levels of government in direct general expenditures shown in Table I-1). In addition, the stability of total tax revenues since 1946, near a level of 22 percent of GNP in four of the five years listed, merits attention.

It is clear from Table I-6 that state governments have been energetic in enacting new taxes. By 1964 these changes, along with numerous rate increases, had produced the highly diversified tax

TABLE I-6. Number of States Adopting New Taxes, by Major Type: Frequency Distributions by Decade, 1901–64

Period	Indi-vidual Income	Corpo-rate Income	Death	Gift	General Sales	Dis-tilled Spirits	Cigar-ettes	Gaso-line	Auto Regis-tration
Pre-1901	—	—	23	—	—	—	—	—	—
1901–10	1	1	15	—	—	—	—	—	33
1911–20	9	8	7	—	—	—	—	5	16
1921–30	5	8	2	—	—	—	8	43	—
1931–40	17	15	2	9	24	29	19	1	—
1941–50	1	2	—	3	5	2	15	1	—
1951–60	—	2	—	—	6	1	5	—	—
1961–64	3	1	—	—	2	—	1	—	—
Totals	36[a]	37[b]	49	12	37	32[c]	48	50	49

Sources: Advisory Commission on Intergovernmental Relations (ACIR), *Tax Overlapping in the United States, 1964* (July 1964), p. 25, and the Tax Foundation, *Tax Review* (October 1964), p. 38.
[a] Includes the partial income taxes of New Hampshire, New Jersey, and Tennessee.
[b] Excludes South Dakota's tax on financial institutions.
[c] Excludes the 17 states that either operate or supervise government liquor stores.

structure shown in Table I-7, and they had created many of the tax coordination problems discussed in Chapter II. Varied though the state tax systems are, they have been dominated for some time by three main kinds of taxes: motor vehicle fuel and registration taxes, general sales levies, and individual and corporate income taxes.

In 1963-64, each of the first two produced one-fourth of state tax collections; the income tax produced one-fifth. Excise taxes on tobacco and alcoholic beverages and property taxes yielded 10 percent. A long list of relatively unimportant levies produced the remaining 20 percent.

TABLE I-7. The Structure of State Tax Collections,[a] Selected Years, 1902–64

Year	Total (Millions)	Percentage Distribution									
		Individual Income	Corporate Income	Death and Gift	General Sales	Motor Fuel	Motor Vehicle Licences	Alcoholic Beverages	Tobacco	Property	Other
1902	$ 156	—	—	4.5	—	—	—	—	—	52.6	42.9
1927	1,608	4.4	5.7	6.6	—	16.1	18.7	—	—	23.0	25.5
1942	3,903	6.4	6.9	2.8	16.2	24.1	11.0	6.6	3.3	6.8	15.9
1948	6,743	7.4	8.7	2.7	21.9	18.7	8.8	6.3	5.0	4.1	16.5
1958	14,919	10.3	6.8	2.4	23.5	19.6	9.5	3.8	4.1	3.6	16.4
1964	24,243	14.1	7.0	2.7	25.1	16.7	7.9	3.6	4.9	3.0	15.0

Sources: Tax Overlapping in the United States, 1964, p. 20, and Governmental Finances in 1963–64, p. 22.
[a] Excludes insurance trust fund revenues.

Local tax systems, in contrast, are much less diversified. Property taxes still dominate, though not nearly to the extent that they did before the Great Depression (Table I-8). Reacting to many problems (see Chapter V), some of the largest cities have been especially active in the search for new revenue sources. While some utilized taxes similar to those existing at higher levels of government to their great advantage, others have gone their own independent ways, frequently adding to both their own and their taxpayers' costs. Various ways of dealing with these important intergovernmental problems are discussed in Chapters II and V.

TABLE I-8. The Structure of Local Tax Collections, Selected Years, 1927–64

Year	Total (Millions)	Percentage Distribution			
		Property Taxes	Sales and Gross Receipts Taxes	Income Taxes	Other Taxes
1927	$ 4,479	97	1	—	2
1942	4,625	92	3	1	4
1948	6,599	89	6	1	5
1958	15,461	87	7	1	4
1964	23,542	87.2	7.7	1.6	3.6

Sources: 1927–58: Tax Overlapping in the United States, 1964, p. 43; 1964: Governmental Finances in 1963–64, p. 5.

State-Local Fiscal Prospects for 1970

How serious the fiscal problems of the U.S. federal system are likely to be in the future depends to a large extent on the difficulties which state and local governments will face. If these are moderate and if they are handled with dispatch in most areas, the federal system of government is not likely to be subjected to undue strains. If, however, the problems are so great, or the will to solve even minor problems so weak, that only halting progress is made in the public sector, U.S. federalism is liable to lose vitality over the next decade. Which prospect is the more realistic is not easy to determine. Some insights can, however, be obtained by systematically examining future needs and demands for the services of state and local governments and by relating these to their future revenue-raising powers. Several projections of this sort have already been made for the early 1970's,[2] but the most detailed and comprehensive are the state-by-state estimates currently being made for 1970 by the Project '70 staff of the Council of State Governments (CSG). These, accordingly, will be used as the basis for the discussion below.

Forecasting in this area is a hazardous undertaking. Given our far-from-adequate knowledge of the determinants of state-local expenditures and tax programs and of the interrelationships between them, the best that one can do is to work out the implications of a number of more or less reasonable assumptions about future fiscal behavior. What emerges from these quantitative exercises is a set of "if-then," or conditional, forecasts. For example, *if* the economy develops in such-and-such a way and *if* present service levels and

[2] See, for example, L. Laszlo Ecker-Racz, "Whither State and Local Finance?" *Journal of Finance,* Vol. 19 (May 1964), pp. 370-81; Otto Eckstein, *Trends in Public Expenditures in the Next Decade* (Committee for Economic Development, April 1959); Robert J. Lampman, "How Much Government Spending in the 1960's?" *Quarterly Review of Economics and Business,* Vol. I (February 1961), pp. 7-17; National Planning Association, *Long-Range Projections for Economic Growth: the American Economy in 1970,* Planning Pamphlet No. 107 (1959); Dick Netzer, "Financial Needs and Resources over the Next Decade: State and Local Governments," in National Bureau of Economic Research, *Public Finances: Needs, Sources and Utilization* (Princeton University Press, 1961); and Outdoor Recreation Resources Review Commission, *Projections to the Years 1976 and 2000: Economic Growth, Population, Labor Force and Leisure, and Transportation,* Study Report 23 (1962).

quality are maintained, *then* state-local expenditures for some particular program can be expected to be $x million in 1970. Such projections, as they have come to be called, do not necessarily represent the forecaster's best guess as to what will in fact happen. Instead they are intended as a basis for improved fiscal programming which, if it does develop to any extent, is itself likely to invalidate any forecast derived mainly from past experience.

State-Local Spending in 1970

Any set of projections must be based on some assumption about the general state of the economy in the year selected for study.[3] For this purpose the CSG projections make use of one of the official macro-models developed for the Interagency Study of Growth in the United States. This assumes a low rate of unemployment in 1970 (not more than 4 percent of the labor force), a GNP of $864 billion, and a population of 208 million. Real output is assumed to increase by 4.1 percent a year on the average between 1962 and 1970; prices are to go up by 1.5 percent a year; and personal income per capita is to rise by 35.5 percent, from $2,366 in 1962 to $3,207 in 1970.[4] There is no need to emphasize the upward push that all of these changes are likely to exert on state and local spending.

The push will have to be a strong one, however, if it is to produce results that match those of the recent past. Between 1953 and 1963 state and local general expenditures rose by 132 percent, from $28 to $65 billion. (For further details see Table IV-12.) Were this same rate of increase to be maintained between 1960 and 1970, general expenditures in 1970 would be about $120 billion, implying an increase in the relative importance of state-local spending from 11.5 percent of GNP in 1964 to 14 percent in 1970 (based on the $864 billion estimate cited above). While at first glance such rapid growth may seem unlikely, it is the forecast of one expert,[5] and in the past forecasters have tended to underestimate increases in state-local expenditures.[6]

[3] In addition, of course, this assumption must be consistent with the specific sectoral projections that are then developed.
[4] Selma J. Mushkin and Eugene P. McLoone, *Public Spending for Higher Education in 1970* (Council of State Governments, February 1965), pp. 61-66.
[5] L. Laszlo Ecker-Racz, *op. cit.*
[6] Between 1957 and 1963, for example, state-local expenditures rose at an

Whether past growth rates will in fact be continued is, needless to say, an exceedingly complex question. For one thing, future needs are not likely to be the same as past needs. As Table IV-12 shows, local school expenditures accounted for no less than 30 percent of the total 1953-63 increase in state-local spending, but in the decade ahead enrollments can be expected to rise more slowly, thereby lessening the pressure on local school boards. This situation is shown in the following population projection:[7]

Age Group	Population (Millions)		Percentage Increase
	1963	1970	1963 – 70
Under 10	41	45	10
10–14	18	20	11
15–19	16	19	19
20–24	13	17	31
25–44	47	48	2
45–64	38	42	10
Over 65	18	20	11

Large quality gaps will remain among schools, but these are more difficult to recognize than quantitative deficiencies, and many of them will be in large cities where the problems of financing needed improvements, as noted in Chapter V, are especially acute. Therefore, local school expenditures may rise much less rapidly in the future than they have in the past.

This is not likely to be the case, however, with public higher education. Not only is the large group of postwar babies just beginning to reach college age, but there have also been steady increases in the percentage of high school graduates, in the proportion of them going to college, and in the proportion of college graduates continuing their academic studies. The Mushkin-McLoone estimate of the result of all of these factors is an increase in degree-credit enrollment in colleges and universities from less than 4.5 million in 1963 to nearly 7.7 million in 1970.[8]

---

average annual rate of 7.9 percent, whereas the Eckstein and Netzer projections cited in footnote 2 above were only 4.3 percent and 4.8 percent, respectively.

[7] U.S. Bureau of the Census, *Current Population Reports,* Series P-25, No. 279 (Feb. 4, 1964), p. 5. These projections are the Census Bureau's Series A, which is based on the continuation of the average annual level of age-specific fertility rates in 1960-63.

[8] *Op. cit.,* p. 45. This assumes that more than half of the 18-to-21-year-old group will go to college in 1970, compared to 40 percent in 1960 and only 30 percent in 1950 (*ibid.,* p. 2).

Unfortunately, estimating enrollments is only the first and also the least difficult step in projecting governmental expenditures on higher education. Among the many problems encountered, the most troublesome appear to be: (1) forecasting future increases in rates of pay for faculty and nonacademic personnel (payrolls constitute about 75 percent of total expenditures for student higher education); (2) estimating what will happen to student-faculty ratios; (3) guessing the extent to which improved teaching methods, more effective use of space, and so forth, will raise university productivity; and (4) forecasting the extent to which university facilities and state funds will become involved in upgrading the skills of adult workers.

TABLE I-9. Expenditures of Public Colleges and Universities, by Major Type, Actual 1962 and Projected 1970[a]

Type of Expenditure	Amounts (Millions)		Percentage Increase 1962–70
	1962	1970	
Student Higher Education	$1,792	$4,589	156
Research, Public Services, and Other Current Costs	1,302	3,981	206
Capital Outlays	949	3,527	272
Total	4,043	12,098	199

Source: Selma J. Mushkin and Eugene P. McLoone, *Public Spending for Higher Education in 1970* (Council of State Governments, February 1965), pp. 48–52.
Note: Figures are rounded and may not add to totals.
[a] Data are for fiscal 1962 and calendar 1970.

With regard to the first two, the CSG projections, which are summarized in Table I-9, assume that academic salary rates will rise by 50 percent between 1962 and 1970 (compared to a 33 percent increase for wage and salary rates in general) and that student-faculty ratios will have risen by 20 percent by 1970.[9] The projection shown on the first line of Table I-9 is highly sensitive to both of these assumptions. If student-faculty ratios were to remain stable,

[9] *Ibid.*, p. 17. A rise in student-faculty ratios may represent, of course, either a decline in educational quality or an improvement in teaching methods so that a given quality can be maintained at lower cost. This appears to be the only explicit allowance made in the CSG projections for item 3 in the list above. Lack of reliable data at the time the preliminary estimates were made also precluded any quantitative treatment of item 4. *Ibid.*, pp. 26-27.

for example, higher education expenditures per full-time student equivalent in 1970 would be $1,259 instead of $1,058—a 41 percent increase over 1962 per student costs of $895 rather than an 18 percent rise.[10] Similarly, since three-quarters of student higher education expenditures goes into faculty and other academic payrolls, the realism of the $4.6 billion figure projected for 1970 will depend very much on whether a 50 percent increase in salary rates is sufficient to attract the large and highly qualified staff needed to handle the forthcoming enrollments. Opinions on this question will differ, but it seems clear that some of the most important fiscal problems state governments are likely to face during the next decade will be in the field of higher education.

Cities, on the other hand, are likely to encounter some of their greatest difficulties in dealing with poverty and with transportation systems. It is still too early to tell how rapidly the economic opportunity program, inaugurated in August 1964, by PL 88-452, will develop; but if it proves to be an effective way of dealing with underdeveloped human resources and if federal shares of total costs, currently extending up to 90 percent, are reduced as scheduled in the law,[11] state-local expenditures in this area may be substantial by 1970. Michael Harrington, for example, has estimated that a minimum of $100 billion is needed over the next ten years to deal adequately with the economic problems of disadvantaged groups.[12] How realistic this particular estimate is, and how rapidly it, or some other level of operations, will be achieved remain to be seen. As shown in Table I-10, for example, the CSG projections show public welfare expenditures growing more slowly between 1962 and 1970 than they did between 1957 and 1962, primarily because older people will qualify for increasing amounts of Social Security and Medicare benefits. Even so, total public welfare expenditures are expected to approach $9 billion in 1970, with state and local governments contributing nearly $4 billion of their own funds.

It is difficult enough, as will be seen in Chapter V, to determine the best solution to urban transportation problems, to say nothing of forecasting what expenditures cities will make for this purpose in

[10] *Ibid.*, p. 47.

[11] To 75 percent for work-study programs and to 50 percent for work-training, community action and adult basic education programs.

[12] *New York Times,* Nov. 16, 1964. See also his *The Other America: Poverty in the United States* (Macmillan, 1962).

TABLE I-10. Expenditures for Public Welfare, by Major Type, Actual 1957 and 1962 and Projected 1970[a]

Type of Expenditure	Amounts (Billions)			Average Annual Growth Rates	
	1957	1962	1970	1957–62	1962–70
Cash Assistance	$2.7	$3.5	$4.5	5.3%	3.0%
Other Assistance[b]	0.8	1.6	4.4	15.5	12.8
Total	3.5	5.1	8.9	7.8	6.8
Financed by:					
Federal Aid	1.6	2.5	5.1	9.6	8.8
State-Local Funds	1.9	2.6	3.8	6.4	4.6

Source: Selma J. Mushkin and Robert Harris, *Financing Public Welfare: 1970 Projections* (Council of State Governments, July 1965), p. 49.
[a] Data are for fiscal 1957 and 1962 and for calendar 1970.
[b] Includes vendor payments, administration services and training, and the poverty program.

1970. That substantial increases can be expected, however, is indicated by the number of detailed studies of transit systems that have already been made or commissioned. The CSG projections for public transportation outlays, which are summarized in Table I-11, allow for this by raising the 3.4 percent average annual growth rate in 1957-62 to 13.2 percent for 1962-70. This is based on the assumption, which appears reasonable in the case of capital expenditures for highways,[13] that mass transit expenditures will be closely related to federal aid, which in turn is projected to rise from $150 million in fiscal 1966 and 1967 to $300 million in 1970.[14] Given the financial difficulties which many of the largest cities face, urban transportation spending is also likely to depend on the extent to which the federal and state governments shoulder an increasing share of the responsibility for promoting education, public welfare, and the development of human resources generally. As will be seen

[13] A cross-sectional regression analysis for 1961-63 produced the following equation, which was used in deriving the 1970 CSG projections:

$$X_1 = 11.09 + 0.40X_2 + 1.16X_3,$$

where X_1 = per capita capital expenditures for highways,
     X_2 = per capita personal income, and
     X_3 = per capita federal aid for highways.
For this equation, $R^2 = 0.90$. Selma J. Mushkin and Robert Harris, *Transportation Outlays of States and Localities: Projections to 1970* (Council of State Governments, May 1965), p. 12.
[14] *Ibid.*, p. 27. As the authors stress, their projections for mass transit expenditures are based much more on political feasibilities than on economic needs.

TABLE I-11. Expenditures for Public Transportation, by Major Type, Actual 1957 and 1962 and Projected 1970[a]

Type of Expenditure	Amounts (Billions)			Average Annual Growth Rates	
	1957	*1962*	*1970*	*1957–62*	*1962–70*
Highways	$7.8	$10.4	$15.1–$16.2[b]	5.7%	4.5%–5.4%
Transit Systems	0.6	0.7	2.0	3.4	13.2
Water Transit	0.2	0.3	0.5	9.1	5.5
Airports	0.2	0.4	0.7	9.7	8.2
Total	8.9	11.7	18.3–19.4	5.7	5.4–6.1

Source: Selma J. Mushkin and Robert Harris, *Transportation Outlays of States and Localities: Projections to 1970* (Council of State Governments, May 1965), p. 39.
[a] Data are for fiscal 1957 and 1962 and for calendar 1970.
[b] The higher projection assumes that federal highway aid is increased from the scheduled $3.9 billion to the $4.9 billion which the Bureau of Public Roads estimates will be needed to complete the Interstate Highway System on time.

in Chapter III, the high mobility of the U.S. population provides a strong argument for operating all of these programs on a shared cost basis. To increase the extent to which this is done would release local funds for other purposes; and if, in addition, some of the revenue reforms discussed in Chapter V were enacted, still more public needs could be met in metropolitan areas.

In sum, then, all projections of future state-local spending levels represent an uneasy compromise between the economic needs for public services and the political and financial constraints within which governments must operate. Therefore, it seems best to give here no more than a rather wide interval estimate of 1970 state-local general expenditures. For the lower limit a figure of $100 billion seems appropriate, that being a good round sum and one that would be a slightly lower percentage of the projected 1970 GNP of $864 billion than state and local expenditures actually were in 1962-63. Since state-local tax systems, as will be seen in the next section, have a GNP elasticity of approximately unity, it seems unlikely that their 1970 spending will fall below $100 billion. How far it will rise above that mark will depend upon how impatient people are about fulfilling public needs and on how well, and in what ways, the various fiscal problems to be discussed in later chapters are handled. The CSG preliminary estimate for 1970, for example, is $108 billion, and as already noted, a level of $120 billion would be produced by a simple continuation of past trends. Since

other expert projections fall in this same range, it seems reasonable
to suppose that the level of general expenditures with which state
and local governments will have to contend in 1970 will lie some-
where between $100 and $120 billion.

State-Local Tax Receipts in 1970

The next question, of course, concerns the amount of assistance
state and local governments can expect to get in 1970 from their
existing tax systems. While all major taxes must be analyzed for this
purpose, the property tax stands out because of its relative
importance:[15]

Tax	Percent of State and Local Tax Receipts, Fiscal Year 1965
Property	44.7
General Sales and Gross Receipts	15.4
Motor Fuel Sales	8.4
Individual Income	8.0
Corporate Income	3.7
Motor Vehicle and Operators Licenses	4.1
All Other	15.7

Unfortunately for forecasters, neither the tax nor its base has be-
haved in a very regular fashion in the past. As Table I-12 shows,
GNP elasticities have varied considerably both for different types of
property during any given period of time and for any given type of
property over different periods of time. Especially notable are the
significantly higher elasticities that have prevailed during the last
ten or so years.

Projection of 1970 property tax receipts, therefore, requires a
disaggregation of the tax base into those types of property that can
be expected to increase in value at different rates in the future.
(This means, of course, forecasting both price changes on existing
property and the value of new construction.) Ideally, one should
also take into account the wide interstate variations in the treatment
of different kinds of tangible and intangible personal property. To
do so, however, might yield only small increases in reliability at
considerable extra cost, and in making their projections the Project
'70 staff of the Council of State Governments has simply used a

[15] U.S. Bureau of the Census, *Quarterly Summary of State and Local Tax
Revenue, April-June 1965* (September 1965), p. 1. The data are for the twelve
months ended with June 1965.

TABLE I-12. GNP Elasticities of the Market Value of the Property Tax Base and its Major Components, Selected Periods, 1899–1961

Type of Property	Period					
	1899–1957	1899–1929	1929–48	1948–57	1953–57	1956–61
Nonfarm Residential	0.9	1.0	0.6	1.0	1.2	1.6
Nonfarm Nonresidential	0.8	0.9	0.3	1.1	1.8	1.9
Farm	0.5	0.6	0.6	0.8	1.0	1.0
All Real	0.8	0.9	0.7	1.0	1.4	1.6
Personal	0.9	0.9	0.9	1.1	1.3	—
All	0.9	0.9	0.7	1.0	1.4	1.5

Source: Benjamin Bridges, Jr., "Income Elasticity of the Property Tax Base," *National Tax Journal,* Vol. 17 (September 1964), pp. 255 and 260–62.

representative general property tax base that is kept uniform from one state to another.[16] By dealing separately with nine categories of property[17] and relying heavily on 1956-61 relations between property values and personal income, they estimated that total 1970 property tax receipts would be $33 billion if effective tax rates remain constant. Constant effective rates imply, of course, rising nominal tax rates as long as assessed values of existing properties lag behind rising market values. To some extent assessed values did lag between 1956 and 1961[18] and if during the late 1960's a similar lag should be combined with constant nominal tax rates, 1970 property tax revenues would, according to CSG calculations, be only $30.9 billion.

Both of these estimates, which imply GNP yield elasticities for state-local property taxes between 1.0 and 1.2, lie at the high end of the range of elasticity estimates recently given by the Advisory Commission on Intergovernmental Relations (ACIR) as shown in Table I-13. Should their GNP elasticity be only 0.7, for example,

[16] Selma J. Mushkin, *Property Taxes: 1970 Outlook* (Council of State Governments, October 1965), p. 19. The representative tax base excludes both household goods and intangible personal property.

[17] Residential realty, commercial and industrial realty, farm realty, vacant lots, public utility properties, inventories, farm personal property, nonfarm producers' durables, and motor vehicles. In addition, the yields of special property taxes were projected separately, but at $1.2 billion they made up less than 4 percent of the total 1970 property tax revenue.

[18] See U.S. Bureau of the Census, *1957 Census of Governments,* Vol. V, *Taxable Property Values,* and *1962 Census of Governments,* Vol. II, *Taxable Property Values.*

TABLE I-13. Gross National Product Elasticities of the Major Categories of State General Revenue Sources

Revenue Source		Elasticity Estimates		
		Low	Medium	High
Property Taxes		0.7	0.9	1.1
Income Taxes:	Individual	1.5	1.65	1.8
	Corporate	1.1	1.2	1.3
Sales Taxes:	General	0.9	0.97	1.05
	Motor Fuel	0.4	0.5	0.6
	Alcoholic Beverage	0.4	0.5	0.6
	Tobacco	0.3	0.35	0.4
	Public Utilities	0.9	0.95	1.0
	Other	0.9	1.0	1.1
Auto License and Registration		0.2	0.3	0.4
Death and Gift Taxes		1.0	1.1	1.2
All Other Taxes		0.6	0.65	0.7
Higher Education Fees		1.6	1.7	1.8
Hospital Fees		1.3	1.4	1.5
Natural Resources Fees		0.9	1.0	1.1
Interest Earnings		0.6	0.7	0.8
Miscellaneous Fees and Charges		0.6	0.7	0.8

Source: ACIR, *Federal-State Coordination of Personal Income Taxes* (October 1965), p. 42.

property taxes would yield state and local governments only $27.6 billion in 1970.[19] Which end of this rather wide range the actual

[19] From the definition of yield elasticity we have:

$$\Delta T = \frac{T_0}{GNP_0} \cdot \Delta GNP \cdot \epsilon$$

where

T_0 = tax revenue in the base year,

GNP_0 = gross national product in the base year,

ΔT = change in tax revenue between the base year and the year of forecast,

ΔGNP = change in gross national product between the base year and the year of forecast, and

ϵ = yield elasticity.

Substituting values for fiscal 1964 and 1970 in the above equation we have:

$$\Delta T = \frac{21.2 \times 261}{609} \epsilon$$

$$= 9.1\epsilon$$

According to this computation, therefore, a change of one-tenth of a point in the *GNP* yield elasticity for state-local property taxes would change projected 1970 tax revenues by $0.91 billion.

yields approach will depend not only upon the volume of future new construction and the rate at which prices rise on existing properties but also upon the effects which existing property tax inequities have on the willingness of local electorates to support steadily rising nominal tax rates. It may be, as some have hinted, that the general property tax has recently been basking in an Indian summer

TABLE I-14. Percentage Increases in State and Local Tax Collections by Major Type of Tax, 1953–63, 1957–63, and 1964–65

Tax	Average Annual Percentage Increase in Yield		
	1953–63	1957–63	1964–65
Property	11.5	10.5	7.9
General Sales and Gross Receipts	10.8	11.6	8.5
Motor Fuel Sales	—	6.6	5.9
Individual Income	20.7	15.2	10.9
Corporate Income	8.6	6.0	13.9
Motor Vehicle and Operators Licenses	—	4.9	4.4
All Other[a]	7.6	8.6	6.9
Total	11.1	9.8	7.9

Source: U. S. Bureau of the Census, *Census of Governments, 1962*, Vol. VI, No. 4, *Historical Statistics on Governmental Finances and Employment; Summary of Governmental Finances in 1963* and *Quarterly Summary of State and Local Tax Revenue, April–June 1965* (September 1965), p. 1.
[a] 1953–63 includes motor fuel sales and motor vehicle and operators license taxes.

of prosperity which, unless some of the reforms discussed in Chapter V are adopted, will soon be followed by a long winter of relative stagnation.

Property tax receipts have not been alone in their rapid growth in recent years (Table I-14). Between 1953 and 1963 state-local individual income tax yields rose by an average of nearly 21 percent a year, and from 1957 to 1963 general sales tax receipts grew by nearly 12 percent a year. These figures, of course, reflect rising tax rates, new adoptions, and base expansions in addition to the automatic response of established taxes to an expanding GNP. Some indication of the difference between the two sets of influences may be obtained by comparing the 1957-63 and 1963-70 GNP elasticities given in Table I-15. With both automatic and discretionary tax changes at work in 1957-63, state-local tax collections expanded by 17 percent for every 10 percent increase in GNP; as projected by the CSG staff at constant tax rates, however, between 1963 and

TABLE I-15. GNP Yield Elasticities of Major State-Local Taxes, Actual 1957–63 and Projected 1963–70 at Constant Tax Rates

Tax	Yield Elasticity	
	1957–63	1963–70
Property	1.8	1.2
General Sales and Gross Receipts	2.0	1.0
Motor Fuel Sales	1.1	0.6
Individual Income	2.6	1.9
Corporate Income	1.0	1.2
Motor Vehicle and Operators Licenses	0.8	0.5
All Other	1.5	0.8
Total	1.7	1.1[a]

Source: Council of State Governments, *Projections of Tax Revenues: Preliminary Tables* (October 1964), Table 3
[a] If the 1963–70 GNP elasticity of the property tax were taken as 1.0 or 0.8, the elasticity of the total state-ocal system would be 1.0 and 0.9, respectively.

1970 total yields are to rise by only 11 percent for every 10 percent increase in GNP. On this latter basis, 1970 tax revenues of state and local governments would be $70 billion. Variations of one-tenth of a point in the GNP yield elasticity used for state-local tax systems as a whole would raise or lower that figure by approximately $2 billion.[20] As shown in Table I-16, ACIR estimates of the GNP elasticity of total state general revenue (taxes plus user charges and fees) in the 1964-70 period extend from a low of 0.8 to a high of 1.1. If a similar range is applied to taxes alone, 1970 tax receipt projections would fall between $64 and $70 billion.

State-Local Fiscal Pressures in 1970

The preliminary projections in the preceding two sections show a gross gap between expenditures and taxes in 1970 for state and local governments ranging from $30 to $56 billion. This gap could be filled in any one of four major ways: (1) by state-local user charges and miscellaneous fees; (2) by federal grants-in-aid; (3) by an increase in state-local indebtedness; and (4) by structural changes in state-local tax systems brought about by the adoption of

[20] Using the equation given above in footnote 19 and taking fiscal 1964 as the base year, we have:

$$T = \frac{48 \times 261}{609}\epsilon = 20.6\epsilon$$

TABLE I-16. Estimates of the GNP Elasticity of Total State General Revenue in 1947, 1954, 1964, and 1970

Fiscal Year	Elasticity Estimate		
	Low	Medium	High
1947	0.74	0.83	0.93
1954	0.75	0.85	0.94
1964	0.82	0.92	1.01
1970	0.89	0.99	1.09

Source: ACIR, *Federal-State Coordination of Personal Income Taxes*, p. 43.

new taxes, by expansions of the bases of existing taxes, or by the enactment of higher tax rates.

A rough indication of what might be expected in 1970 from the first two sources, on the basis of past experience, is given in the tabulation below. The "A" projections were derived by taking the 1962-63 ratios of each source of receipts to GNP and applying them to a projected 1970 GNP of $870 billion; the higher set of "B" projections was obtained by simple extrapolation of 1952-62 trends in the receipts-to-GNP ratios. In each case the GNP ratios used are given in the tabulation of alternative projections of nontax state-local revenues in 1970:

	Projection A		Projection B	
Type of Revenue	Revenue/GNP Ratio Used	Projected Revenue (Billions)	Revenue/GNP Ratio Used	Projected Revenue (Billions)
User Charges and Miscellaneous Fees	.016	$14	.02	$17
Federal Grants-in-Aid	.014	12	.02	17

Projecting the contribution that state-local borrowing is likely to make to the financing of general expenditures in 1970 is made particularly difficult by several factors: the widespread existence of constitutional and statutory debt limitations; the close relation between long-term debt issues and state-local capital expenditures; and the dependence of state-local borrowing powers on the market for tax-exempt securities, a market which may well not expand in the future at the same rate as other financial markets. Suffice it to note here that in recent years state and local governments have increased their outstanding long-term indebtedness by about $6 billion a year. If this amount is added to the figures given in the preceding paragraph, nontax receipts in 1970 would range between $32 and $40 billion, or within the lower half of the projected gross expenditure-tax gap. There is, in short, a definite possibility that fiscal pressures in the next five years will not rise beyond the ability of state and local governments, operating mainly within the present federal fiscal framework, to deal with them. There is, however, at least an equal possibility that the pressures will soon be too great to be met in conventional ways; it is this prospect that brought about this study.

The Fiscal Problems of Federalism

State and local governments now stand at one of the most important crossroads in their development. While citizens have been demanding more and better public services, governments often have been dominated by rural electorates with little interest in emerging urban problems and run by unimaginative officials with the help of inferior staffs. Signs at the crossroad point in one direction to a neglect of urgent public needs and in the other to a steady decline in state and local responsibilities as civic needs are increasingly satisfied from Washington. On the other hand, the legislative reapportionments now under way promise to create state governments that will be more responsive to the problems of the times. With sufficient funds they can then begin to attract the talent that they need to get on with the job. Whether the required revenue sources will be developed in time is still an open question. The major problems and possibilities are summarized briefly in the remaining sections of this chapter and discussed in detail in Chapters II-V.

Tax Coordination

Use of the same tax by two or more levels of government poses obvious threats to the efficient operation of a federal system of government. With the proper use of some of the coordinating devices discussed in Chapter II, however, this threat can be turned aside and an efficient and equitable tax system designed that, at least po-

tentially, places ample sources of tax revenue within the reac
but the poorest state and local governments.

Tax Competition

Whether they can obtain these revenues, however, is another
question. The trouble is that state and local governments have been
engaged for some time in an increasingly active competition among
themselves for new business. If there is, as Edwin C. Gooding suggests, a "New War Between the States,"[21] the main weapons are
state guarantees of private loans to new business, direct state loans
for the same purpose, local bonds issued to finance the construction
of industrial facilities for lease to private firms, tax exemptions and
concessions, and statewide, privately financed development credit
corporations. Between 1960 and 1962 one or more of these inducements were put into operation by nineteen states, and nine additional ones were authorized in 1963.[22] On September 30, 1963, only
five states were not using any of the devices, and twelve states had
authorized three or more.[23]

In such an environment government officials do not lightly pro-
pose increases in their own tax rates that go much beyond those
prevailing in nearby states or in any area with similar natural attractions for industry. They may do so if the additional revenues
are required to finance programs with localized benefits known to
be highly desired by business firms or their employees, but there are
many situations in which the benefits are too intangible or too
diffused geographically to have much drawing power, or at least so
they appear to the average state or local legislator. If such programs
are to be provided at all, they must be financed either by taxes that
are not highly objectionable to business managers or by generous
federal grants-in-aid. Active tax competition, in short, tends to pro-

[21] See his four-part article with that title in the Federal Reserve Bank of Boston's *New England Business Review* (October and December, 1963, and July and
October, 1964).

[22] *Ibid.* (October 1963), p. 2.

[23] Benjamin Bridges, Jr., "State and Local Inducements for Industry. Part I,"
National Tax Journal, Vol. 18 (March 1965), pp. 3-4. The five states using none
were Arizona, California, Nevada, Texas, and Utah, and the twelve that had
authorized three or more were Arkansas, Hawaii, Kentucky, Maine, Maryland,
Minnesota, Mississippi, Oklahoma, Rhode Island, Tennessee, Vermont, and West
Virginia.

duce either a generally low level of state-local tax effort or a state-local tax structure with strong regressive features. Paradoxically, the more widespread it is, the more likely it is to produce these debilitating fiscal effects without creating the stimulating economic effects sought by the tax competitors.

It is difficult to judge exactly how much state and local taxing powers are weakened by tax competition. Several regions have already been highly successful in attracting certain kinds of business by spending money on higher education and research. As worker skills continue to be upgraded, more and more people may shift their attention from the height of tax rates to the quality of local public services. The difficulty is that such changes in human attitudes develop slowly. In the meantime the familiar alternating movement of hesitant tax rate advances, followed by a gradual matching of them on the part of other state and local governments, followed by further rate advances, and so forth, is likely to continue. If speed is of the essence, as it may well be, other means of financing high-priority state-local programs will have to be found. Some help can be obtained through the right kind of tax coordination; for the rest it may be necessary to turn to intergovernmental grants.

Intergovernmental Grants-in-Aid

The case for functional grants from one level of government to another rests on the existence of public benefits that spill over the boundaries of the governmental unit operating the program in question. That these externalities are important in various fields, such as education, health, and public welfare, is the theme of Chapter III, where it is argued that an economically optimal solution to the problem can be provided only by open-end, matching grants that are carefully restricted to specific programs and that are managed jointly by the grantor and grantee governments. The problems involved in enacting and operating such grant programs are analyzed, and existing federal and state functional grants are then appraised from this point of view. In spite of its rather haphazard and irregular growth, the present system has many desirable features, and new, improved ones are steadily being added. The conclusion is that intergovernmental functional grants have been an important part of the U.S. federal system, and that with further development they can contribute much more.

There are, however, definite limits beyond which they should not be pushed. Well before these limits are approached, serious consideration should be given to a more controversial type of intergovernmental grant—one under which the money is extended with no strings, or with very few strings, attached. As Walter W. Heller and Joseph A. Pechman, among others, have stressed, unconditional federal grants could do much to enable the poorest states and the poorest local governments to bring their public service levels more in line with those prevailing in the rest of the country.[24] In addition, unconditional grants are one way of obtaining the government programs for local benefit which are widely desired by the people but which cannot, because of interstate and interlocal tax competition, be locally financed even in the wealthiest jurisdictions.

Whether a workable program of unconditional federal grants could be designed and whether it would represent a superior or an inferior use of federal funds forms the subject matter of Chapter IV. These questions have already received considerable public attention, and the recent vote of the 1965 governors' conference to ask the federal government to study the matter further is likely to keep the proposal under serious discussion as one important means of solving the fiscal problems of a federal system.

Expenditure Coordination and Analysis

It is in metropolitan areas that some of the most difficult problems of intergovernmental relations arise. Because of the political fragmentation that characterizes most of them, benefit spillovers are a common phenomenon, and action on areawide programs is frequently stymied either by organizational inadequacies or by the lack of an objective basis for cooperative agreements among independent municipal jurisdictions. Both of these problems are discussed in Chapter V. Alternative forms of metropolitan government are suggested to deal with organizational problems. The con-

[24] Walter W. Heller, *New Dimensions of Political Economy* (Harvard University Press, 1966); Joseph A. Pechman, "Financing State and Local Government," in *Proceedings of a Symposium on Federal Taxation* (American Bankers Association, 1965; Brookings Institution Reprint 103, 1965).

tributions which modern systems analysis can make to a workable solution of jurisdictional problems are discussed. In both cases the prospects seem encouraging, particularly if federal and state governments lend their financial and technical assistance to local efforts to deal with such mounting metropolitan problems as traffic congestion, air and water pollution, slums and neighborhood blight, and the underprivileged, undereducated people that represent such a waste of national resources.

Metropolitan Revenue Reform

Part of the metropolitan fiscal problem could be solved by means of metropolitan revenue reform. Property tax inequities and inefficiencies need to be eradicated; local sales and income taxes could be used more extensively and effectively than they now are; and the whole system of user charges and miscellaneous fees could be revised and expanded. Some observers contemplate more radical changes now that the conversion of the general property tax into a local tax on net wealth seems administratively feasible for the first time, thanks to the development of computers and data processing. This shift would materially increase local taxing powers. All of these reforms, which are analyzed in the last section of Chapter V, would require considerable assistance from higher levels of government, but once enacted they would place metropolitan governments in a much better position to handle their own fiscal affairs in their own individual ways.

Economic and Fiscal Variables of States

In the following chapters whenever complete tabulations have been unnecessary, a sample of states has been used to illustrate the point at issue. This sample of nineteen states was selected to provide a broad geographical coverage and to include states exhibiting widely different economic and political conditions. The following table summarizes some of these characteristics for the selected states.

Sample of States Ranked by Selected Economic and Fiscal Variables

State and Region	Rank[a] on the Basis of		
	1963 per Capita Personal Income (1)	1959 per Capita Income Produced (2)	1959–60 Tax Effort Index (3)
New England			
Massachusetts	9	11	27
Mideast			
New York	5	3	18
New Jersey	8	8	43
Delaware	11	18	50
Maryland	3	28	38
Great Lakes			
Indiana	18	13	37
Illinois	7	4	42
Wisconsin	23	25	22
Plains			
Minnesota	24	20	10
Missouri	14	12	49
South Dakota	40	38	1
Southeast			
Virginia	34	34	47
Tennessee	46	47	35
Florida	32	37	26
Alabama	48	48	40
Mississippi	51	51	8
West			
Colorado	22	15	16
California	6	5	15
Oregon	13	29	19

Sources: (1) Appendix Table A-1, Column (2). (2) ACIR, *Measures of State and Local Fiscal Capacity and Tax Effort* (October 1962), pp. 27–28. (3) Appendix Table A-6, Column (1).
[a] From highest to lowest.

CHAPTER II

Tax Coordination

A FEDERAL FISCAL SYSTEM faces two kinds of tax coordination problems. The first arises when two or more different levels of government use the same tax base, as when the federal government and a state government tax the same income (vertical tax overlapping); the second appears when large businesses or mobile individuals carry out economic activities in many different taxing jurisdictions at the same level of government, such as different states (horizontal tax overlapping). Both kinds of overlapping are widespread in the United States today, and both are capable of creating economic inefficiencies and taxpayer inequities which, if allowed to develop, will seriously restrict the spending powers of state and local governments.

The undesirable effects take several forms. A badly designed state and local tax system will soon reach its limit in producing additional tax revenues. At this point, high-priority public needs may go unsatisfied either because few desirable kinds of new taxes are available or because voters cannot agree as to which new tax they find least onerous. In another case regressive taxes, for which state and local governments have shown a strong penchant in the past, may penalize low-income individuals by preventing them from attaining their full productive capacity. The result may be a

28

significant undermining of the state and local economic base needed to support vital public programs. Finally, taxes that are difficult to administer tend to divert government expenditures from more important purposes. It is the task of tax coordination to avoid all of these undesirable developments.

The general background for the discussion can be quickly sketched. Those conditions that make for a large amount of horizontal tax overlapping—businesses operating in many states and taxpayers living in one community and working in another—have long been familiar characteristics of the American economy. Nor is vertical tax overlapping likely to be unfamiliar to the average taxpayer except, perhaps, by name. At the beginning of 1964 individual income taxes were collected by thirty-six states and a large number of local governments, mainly in Ohio and Pennsylvania. Death taxation was shared by the federal government and forty-nine states, and excises on gasoline, tobacco, liquor, and amusements were used in varying degrees by all three levels of government.

TABLE II-1. Federal, State, and Local Tax Collections, by Major Type of Tax, 1963–64

Tax	Percentage Distribution[a]			Total Yield (Billions)
	Federal	State	Local	
Customs Duties	100	0	0	$ 1.3
Property	0	3	97	21.2
Corporation Income	93	7	—[b]	25.2
Individual Income	93	6	1	52.5
Motor Vehicle and Operators' License Fees	0	94	6	2.0
General Sales and Gross Receipts	0	84	16	7.3
Alcoholic Beverage Excises	80	20	1	4.4
Tobacco Excises	62	36	2	3.3
Motor Fuel Excises	40	60	1	6.8
Public Utility Excises	54	27	19	1.9
Other Excises	75	22	2	5.7
Death and Gift	78	22	—[c]	3.1
All Other Taxes	31	50	19	3.7

Source: Computed from data given in U. S. Bureau of the Census, *Governmental Finances in 1963–64* (1965), p. 22.
[a] Percentages are rounded and may not add to 100.
[b] Minor amount included in individual income tax figure.
[c] Minor amount included in "all other taxes."

In spite of these multiple usages, which have increased over time, the major tax sources have remained highly concentrated in the hands of one level of government. As Table II-1 shows, almost all property tax receipts flowed into the hands of local governments in 1963-64; 93 percent of income tax revenues went to the federal government; and the states collected the dominant share of motor vehicle, general sales, and motor fuel taxes. These, of course, are national patterns which conceal the great diversities which exist among states and local areas. Complex as the picture may be, there is no doubt that vertical tax overlapping is important enough to warrant serious consideration.

Separation of Tax Sources

The most obvious solution to vertical overlapping would be to divide the major tax sources among the different levels of government, granting each of them exclusive jurisdiction over its own type of tax. Suppose, for example, that tax collections in a given year were as follows:

	Federal	State
Tax A	80	10
Tax B	10	50

Under these circumstances, would it not be more efficient for the federal government to relinquish its share of tax B in return for state abandonment of tax A? With revenue maintenance, the tax structure would then be:

	Federal	State
Tax A	90	
Tax B		60

There are two basic difficulties in this solution. The first is that tax B might be such that it could not be effectively administered by the states acting alone. If so, the move would be precluded on grounds of efficiency. The second difficulty is that the shift might interfere unduly with the states' freedom to design their own tax structures. It would be one thing if all states used both taxes A and B and were more or less indifferent to small changes in their relative importance, but quite another if some states used A but not B and strongly preferred that pattern to the alternative. Finally, though the plan involves no change in national tax revenues, it is almost certain to have diverse effects among the states. The states that experience a net increase in federal tax burdens can be expected to be less than enchanted with the reform.

It may be thought that we have biased the case against tax separation by choosing an example in which vertical tax overlapping already existed. Suppose, then, that tax A is used only by the federal government and B is used exclusively by the state governments. Then suppose that state governments find themselves in need of additional revenue. Under these conditions, additional administrative and compliance costs will have to be incurred at the state level and they may well be less (or at least not significantly more) with tax A than with its principal competitors. If, in addition, tax A is judged high on equity grounds and is relatively free of undesirable economic effects, the choice should go to it, even though its adoption increases the amount of vertical overlapping in the tax system.

In view of these drawbacks it is not surprising to find that tax separation has so far had only limited success in this country. Property taxes, it is true, have been increasingly reserved for local governments, but the federal government has not been highly successful in shifting either spending programs or revenue sources to state and local governments. A concerted effort to do both, by the Eisenhower Administration's Joint Federal-State Action Committee in 1957-59, produced only the modest proposal that the states take over full responsibility for vocational education and the construction of waste treatment plants (then being supported by a federal grant of some $80 million a year) in return for a tax credit against part of the federal excise on local telephone service. Though the plan was carefully designed so that no state would have lost money from the shift, at least in the short run, Congressional approval was not forthcoming. During the 1950's the federal government also repealed its tax on electrical energy and substantially reduced its excises on admissions. Both levies are generally regarded as well suited for use by state and local governments, but in neither case was much of the slack taken up.[1] Nor is it likely that the federal ex-

[1] I. M. Labovitz and L. L. Ecker-Racz, "Practical Solutions to Financial Problems Created by the Multilevel Political Structure," in National Bureau of Economic Research, *Public Finances: Needs, Sources and Utilization* (Princeton University Press, 1961), p. 172.

cises eliminated in 1965 will reappear to any large degree in state-local tax systems. The resulting reduction in federal tax burdens may, of course, stimulate some increases in other kinds of state and local taxes, but it remains to be seen how important these will be.

Complete tax separation, it would appear, is neither attainable nor desirable. Too many of the taxes usually listed as suitable for exclusive state and local use[2] are inequitable or inefficient or both, and some of the most important ones seem firmly entrenched at the federal level. Limited gains in this area will probably continue to be made, but most of the problems of tax coordination will need to be solved by other means.

Coordinated Tax Administration

One means of coordinating taxes that has the attractive feature of allowing each government considerable freedom in designing and levying its own taxes is cooperative or joint tax administration. In the income tax field, federal-state cooperation began as early as 1931, but for a long time its accomplishments were limited, partly for lack of appropriate economic incentives.[3] State officials could, and did, examine federal tax returns with profit to their governments, but in the process they imposed costs on the Internal Revenue Service (IRS) for which it was not reimbursed (state payments for audit abstracts and photostatic copies accrued to the Treasury's General Fund). As a result, the IRS did not seek to expand the cooperative arrangements. Again, in 1949, when a plan was developed for the coordinated use of federal-state income tax audits, it was found that the states had little *quid* to offer for the federal *quo*.

The real breakthrough came in 1957, when the first of a new

[2] The list includes general sales taxes, death and gift taxes, and excises on amusements, cigarettes, club dues, coin-operated machines, gasoline, motor vehicle registration, local telephone service, and safe deposit boxes. See Douglas H. Eldridge, "Equity, Administration and Compliance, and Intergovernmental Fiscal Aspects," in *The Role of Direct and Indirect Taxes in the Federal Revenue System*. A Conference Report of the National Bureau of Economic Research and the Brookings Institution (Princeton University Press, 1964), p. 191.

[3] Advisory Commission on Intergovernmental Relations (hereafter cited as ACIR), *Intergovernmental Cooperation in Tax Administration* (June 1961), pp. 2-7.

series of "agreements on the coordination of tax administration" was signed with Minnesota. These agreements (thirty-five had been signed by early 1965) are distinguished by their breadth of scope and flexibility of terms. Exchange of information is not confined to income taxes, and the states have found that they can supply the IRS with a wide variety of useful data from their administrative files. This agreement forms a basis for federal-state coordinated tax administration on a mutually beneficial basis. In 1960, for example, the IRS reported receipts of $10.6 million and costs of only $50,000 from the agreements. States can expect to gain in several ways. The direct revenue gains should be substantial—in 1959 California reported a net income of over $4 million from its use of federal audit adjustments and its comparisons of federal and state income tax returns.[4] Moreover, there are prospects of improved taxpayer compliance with the law and the likelihood that, with federal technical assistance, the quality of state auditing will be greatly improved. Finally, it should be possible, particularly if federal and state income tax laws are made as nearly alike as possible, to set up joint audit procedures, with savings to both governments.

Coordinated tax administration need not be confined to federal-state fiscal relations. States can help their local governments deal with both property and nonproperty taxes; counties can assist smaller jurisdictions within their boundaries; and several adjoining units can cooperate to set up a more efficient, pooled administration of their common taxes. All of these means of increasing state-local spending powers were included in the 1966 State Legislative Program of the Advisory Commission on Intergovernmental Relations (ACIR).[5]

Coordinated Tax Bases

The use of similar, or even identical, income tax bases by federal, state, and local governments would not only facilitate joint tax administration but also reduce the time and money spent by taxpayers in meeting their fiscal obligations. In recent years the federal definition of adjusted gross income, or net income, or taxable in-

[4] Federation of Tax Administrators, *Federal-State Exchange of Tax Information* (1962), pp. 15, 19.
[5] ACIR, *1966 State Legislative Program* (October 1965), pp. 45-57.

come has been increasingly adopted as the basic figure from which the state income tax base is to be derived by a limited number of additions and subtractions.[6] If these involve only such simple alterations as the addition of interest income from state and local bonds and the subtraction of interest income from federal bonds, the taxpayer is put to little additional trouble by the existence of a state income tax. Much more burdensome, however, are separate state rules for depreciation deductions, because in most cases these would require extensive alterations in the firm's accounting records.[7]

Close conformity to federal income tax law is not without its costs. Whenever that law changes significantly, state income tax authorities either have to incorporate those changes in their own law, or if their law is set up so as to conform automatically to the federal tax base, they must decide which of the changes they wish to keep out of their own law. For example, New York State found that during the first few years of its new automatically conforming state income tax, approved by its voters in November 1959, it was necessary to pass more than thirty laws providing for differences between the federal tax base and its own.[8]

A second potential problem is that it may be more difficult for state authorities to predict the revenues that will be yielded by a coordinated tax system than by an independent, and more structurally stable, state income tax. Should this be so, an evaluation of coordinated tax policy should take account of the extra costs of state revenue projections which must be credited against the administrative and compliance cost savings. Finally, state legislators may be reluc-

[6] In 1964 fifteen states were making use of the federal individual income tax base in this way: Alaska, Colorado, Hawaii, Idaho, Indiana, Iowa, Kentucky, Minnesota, Montana, New Jersey, New Mexico, New York, North Dakota, Vermont, and West Virginia. Sixteen were using the federal corporate income tax base. In addition, California achieves a considerable degree of conformity by having its own separate income tax law but keeping its provisions similar to, or identical with, the corresponding provisions of the federal law. See ACIR, *Tax Overlapping in the United States, 1964*, pp. 121, 142, and *Federal-State Coordination of Personal Income Taxes* (October 1965), pp. 167ff.

[7] For two detailed comparisons of federal and state definitions of individual and corporate taxable income see *Federal-State Coordination of Personal Income Taxes*, and *State Taxation of Interstate Commerce*, H. Rept. 1480, 88 Cong. 2 sess., Vol. I, pp. 255-80.

[8] California Legislature, Assembly Interim Committee on Revenue and Taxation, *Conformity of State Personal Income Tax Laws to Federal Personal Income Tax Laws*, A Major Tax Study, Pt. 3 (September 1964), p. 11.

tant to make state income taxes conform closely with the federal tax base for fear that statutory reductions will be made in the latter from time to time, thereby presenting them with the politically painful task of raising state tax rates in order to maintain revenues. How serious a problem this will be depends upon the future strength of the forces that have worked to erode the federal individual income tax base. Predictions of this sort are always hazardous, but Joseph A. Pechman, an astute observer, declared of the Revenue Act of 1964, "[It] can be said to have finally halted the erosion of the individual income tax base which had been characteristic of almost every major tax law enacted since 1913 and to have reversed it to a small extent."[9]

To a considerable degree, then, federal-state coordination of income tax bases imposes additional burdens on state legislators and removes them from state tax administrators and state taxpayers. Nevertheless, it seems clear that state legislators have become increasingly well-disposed toward tax base coordination;[10] and the experience with it gained by such pioneering states as Alaska, Montana, New Mexico, and New York, all of which have adopted federal taxable income on a prospective basis, should enable others to judge more realistically the benefits and costs resulting from specific moves toward greater conformity.[11]

[9] "Individual Income Tax Provisions of the Revenue Act of 1964," *Journal of Finance,* Vol. 20 (May 1965), p. 259. The 1964 Act actually made a small reduction in taxable income as defined in the Internal Revenue Code (less than 4/10% for tax returns filed in 1962, *ibid.,* p. 258), but Pechman's conclusion rests on the argument that adoption of the minimum standard deduction represents not an erosion of the tax base but an increase in personal exemptions and that elimination of the dividend credit, which had no impact on taxable income, should be regarded as a strengthening of the federal tax base. Both of these points seem well taken.

[10] The four states adopting individual income taxes since World War II— Alaska in 1949, New Jersey and West Virginia in 1961, and Indiana in 1963—all based their laws explicitly on the federal IRC, and Wisconsin recently completed a major tax revision designed to achieve greater conformity. See ACIR, *Federal-State Coordination of Personal Income Taxes,* Chapter 7. It should be noted that the New Jersey tax is a very restricted levy that applies only to New York residents who derive income from New Jersey sources.

[11] From its detailed study of the problem the California Assembly's Interim Committee on Revenue and Taxation concluded that there should be a presumption in favor of the adoption of some coordination method but that more information was needed about its likely impact on the ability of the state to predict and control its own income tax revenues. See their *Conformity of State Personal Income Tax Laws to Federal Personal Income Tax Laws,* p. 8.

Municipal income taxes, which provide one of the solutions to the metropolitan fiscal problems discussed in Chapter V, can also be closely coordinated with the federal or, in income-tax states, the state tax base. That such integration is still the exception rather than the rule in this country appears to be largely an historical accident. The first city income tax, that enacted by Philadelphia in 1938, had to be restricted, because of state legal requirements, to wages and salaries and to the profits of sole proprietors and partners; and subsequent municipal income taxes levied in Ohio, Kentucky, and Missouri were all patterned on the Philadelphia model.

In 1962, however, Detroit broke away from this tradition by assessing all of the income of its residents. The Detroit tax was closely tied to the federal definition of adjusted gross income, and in mid-1964 this feature was made general throughout the state by a law requiring all city taxes to be based on the Uniform City Income Tax Ordinance specified in the legislation. Michigan municipal income taxes, therefore, should involve relatively few taxpayer compliance costs, and city officials should find it relatively easy to work out joint administrative procedures with the Internal Revenue Service. Whether the Michigan levies, or any other kind of local income tax, can be developed into productive revenue sources, however, is likely to depend upon how well intergovernmental competition for business and for wealthy taxpayers is controlled. Various ways of doing so are discussed in Chapter V.

Tax Supplements

The ultimate in coordinated tax bases is provided by tax supplements. This device, which is an important part of local finance in Scandinavian countries,[12] has several attractive features:

1. The enacting government, say at the local level, uses the tax base defined by some higher level of government (state or federal), but applies its own rates to that base. The municipality, therefore, remains free to vary its tax receipts each year in accordance with its financial needs.

[12] Harold M. Groves, "New Sources of Light on Intergovernmental Fiscal Relations," *National Tax Journal*, Vol. 5 (September 1952), pp. 234-38, and Harvard Law School, International Program in Taxation, *Taxation in Sweden* (Little, Brown, 1959), pp. 519*ff*.

2. The local tax is collected by the higher level of government, along with its own tax, and the local proceeds are then returned to their source. Municipalities, therefore, need not have their own separate administrative staffs but will simply pay for the services provided to them by the collecting government.

3. Taxpayers fill out only one tax form, and in some cases they will probably be unaware that they are paying two different taxes.

Tax supplements have been most successfully used in this country to integrate state and local sales taxes. Pioneered by Mississippi in 1950, the arrangement is now (1964) generally available in six states—California, Illinois, Mississippi, New Mexico, Tennessee, and Utah. In California both counties and cities can attach a 1 percent supplement to the state tax base, but counties must allow a credit for whatever taxes are imposed by cities within their boundaries. Though this arrangement does favor cities,[13] counties have some bargaining power because their refusal to enter the uniform state sales tax system precludes the cities' enjoying its administrative advantages. In 1963-64 all of the cities in populous Los Angeles, Orange, and San Diego Counties used the maximum rate of 1 percent, but more than two hundred other cities in the state used lower rates.[14]

Similar jurisdictional problems would occur for local supplements to state individual income taxes, though it does not appear that their solution would involve significant administrative complexities. State taxpayers are ordinarily required to itemize their income by type and to report both their place of residence and their place of business. For those living in one municipality and working in another, therefore, it should be a simple matter for the state, in return for an appropriate fee from local governments, to allocate each person's income according to an agreed-upon formula, to

[13] In 1962-63, for example, California cities, though they had less than 70 percent of the population, received 84 percent of the total sales tax revenue returned to local jurisdictions. It should be stressed that both percentages exclude the combined City and County of San Francisco. See California Legislature, Assembly Interim Committee on Revenue and Taxation, *Financing Local Government in California,* A Major Tax Study, Pt. 6 (December 1964), pp. 69-77.

[14] California State Board of Equalization, *Annual Report 1963-64,* pp. A-46—A-49.

apply to each portion the relevant local tax rates, and then to return the net proceeds to the appropriate governments. The problems involved in designing such allocation formulas are discussed later.

Another difficulty with income tax supplements is the lack of a rational and equitable base to which to attach them. There is no need at this point to discuss the well-known deficiencies of federal tax law[15] (which, as noted earlier, has had an important influence on state statutes) or to speculate about the probabilities of their removal in the near future. In the meantime, most state and local governments will probably wish to continue to make their own alterations in the federal definition of taxable income. Their task in doing so, however, is far from simple. Each departure from the federal base must be evaluated by comparing the increased complexity it generates with the gains in interpersonal equity and in state economic performance it is likely to produce. Though recent technical studies of these matters do provide helpful guidance,[16] much research remains to be done. As it progresses, the Advisory Commission on Intergovernmental Relations might well make the results available to state and local officials in the form of periodic analyses of specific issues concerning intergovernmental conformity in the definition of taxable income.[17]

The highest degree of federal-state income tax coordination, attained by Alaska between 1949 and 1964 and by West Virginia between 1961 and 1964, is achieved by making each person's state tax a flat percentage of his federal income tax liability. Though this is a simple way of incorporating federal tax rate progression into state law, it has the disadvantage of making state income tax revenues highly sensitive to federal tax policy. While the Revenue Act of 1964, for example, maintained the federal tax base virtually unchanged, it reduced federal tax liabilities in that year by nearly $10

[15] See, on this point, Richard Goode, *The Individual Income Tax* (Brookings Institution, 1964), Joseph A. Pechman, "Erosion of the Individual Income Tax," *National Tax Journal,* Vol. 10 (March 1957), pp. 1-25, and the papers by Pechman and William F. Hellmuth in U. S. Congress, House Committee on Ways and Means, *Tax Revision Compendium,* Vol. I (1959), pp. 251-316.

[16] See, for example, Richard Goode, *op. cit.,* and the already-cited California Assembly's *Conformity of State Personal Income Tax Laws to Federal Personal Income Tax Laws.*

[17] A modest beginning has already been made in its publication on *Federal-State Coordination of Personal Income Taxes,* Chapter 7.

billion,[18] thereby creating serious revenue deficiencies in Alaska and West Virginia and helping to induce their shift to conformity on the basis of federal taxable income, rather than federal tax liabilities.

In summary, then, tax supplements appear to be a promising coordination device whose chief use so far in this country has been to integrate state and local sales taxes. Similar linkages between state and local individual income taxes also seem feasible, and may stimulate further diversification of property-dominated local tax systems. Though constitutional and other impediments make supplements to the federal income tax less likely, virtually the same effects can be achieved by the use of the various means of coordinating tax bases discussed in the preceding section.

Tax Deductions

The distinguishing characteristic of the coordinating devices so far considered is the great freedom they give each level of government to act independently. The freedom to act, however, is also the freedom to miss important opportunities. If intergovernmental competition is, as many believe, a major constraint on the taxing powers of some state and local governments (see Chapter I), their citizens, if given the choice, might well prefer a little less fiscal freedom and a few more high-priority public services. Three different ways in which the federal government can help in this regard, all involving tax coordination, are discussed in this and the following two sections.

By allowing the deduction of state and local income, property, gasoline, and general sales taxes under its own individual income tax, the federal government mitigates the impact on taxpayers of any increases in those four taxes, and thereby presumably strengthens the fiscal powers of state and local governments. The loss of freedom in this case is all at the federal level—in effect, the Treasury agrees to pay part of any state or local tax increases in the four selected areas. Professional evaluations of this situation differ widely,[19] but in general one can say that the deductibility of gaso-

[18] This was 19 percent of the 1964 liabilities that would have been incurred under the 1954 Code. See Pechman in *Journal of Finance, op. cit.,* p. 259.

[19] Compare, for example, the papers by Harvey Brazer and Walter W. Heller in *Tax Revision Compendium,* Vol. I, pp. 407-18 and 419-33; Goode, *op. cit.,* p. 178; James A. Maxwell, *Tax Credits and Intergovernmental Fiscal Relations*

line taxes has the least support and the deductibility of income taxes the most.

The important question here is to what extent deductibility reduces opposition to state and local tax increases, either from taxpayers resisting additional tax burdens or legislators fearful of a loss of business to lower-tax areas. Although there is little or no concrete evidence in this area, three propositions and the policy guidelines they provide are worth considering.

The first proposition is that, other things being equal, taxpayers oppose benefit levies, such as gasoline taxes earmarked for highways, less than other kinds of taxes; federal deductibility, therefore is less important for benefit taxes. The argument here is that taxpayers see in ordinary tax rate increases only, or mainly, the additional burden to themselves. The more informed among them, however, will recognize the mitigating effects of federal deductibility. For benefit levies, on the other hand, the taxpayer and voter considers mainly the value of government services financed by the tax. Federal deductibility is a minor part of the whole picture.

The second proposition is that awareness of, and sensitivity to, federal provisions for deducting state and local taxes is greater among high-income than among low-income taxpayers. This should be true not only because the tax value of deductions increases with income but also because high-income taxpayers typically itemize their deductions, whereas low-income taxpayers typically do not.[20] In addition, tax consciousness in general probably increases with income level. A recent study of this question for high-income taxpayers in this country found that whereas 35 percent of the total income of the subgroup with adjusted gross incomes between $10,000 and $30,000 was received by those who were unaware of their marginal tax rates, only 15 percent of the income of those receiving over $30,000 went to people who were unaware of their marginal rates.[21]

(Brookings Institution, 1962), p. 105; and William Vickrey, *Agenda for Progressive Taxation* (Ronald, 1947), pp. 93-100.

[20] In 1960, for example, 75 percent of taxpayers with adjusted gross incomes between $2,000 and $3,000 took the standard deduction, but the percentage dropped to 29 percent between $10,000 and $25,000 and to well below 10 percent above $25,000. See Goode, *op. cit.,* p. 182.

[21] Bruce L. Gensemer, Jane A. Lean, and William B. Neenan, "Awareness of Marginal Income Tax Rates Among High-Income Taxpayers," *National Tax Journal,* Vol. 18 (September 1965), p. 263.

The third proposition is that uncertainty as to the burdens to be imposed by a given tax increase tends to blunt both opposition to the tax change and the offsetting effects of federal tax deductibility. Indirect taxes have long been felt to possess superior political appeal for this reason, though deductibility itself may well increase taxpayer awareness of sales and gasoline taxes, particularly if more and more people continue to itemize their deductions under the federal tax.[22] Even so, changes in an individual income tax that is withheld at the source are likely to make more of an impression on the average taxpayer than equal changes in a general sales tax that excludes food, rentals, and many consumer services from its base.

Taken together, these three propositions throw doubts on the revenue-stimulating powers of all existing federal deductibility rules except the one applying to state and local income taxes. Not only is the gasoline tax a benefit levy, but both gasoline and general sales taxes impose burdens that are difficult to estimate quantitatively and their significance in relation to adjusted gross income is not high for families above $10,000. The following tabulation shows the relation of personal deductions for selected types of state and local taxes to adjusted gross income on taxable individual income tax returns with itemized deductions in 1960:[23]

Percent of Adjusted Gross Income

Adjusted Gross Income Class ($000)	Real Estate Taxes	Sales Taxes	State Income Taxes	Gasoline and Other Taxes
Under 2	2.1	1.5	0.3	2.6
2– 3	2.1	1.3	0.3	2.2
3– 5	2.1	1.2	0.4	2.0
5– 10	2.4	1.2	0.6	1.6
10– 25	2.3	1.0	1.2	1.1
25– 50	1.7	0.6	2.5	0.7
50–100	1.3	0.4	3.0	0.7
100–500	1.1	0.2	3.6	0.8
500 and over	0.6	0.1	3.3	0.7

Property taxes, in contrast, are highly visible to home owners, and their amounts are seldom insignificant. Moreover, they have many of the features of a benefits-received levy especially for fam-

[22] Between 1944 and 1960 the proportion of taxpayers doing so rose from under one-fifth to nearly one-half. Goode, *op. cit.*, p. 181.
[23] Goode, *op. cit.*, p. 177.

ilies with children in the public schools. As a result, federal deductibility for property taxes may well do little to strengthen the taxing powers of residential suburbs, especially those populated mainly by young families. The sole survivors of the three tests of effectiveness are deductions for state and local income taxes. Even they, however, may fall short of what is needed. Interstate and interlocal tax differentials are reduced but not eliminated by them, and they have so far failed to induce some of the most prosperous and industrialized states (Connecticut, Illinois, Michigan, New Jersey, Ohio, and Pennsylvania) to enact their own income taxes.[24] As a result, over one-third of the U.S. population is still free of state income taxation from its home states. For many observers who regard this as unfortunate the tax credit represents a promising reform measure.

Tax Credits

Tax credits are a highly flexible fiscal device that can be used either to prevent excessive taxation of the same base by competing jurisdictions at the same level of government (to be discussed in a later section) or to strengthen the revenue bases of state and local governments. In their basic form, credits simply allow the deduction of one tax from another; but restrictions, which can be defined in terms of either of the two taxes involved, are frequently used to limit the amount of tax offsetting that can take place. The available formulas may be classified as follows:

1.   *Proportional tax credits.* Here the taxpayer would be allowed to deduct x percent of his state tax against his federal tax liability.

2.   *Graduated tax credits.* These would divide state tax liabilities into brackets and allow the deduction of differing portions of each: for example, x percent of the first $100, y percent of the second $100, and z percent of the remainder. Regressive credits $(x > y > z)$ include flat-sum allowances as a special case, and progressive credits $(x < y < z)$ are similar in their distributional effects to tax deductions.

3.   *Unlimited credits subject to a proportional ceiling.* Here

[24] Local income taxes do, however, flourish in three of these states. ACIR, *Tax Overlapping in the United States* (1964), pp. 134-38.

the taxpayer would be allowed to deduct all of his state tax but only up to x percent of his total federal tax liability.

4. *Unlimited credits subject to a graduated ceiling.* An example is the proposal made by Walter W. Heller in 1959 that state income taxes be made fully deductible from the federal individual income tax up to 20 percent of the first $200 of liability, 10 percent of the next $300, and 1 percent of the remainder.[25]

There is no need at this point to discuss both the two existing federal tax credits (those in the death tax and unemployment insurance fields) and the type most frequently urged for future adoption (a corporate and individual income tax credit). Since detailed analyses of the former are already available,[26] we shall use the latter to illustrate the principal strengths and weaknesses of tax credits in general.

Before a federal income tax credit can be evaluated, its effects on state and local revenues must be predicted. The diversity of state attitudes to, and use of, income taxes is so great that this is no easy task. If the credit were of the unlimited variety (subject to a ceiling), it would clearly provide a strong, and probably irresistible, incentive to all states without income taxes to adopt them since they could do so, up to the amount of the ceiling, without cost to their own taxpayers. Some states, it is true, might hold back on the grounds that a progressive income tax is an iniquitous levy that ought not to be admitted to the state treasury and, if admitted, would inevitably grow beyond the limits of the federal credit ceiling. The price of these fears, however, would be high, and even constitutional restrictions might crumble in the face of public pressures on the legislature to enact a state income tax, at least designed to absorb the full federal credit.[27] Maxwell estimated that in 1958 nearly half of a 7 percent federal income tax credit would have accrued to the nineteen states then lacking an individual income tax.[28]

[25] *Op. cit.,* p. 425.

[26] Labovitz and Ecker-Racz, *op. cit.,* pp. 157-69; Maxwell, *op. cit.,* pp. 19-65; and ACIR, *Coordination of State and Federal Inheritance, Estate, and Gift Taxes* (January 1961).

[27] If the federal credit ceiling were a flat x percent of federal liabilities, such a "pick-up" tax would duplicate the federal tax in every respect except that its bracket rates would be x percent of the federal marginal rates.

[28] The amount was $1.1 billion out of a total credit of $2.4 billion. *Op. cit.,* p. 73.

At the other end of the spectrum would be the states already levying income taxes greater than the credit ceiling.[29] Their taxpayers would enjoy an immediate tax benefit, and it would be up to the states to divert part, or all, of these gains to themselves by raising tax rates. How successfully they would be able to do this, and what state taxes would be affected, is difficult to predict. These problems could be avoided by combining the tax credit with a revenue-maintenance requirement. In order to qualify states would then have to restructure their income taxes so as to raise their revenues from them by the full amount of the federal credit.[30]

Such a credit, then, could bring important financial aid to state and local governments. Supporters also stress the opportunity it would provide for improving tax coordination by requiring, say, that eligible state income taxes be similar in structure to the federal levy, that residents and nonresidents and multistate corporations be taxed in uniform ways, and so forth. These would be important gains, though they are probably attainable in other ways as well. Compared to straight federal tax reduction, a proportional income tax credit would not only induce a greater increase in state and local revenues, but it would probably also keep the nation's tax system more progressive. The reason is that when states are left free to choose their own tax increases, they can be expected to expand sales and property taxes more than income taxes. Of course, opinions differ as to the desirability of this state policy. A tax credit would also complicate federal policymaking, though not seriously. Future changes in the income tax would simply have to be evaluated in terms of their effects, through the credit, on state tax revenues and the credit then changed to achieve the results desired.

The most serious criticism of tax credits is that they are not well adapted to solving two of the most important fiscal problems of a federal system—unequal state and local fiscal capacities and the existence of state and local expenditure programs with significant spillover effects. Maxwell's calculations, for example, show that both proposals—a flat 7 percent ceiling credit and a graduated Heller-type credit—are positively correlated with state per capita

[29] Eighteen such states in fiscal 1959 levied income taxes of $1.4 billion, compared to their maximum credit of $0.8 billion. *Ibid.*, p. 76.
[30] *Ibid.*, pp. 77-81.

incomes, though the Heller credits are somewhat more favorable to the poorer states.[31]

Unlike functional grants, tax credits leave the recipient free to spend the proceeds as he wishes; therefore, they would probably be devoted to programs of local, rather than regional or national, interest. Nevertheless, adoption of a proportional federal tax credit has much appeal to those who believe that state use of individual income taxes has been unduly hampered by fears of interstate tax competition and by the heavy reliance placed on the tax by the federal government. A fractional credit, they argue, would help overcome these obstacles and would shift state tax systems toward greater equity and built-in sensitivity to economic growth. The Advisory Commission on Intergovernmental Relations, for example, recently recommended that Congress amend the Internal Revenue Code so as to give taxpayers the choice of continuing to itemize and to deduct their income tax payments to state and local governments or of claiming a "substantial percentage of such payments as a credit against their Federal income tax liability."[32]

Centralized Tax Administration

Though tax credits are frequently criticized for being unduly coercive, they actually leave receiving governments a great deal of fiscal freedom.[33] Strong-minded states may refuse to partake of a federal credit—witness Nevada in the death tax field. Even those who do partake fully remain completely free to expand their revenues beyond the ceiling amounts subject to credit. That the federal death tax credit has not set up an artificial barrier to tax increases is indicated by the fact that in recent years state death taxes have averaged 2.8 times the amount of the credit.[34] Such tax freedoms, however, are not without their costs. Duplicate tax administrations

---

[31] The correlation coefficients for 1958 were + .865 for the 7 percent credit and + .586 for the Heller credits. *Ibid.*, p. 89.

[32] *Federal-State Coordination of Personal Income Taxes* (October 1965), p. 19.

[33] This is not to deny that a very generous ceiling-type credit, applied to a federal tax that had already been pushed to, or near, its revenue limit, would in effect freeze states into enjoyment of the revenues from that tax. Tax credits, however, need not be carried to such extremes.

[34] ACIR, *Coordination of State and Federal Inheritance, Estate, and Gift Taxes*, p. 49.

are necessary, and without close coordination they can be highly wasteful of resources or taxpayer equities. Worse still, if interstate competition is serious, the freedom to raise one's own tax rates may be an empty privilege indeed.

It is in situations of this sort that centralized tax administration has its greatest appeal. The tax in question is imposed and administered by only one level of government, say the federal, and the net revenue or a portion of it is then returned to the various jurisdictions, say the states, from which it came. In essence, the states contract to have one of their taxes administered for them at that level of government where it can be done most efficiently.[35] At the same time, tax rates are made uniform throughout the country and the dangers of interstate tax competition are avoided. While the arrangement may be both productive and efficient, it does reduce the flexibility of state tax systems. To alter their receipts from the centrally administered tax, states must first agree among themselves as to what should be done and then have the desired changes made by the federal government.

An interesting proposal for centralized administration of cigarette taxes which involves both taxpayers and the federal government has recently been made by the Advisory Commission on Intergovernmental Relations.[36] Imposed independently by the federal government and 49 states,[37] cigarette taxes yielded $3.2 billion in fiscal 1963, 63 percent going to the federal government, 36 percent to the states, and 1 percent to local jurisdictions. While the federal tax is collected from the few manufacturers at a very low cost—less than one-thirtieth of one percent of the revenue yield—the state taxes are collected from a large number of jobbers, wholesalers, and retailers at an average cost of 5 percent of revenue.[38] Clearly, there should be much to gain from improved administration of state

[35] Some writers refer to this arrangement as a type of tax sharing. However, centralized administration seems a more precise description, since the tax revenues are returned to their source, and the term "tax sharing" will be reserved for plans, to be discussed in Chapter IV, which take the proceeds of some taxes and distribute them to state or local governments on a basis other than source.

[36] ACIR, *State-Federal Overlapping in Cigarette Taxes* (September 1964).

[37] Includes the District of Columbia. North Carolina and Oregon were the two nontaxing states.

[38] For an analysis of these costs see ACIR, *State-Federal Overlapping in Cigarette Taxes,* pp. 32-50.

and local cigarette taxes.

After examining all of the standard coordination devices and finding them lacking, largely because of the wide diversity in cigarette tax rates among the states,[39] the Commission concluded that the most promising solution would be to dispense with the use of stamps and have each manufacturer add to his invoice the amount of tax imposed by the state to which the shipment was to go.[40] If both expert assistance from the Internal Revenue Service and cooperation from tobacco manufacturers were available, the states could save an estimated sum of at least $30 million a year by adopting the plan.

Centralized administration of existing state taxes is not likely unless the taxes are relatively uniform from one state to another. In its report on death tax coordination, for example, the Advisory Commission regarded such an arrangement as a desirable long-term objective, but they recognized that the states would first have to eliminate most of the many idiosyncrasies that now characterize their inheritance and estate taxes. To this end, the Commission recommended that any future liberalization of the federal death tax credit be applied only to state taxes of the estate type, preferably modeled on the federal law.[41]

Another set of taxes for which centralized administration is very attractive, at least in principle, are state and local levies on corporate profits. These taxes are characterized by important inefficiencies and inequities, but their conversion into a single, nationwide tax

[39] *Ibid.*, pp. 17-31.

[40] Reshipments out of that state would then be subject to tax adjustments made by the reshipper, under the supervision of state tax administrations. For further details see *ibid.*, pp. 53-62.

[41] ACIR, *Coordination of State and Federal Inheritance, Estate, and Gift Taxes,* pp. 10-24. Since states currently draw a significant amount of revenue from estates too small to be subject to federal taxes, some broadening of the federal base would presumably be necessary. Comprehensive reform of the federal tax, designed to improve both horizontal and vertical equity, has long had wide support among tax experts. In the process, the revenue-producing powers of the federal tax could be significantly increased and a large part of the gains returned to the states. Bowen's estimates for 1953, when federal-state death taxes yielded only $1.1 billion, indicated potential yields ranging from $2 to $9 billion a year, and in recent years actual yields have exceeded $2.5 billion. See John C. Bowen, "Some Yield Estimates for Transfer Taxes," *National Tax Journal,* Vol. 12 (March 1959), pp. 54-68.

that is returned to the jurisdiction of source would involve two major difficulties. The first would be to define a practicable and equitable allocation formula. Net value added by corporate enterprises might be considered for this purpose, on the argument that income is created wherever the productive activity of the corporation takes place, but only rough estimates of its geographical distribution are currently available.[42] To serve as tax allocators these estimates would need to be refined and their computation placed on an annual, or some other regular, basis.[43] Alternatively, a federally collected corporate income tax might be returned to the states whose residents actually bear the burdens of the levy. Here, of course, the problem would be to obtain a consensus on the extent to which corporate tax incidence falls on consumers, on workers, or on shareholders. Since economists are far from agreed on this question, whatever allocation formula was adopted would be a highly arbitrary one.

The second major problem would be to induce all corporate-income-tax states to give up their own levies in return for an appropriate share of the federal corporate tax. Exactly what portion of the latter would have to be distributed so that no state lost as a result of the interchange would, of course, depend upon the specific allocation formula that was chosen. Table II-2 shows the solution that would have resulted in 1959-61 from the use of a formula allocating 50 percent of the federal corporate income tax to the states on the basis of retail sales and 50 percent on the basis of the dividends received by their residents, thereby allowing for an approximately equal split of the total incidence between consumers and shareholders. In the case of North Carolina a distribution of at least 15.4 percent of federal tax collections would have been required to leave the state's fiscal position unaltered (neglecting whatever saving in administrative costs the state might enjoy as a result of the change). At the level of administrative budget receipts from corporate income taxes projected for fiscal 1966 ($27.6 bil-

---

[42] For a brief discussion of some of the problems involved see ACIR, *Measures of State and Local Fiscal Capacity and Tax Effort* (October 1962), pp. 23-25.

[43] Unless reallocations were made at least as frequently as every five years, significant interstate discriminations would probably develop, because the centrally administered part of the federal corporate income tax would tend to favor static and declining states at the expense of those growing more rapidly.

TABLE II-2. Corporation Income Taxes: State Collections as a Percentage of Federal Collections,[a] Averages for 1959–61

Under 5 percent		5 to 10 percent		10 to 15 percent		15 percent and over	
Alabama	4.7	Arkansas	9.3	Alaska	12.6	North	
Arizona	4.6	Colorado	7.3	California	11.3	Carolina	15.4
Delaware	4.0	Connecticut	6.6	Hawaii	10.8		
Iowa	1.5	District of		Minnesota	10.1		
Kansas	4.4	Columbia	6.4	Mississippi	14.0		
Massachusetts[b]	4.1	Georgia	8.3	Oregon	12.3		
Missouri	2.1	Idaho	9.9	Pennsylvania	10.0		
New Jersey	3.1	Kentucky	9.4	South			
New Mexico[c]	3.2	Louisiana	7.8	Carolina	14.2		
North Dakota	3.3	Maryland	5.7	Wisconsin	13.1		
Vermont	4.9	Montana	6.2				
		New York	8.9				
		Oklahoma	7.1				
		Rhode Island	7.7				
		Tennessee	8.2				
		Utah	8.0				
		Virginia	8.3				
Number of States	11		16		9		1

Source: ACIR, *Tax Overlapping in the United States,* 1964, p. 146.
[a] Allocated among the different states in the manner discussed in the text.
[b] State collections do not include corporation excise taxes and surtaxes measured in part by net income and in part by corporate excess, which are classified as licenses.
[c] Since state income tax collections include both the individual and the corporate tax, the computation is based on federal and state collections from both taxes.

lion), such a distribution would require a return of $4.25 billion to the states and would generate large windfall gains in the states shown in the first column of Table II-2, to say nothing of the thirteen that have no taxes at all on corporate income.

These last difficulties could be avoided if a completely new tax were added to the U. S. fiscal system at the federal level, part of its proceeds being retained in Washington and part being returned to the states on the basis of some source-oriented allocation formula. Probably the most discussed candidate in recent years has been a federal tax on the net value added by all business enterprises.[44] Whether such a levy has enough broad support to bring about its

[44] See, for example, House Committee on Ways and Means, *Excise Tax Compendium* (1964), pp. 89-107; Tax Institute of America, *Alternatives to Present Federal Taxes* (Princeton University Press, 1964); and Tax Foundation, Inc., *Federal Non-Income Taxes: an Examination of Selected Revenue Sources* (1965).

enactment in the near future is a moot question. Should that happen, however, the occasion would provide an excellent opportunity for a strengthening of state-local fiscal resources by means of centralized tax administration.[45]

Horizontal Tax Overlapping

In few areas of taxation does the gap between appearance and reality—between the laws as written and the taxes as administered—seem as broad as it is for the state taxation of interstate business income. An intensive, three-year study of the problem, just completed by a special subcommittee of the House Committee on the Judiciary, concluded, among other things, that

> In broad terms the demands of the States upon interstate businesses are largely disregarded. For the unusually scrupulous, the very naive, or the simply unlucky, the legal rules may describe the system; for the great mass of interstate companies, practice bears little relationship to the law . . . it is . . . a system in which the States are reaching farther and farther to impose smaller and smaller liabilities on more and more companies. It is . . . a system which calls upon tax administrators to enforce the unenforceable, and the taxpayer to comply with the uncompliable.[46]

Similar problems plague other taxes and complicate the fiscal interrelationships of local, as well as state, governments. Three aspects of the complex situation, selected for their importance and for the light they throw on other areas, are discussed briefly in the remainder of this section.

Mobile Taxpayers

The metropolitan taxpayer who lives in one jurisdiction and works in another is a familiar figure in the modern world. How should the conflicting claims on his income from the government of

[45] Sharing of a federal value-added tax would, of course, encounter the same difficulties in developing an allocation formula as were discussed above in connection with the federal corporate profits tax.

[46] *State Taxation of Interstate Commerce*, H. Rept. 1480, by the Special Subcommittee on State Taxation of Interstate Commerce of the House Committee on the Judiciary, 88 Cong. 2 sess. (1964), Vol. I, pp. 596, 598.

residence and the government of employment be resolved? To answer, the economist refers to the "benefits-received" theory of taxation, but it must be admitted that no precise solution can be obtained from it. There are, it is true, a number of government programs, such as water supply systems or public parks, that generate only private benefits which can be allocated more or less accurately to specific individuals. However, if services of this type are financed, as the benefits-received doctrine says they should be, by user charges, fees, and prices, they will give rise to no allocation problems among local governments. Our concern, instead, is with the much larger group of public programs which produce major social benefits that cannot be allocated to specific persons. These are public services in the technical sense of the word, and we can say that their benefits accrue, as a whole, to each individual within the jurisdiction of the government that provides them. Satisfactory as this proposition may be for the person who never moves outside of a single jurisdiction, it is not very helpful in identifying the benefits enjoyed by a person who does move. These benefits are clearly some function of the benefits generated by the different governments with which he has some contact. But what is the form of that function?

One relevant consideration, presumably, is the amount of time that the income receiver and his family spend in each jurisdiction. On this basis, let me suggest a simple two-part rule for dividing his taxable income among competing governments:

1. Exclude all governments with which he has only minimal contact—for example, the place where he spends his vacation or where his wife does some of her shopping.
2. Allocate the right to tax his income among the remaining governments in rough proportion to the time spent working and living in each.

In practice, this rule should restrict consideration to two governmental units, those of residence and employment; of these two, the former should normally have the greater claim. Most city workers probably spend more time in their home suburbs than in the city, and this should be even more true for other members of their families.

A second relevant consideration is the structure of local government expenditures. Among these, education ranks supreme, and this fact, too, favors the claim of the government of residence. While public schools, as will be discussed in detail in Chapter III, do create social benefits which accrue to the taxpayer both where he works and where he lives, the private benefits enjoyed by him and his family will normally be provided only by the government of residence. Finally, attention should be given to the interjurisdictional incidence and yield patterns of other local taxes. This means, for example, that the adoption of a local sales tax or the exclusion of business plant and equipment from the property tax may alter the basis on which local income taxes should be allocated among competing metropolitan governments. Specific solutions to this problem are discussed later in Chapter V.

Similar jurisdictional problems apply to state individual income taxes, most of which allow a credit for income taxes paid to a nonresident state, some a credit for taxes paid to a state of residence, some both, and some neither.[47] Not only do the credits for taxes paid to states of nonresidence frequently depend upon the nature of the reciprocity arrangements worked out with these states, but state definitions of "residence" often conflict with one another. As a result, mobile taxpayers can find their incomes subject to taxation in more than one state. Some consistent and uniform solution to these overlapping problems is clearly desirable. As already noted, it could be one of the valuable by-products of enacting a federal income tax credit.

Interstate Sales

The inequitable over- or under-taxation of interstate sales is widely regarded as the most important problem created by state sales and use taxes. Two general principles of tax policy which assign interstate sales either to the state of destination or to the state of origin can be used in solving these problems, though neither is entirely satisfactory.

The destination principle rests squarely on the standard consumer-burden theory of sales tax incidence. According to this theory, prices will be higher in a sales-tax state (by the amount of the

[47] ACIR, *Tax Overlapping in the United States, 1964,* p. 128.

sales tax) than they will be in an income-tax state, the two states being similar in all other respects. From this it follows that the sales-tax state must exempt its exports to keep them from being at a competitive disadvantage in the income-tax state, and tax its imports to prevent them from entering at a competitive advantage over local products. To do this effectively, as the Fiscal and Financial (Neumark) Committee of the European Economic Community noted with regret,[48] requires fiscal frontiers at which all interstate shipments can be intercepted and controlled. Fortunately these frontiers are lacking in this country, so states have combined their sales taxes with use taxes. They have tried to collect use taxes either directly from consumers, with little success except for a few products, or indirectly from out-of-state vendors, also with limited success so far. Though the Supreme Court has helped[49] and serious attempts at enforcement have been made, a considerable amount of undertaxation presumably remains. At the same time, the failure of some states to allow credits for sales taxes paid elsewhere and the use by others of rules that discriminate against out-of-state sellers create some important instances of overtaxation.

Various solutions to these problems, all based on the destination principle, have been proposed. John F. Due, for example, has suggested the following five-point program for federal action:

1. legislation requiring each state to allow a credit for sales taxes paid to the state of delivery, except for motor vehicles, which would be taxable only by the state of initial registration;

2. legislation regulating the interstate sales of one business firm to another so that the tax on them is payable by the purchaser to the state of destination whenever that firm is also registered there as a seller of taxable goods or services;[50]

3. legislation requiring out-of-state sellers to register and to

[48] Commerce Clearing House, Inc., *Tax Harmonization in the Common Market* (1963), pp. 78-83.

[49] Notably by sustaining the right of a state to require out-of-state vendors, with no permanent local establishment but with local independent sales representatives, to collect and remit state use taxes. *Scripto, Inc. v. Carson*, 362 U.S. 207 (1960).

[50] At present such sales may be taxable or not depending upon the use to which the purchaser puts the goods in question. To require the out-of-state seller to inquire into these matters in order to remit the correct amount of sales tax to the state of the purchaser clearly places excess burdens on the interstate seller.

pay sales tax to the state of destination whenever they have property or employees in that state, make regular deliveries of goods into it, or solicit business there either by the use of salesmen or agents or by the use of catalogues or direct-mail advertising;

4. legislation requiring any nonregistered out-of-state seller shipping goods from a sales-tax state to pay tax either to that state or to the state of destination;[51]

5. legislation requiring any nonregistered out-of-state seller shipping goods from a non-sales-tax state either to pay the tax of the state of destination or to pay a tax based on a "model" sales tax law to the federal government which would then remit the net proceeds to the states of destination.[52] Another set of proposals, involving a somewhat more radical departure from existing practice, have recently been made by the House Judiciary (Willis) Subcommittee and are discussed in Chapter VI.[53]

Under the origin principle a retail sales tax would be levied on all goods and services sold to final consumers by businesses operating within the taxing state, regardless of the location of those final consumers. In addition, there would be no use taxes, since imports would already have been taxed in the state of origin. Unless it were widely adopted on a uniform basis, such a system of sales taxation would encounter two major difficulties. The first would be the concern of businessmen operating in high-tax states about unfair competition from untaxed imports and about their own ability to export goods and services to low-tax regions.[54] The second problem would

[51] In the absence of such a mandatory option, the sales would presumably go untaxed; in its presence, the tax would probably go to the state of origin, because of the closer connection between the seller and that state, except where the state of destination had the lower tax rate.

[52] For further discussion of these proposals see John F. Due, "Sales Taxation and the Willis Subcommittee Report," *Illinois Business Review*, Vol. 23 (January 1966), pp. 6-8. See also his "State Taxation of Interstate Commerce—Sales and Use Taxes," *Canadian Tax Journal* (November-December 1965), pp. 519-25.

[53] See pp. 236-38. For the analysis and recommendations of the Willis Subcommittee see *State Taxation of Interstate Commerce*, H. Rept. 565, 89 Cong. 1 sess., Vol. 3 (June 30, 1965), pp. 603-895, and H. Rept. 952, 89 Cong. 1 sess., Vol. 4 (Sept. 2, 1965), pp. 1136-37 and 1177-89, respectively.

[54] These producer worries stem, somewhat paradoxically, from the consumer-burden theory of sales tax incidence. If it could be shown that a state sales tax tended to raise retail prices no more than, say, an equal-yield state individual income tax, there would be no need for sales-tax-paying businessmen to worry about low-priced imports from income-tax states, and exporters from sales-tax

be the strong incentive provided to exporters who had been selling directly to out-of-state consumers to do so through intermediate distributors in a no-tax state, since this change would eliminate retail sales tax liabilities in their home state. Both of these problems become less and less important, however, as the use of an origin-oriented, single-stage sales tax is extended geographically. In the limit, if all states used the same tax rate, the problems would disappear, and there would be a uniform, nationwide retail sales tax which avoided the difficulties states now have in enforcing their use taxes.[55] In the absence of such a general tax—and that appears to be the prospect in this country for some time to come—the destination principle is likely to remain dominant, and further improvements in state sales and use taxes are likely to come, perhaps as a direct result of the projected 1966 Congressional hearings on the subject, from the reforms recommended by the House Judiciary Subcommittee, John Due, and other experts.

Interstate Business Income

The multistate corporation has apparently been the source of a good many multistate tax headaches. In their efforts to tax its income, states have had great trouble answering two fundamental questions. When should a business be taxable in a given state; and if it is taxable, what should be that state's fair share of the corporation's total interstate income?

The first question has to do with nexus, or state tax jurisdiction, about which—as the inquiries of the Special Subcommittee on State Taxation of Interstate Commerce amply demonstrated—there is little agreement among the states, either in practice or in principle.[56] At one end of the spectrum is the maintenance of a factory or retail store, which is universally considered sufficient to create taxability; in the middle is the maintenance of a stock of raw

---

states would tend to enjoy lower input prices than their competitors elsewhere. The extent to which state sales taxes push down factor prices rather than raise product prices, however, is a much debated question among the experts, and until the factor-burden theory of incidence achieves a broader acceptance than it now has, the difficulties mentioned in the text will probably persist.

[55] Enactment of such a tax system would presumably require Congressional action to remove any constitutional barriers imposed by the interstate commerce clause.

[56] H. Rept. 1480, Vol. I, pp. 141-52.

materials or of investment property, about which there is disagreement. Placed at the other end by explicit Congressional action in PL 86-272 (73 Stat. 555 [1959]) is the mere solicitation of orders either by the corporation's own employees or by independent contractors—activities which do not create taxability as long as the orders are approved and filled from outside the state. Despite wide diversity among independently determined administrative practices, however, a broad consensus on a uniform nexus formula is not unobtainable, since many of the differences may be far from fundamental. To satisfy the usual canons of taxation, such a formula should be clear and definite, should entail administrative and compliance costs that are a low percentage of revenues produced, and should be legally enforceable by the states. In addition, it should be integrated with the division-of-income rules to be discussed below so that multistate business income is not assigned to states lacking effective power to tax it.[57]

Multistate business income can be divided up among the prospective claimants by separate accounting, by specific allocation, or by formula apportionment. Separate accounting involves the cracking apart of a single corporate enterprise for tax purposes and may be illustrated by a corporation that has two separate divisions, one in each of two states. If each buys its inputs and sells its output independently of the other, tax officials might be tempted to treat the two divisions as if they were separate enterprises, particularly if the officials belong to the state with the more profitable of the two divisions. Economists, however, object to this procedure because it ignores important economies of scale—in management, advertising, and fund raising—that the two divisions could not realize if they did operate separately. Nevertheless, state tax officials may find it difficult to view a diversified corporation stressing decentralized management in the same way as a corporation engaged in one integrated set of operations and may be willing, therefore, to incur some additional administrative costs in order to treat the two types differently.[58]

[57] *Ibid.*, pp. 485-516.
[58] For a discussion of the problems involved see Arthur B. Barber, "State Income Tax Uniformity Concerning Taxable Units," *National Tax Journal,* Vol. 16 (December 1963), pp. 354-64; and George T. Altman and Frank M. Keesling, *Allocation of Income in State Taxation,* 2nd ed. (Commerce Clearing House, Inc., 1950).

A second distinction that is frequently attempted is that between a multistate corporation's mainstream income, which cannot
be claimed exclusively by any one state, and various kinds of sub-
sidiary income, which can.[59] An example would be a headquarters
building in New York City in which most of the space was rented
out to other businesses. New York (city or state or both) might then
claim the sole right to tax that rental income.[60] This procedure,
known as specific income allocation, involves the greatest difficulty
when applied to intangible assets. Dividend and interest income, for
example, has traditionally been allocated to the state of residence of
the recipient, but claims to residence may be entered by both the
state in which the business is incorporated and any state that views
itself as the corporation's commercial domicile. Nor is it easy to
measure net dividend or interest income since, in obtaining it, the
corporation may incur costs that are difficult to segregate from its
other expenses. One may seriously question whether the gains from
specific income allocation are worth the costs involved.

The basic problem of dividing up multistate business income is
encountered in the unitary, or mainstream, income of an integrated
interstate corporation. It is generally agreed that this income must
be apportioned by formula, but there is great controversy as to
the components of that formula. Current practice for manufacturing corporations favors a three-factor formula based on property,
payroll, and sales,[61] but many experts have been highly critical of
including sales.[62] As the Special Subcommittee put it, "Of all the

[59] In 1963 only six of the thirty-eight income tax states did not provide for
such specific income allocation. H. Rept. 1480, Vol. I, p. 118.

[60] Other states, of course, might seek to combine the rental income with the
corporation's other income which would be then apportioned by formula among
all the states in which the corporation carried out business operations. For a
detailed description of state practice in this area see *ibid.*, pp. 197-232, and for
an analysis of the problem see Arthur B. Barber, "'Nonapportionable Income'
Under a Uniform State Net Income Tax Law Imposed by Congress," *National
Tax Journal*, Vol. 16 (June 1963), pp. 147-58.

[61] This formula was used in 1963 by 26 of the 38 states then taxing corporate
net income. H. Rept. 1480, Vol. I, p. 119.

[62] Arthur B. Barber, "A Suggested Shot at a Gordian Knot of Income Appor-
tionment," *National Tax Journal*, Vol. 13 (September 1960), pp. 243-51; Charles
E. Ratliff, Jr., *Interstate Apportionment of Business Income for State Income
Tax Purposes* (University of North Carolina Press, 1962); and Paul Studenski,
"The Need for Federal Curbs on State Taxes on Interstate Commerce: An
Economist's Viewpoint," 46 *Virginia Law Review* 1121 (1960).

steps involved in the process of dividing income for tax purposes, the attribution of sales presents more problems than any other."[63]

The most popular procedure, which has become increasingly so in recent years, is to allocate sales on a destination basis, to the state of the consumer.[64] Unfortunately, this appears to be the most troublesome of all the available standards. The reason is that it greatly expands the number of companies that are, potentially at least, subject to income taxation in more than one state. In the Special Subcommittee's sample of interstate companies, for example, 66 percent of the manufacturing and 74 percent of the mercantile companies had places of business in only one state.[65] Under a rule that allocated sales by origin rather than destination (as well as under an income-apportionment formula based only on property and payroll), most of these companies would be taxable in one state only. The saving to them in compliance costs could be substantial.[66]

A second criticism of the destination sales factor is that it allocates income to many states that lack sufficient nexus, or jurisdictional connection, to tax it. While in some cases a throwback rule is used to reallocate the income in question to the state of origin,[67] in others interstate corporations simply go undertaxed, compared to other companies with like amounts of income. Among thirteen undertaxed multistate companies studied by the Special Subcommittee, two were taxed on less than half their incomes and the rest on percentages varying from 98½ to 52½.[68] Undertaxation, of course,

[63] H. Rept. 1480, Vol. I, p. 181.

[64] Such a market-oriented sales factor was used in 1963 by 24 states, compared to only 10 in 1955. The next most popular rule, which assigned sales according to the location of the office through which the sales transaction was made, was used by 18 states in 1955 and only 12 in 1963. *Ibid.*, p. 122.

[65] *Ibid.*, pp. 77-78.

[66] As would be expected, most of the one-state-place-of-business companies were small in size, and the Special Subcommittee's studies showed that income allocation by means of a sales factor was particularly burdensome to such companies. These compliance burdens would be substantially lessened, however, if sales below a certain minimum annual amount—the Subcommittee used $100,000 in its studies—were allocated to the state of origin rather than of destination. *Ibid.*, pp. 508-13, 526.

[67] In 1963 ten of the states using a destination sales factor in their apportionment formulas had also a throwback rule, typically requiring that sales be assigned to the state of origin if the corporation was not taxable in the state of destination. *Ibid.*, p. 243.

[68] *Ibid.*, p. 395.

is by no means a fortuitous phenomenon. States adopting a destination sales factor have frequently done so mainly to attract new business by offering it a "favorable tax climate."[69] It seems unlikely, therefore, that the states will give up these market-oriented sales factors voluntarily. If they do not, corporate income taxation will remain an unreliable source of additional state and local revenue or a major overhaul of jurisdictional and apportionment rules will be necessary.

Some experts believe that such an overhaul would involve the complete elimination of the sales factor from income apportionment formulas. Logically, they argue, income should be apportioned according to the location of the land, labor, and capital goods that produce it. According to this test, sales would be entitled to consideration only to the extent that the company's own labor and property were involved in the transactions; otherwise the value added in selling should be attributed to other businesses and their incomes taxed accordingly. To some, then, logic calls for a two-factor income apportionment formula based on tangible property and payrolls, and they also note that practical considerations reinforce their choice. Not only would nexus problems be greatly simplified, but administrative and compliance costs would be reduced as well.[70]

The problem, of course, is to persuade the nonindustrial states that a production-oriented apportionment formula would not unduly compromise their interests. To this end the Special Subcommittee undertook a detailed quantitative comparison of the revenue effects of the three leading types of formulas—property and payrolls only; property, payrolls, and a destination sales factor; and property, payrolls, and an origin sales factor. Their conclusion was that the revenue importance of the choice of formula is not great now and can be expected to become even less in the future. Nevertheless some states would lose,[71] and compromises would be needed to sell

[69] *Ibid.*, pp. 122-27.

[70] *Ibid.*, pp. 521-63.

[71] The Subcommittee's calculations showed that by shifting from their present tax laws to one of the Subcommittee's three apportionment formulas ten states would lose .5 percent or more of their total tax revenues. Four of them had above-average per capita personal income in 1963 (Alaska, District of Columbia, Massachusetts, and New York), three were close to the average (Colorado, Oregon, and Pennsylvania), and three were below average (Georgia, Iowa, and Montana). *Ibid.*, pp. 554-57.

them the two-factor formula as a uniform income apportionment standard.

The logic behind the payroll-property formula, however, is not as unassailable as its supporters like to claim. The importance of demand is recognized only insofar as it is created by advertising and other selling activities on the part of business. If, in the spirit of Alfred Marshall's famous example involving the two blades of a pair of scissors,[72] aggregate demand and supply are equally important in the creation of value, sales surely deserve more attention than they receive in the two-factor formula.

The situation calls for a pragmatic solution that would pay considerable attention to existing practice and would sacrifice some elements of the ideal solution—whatever that may be—to obtain an early agreement by the states on uniform jurisdictional and income-allocation rules. The range of possibilities is, of course, large, but the following broad rules seem worthy of special consideration:

1.   Make the right to tax corporate profits depend upon either some physical presence in the state—for example, property or payroll—or the completion of some above-minimum amount of sales there—perhaps $100,000 a year as suggested by the Judiciary Subcommittee.

2.   Use a uniformly defined, three-factor, destination-sales apportionment formula.

3.   Either exclude any sales made in states that lack taxing jurisdiction from the denominators of the income allocation formulas of other states or provide for the recapture of those sales by the states of origin.

4.   Include all other sales in the income-apportionment formulas. Specifically, a state with below-minimum sales but with jurisdiction to tax because of the location in it of property or payroll would include those sales in the numerator of its apportionment formulas, and above-minimum sales made in nontaxing states would be included in the denominators of the formulas used by all taxing states.

[72] "Thus again we see that demand and supply exert coordinate influences on wages; neither has a claim to predominance, any more than has either blade of a pair of scissors, or either pier of an arch." Alfred Marshall, *Principles of Economics,* 8th ed. (London: Macmillan, 1938), p. 532.

Once uniform rules of this or some other sort have been adopted, it should be possible to promote greater efficiency by establishing some central agency to collect state profits taxes from all interstate corporations, remit the proceeds—minus administrative costs —to the proper jurisdictions, and handle disputes between taxpayer and tax collector. The operations of such an agency would be greatly simplified if some uniform definition of taxable income were also adopted at the time it was established. The potential gains from such a solution to the taxing problems states now have with corporate income seem well worth the effort needed to develop the necessary uniform rules. Early action seems preferable to a lengthy and perhaps fruitless search for some ideal solution on which all could agree.

CHAPTER III

Functional Grants-in-Aid

IN BROADENING THEIR HORIZONS far beyond the local community, modern producers and consumers have greatly complicated the fiscal problems of state and local governments. Previous chapters have concentrated on the political and economic risks faced by legislators who seek to raise state and local tax rates and the difficulties governments have had in treating overlapping tax bases equitably. Other problems, of special concern to large metropolitan areas, will be dealt with in Chapter V. Here the discussion turns to an important source of relief for harried state and local officials—one that, paradoxically, was created by the same forces that have seriously weakened state and local taxing powers. In the modern world some of the most important local governmental programs generate benefits that accrue to people living in other parts of the country. These spillovers, unless offset by forces to be discussed later, justify federal aid in the form of functional, matching grants to state and local governments, as well as state aid of the same kind to cities and counties.

These aid programs are discussed in seven main parts. The first deals with the external public benefits that provide the basic rationale for intergovernment action. Though our knowledge of these spillovers is limited, recent economic research has greatly clarified their role in the field of education, the single most important kind of state and local activity. Education is accordingly used as an example to identify the factors that must be considered by intergovernmental policy makers and to illustrate the importance and probable geographical scope of the external benefits that result. The conclusion is that external benefits, which will probably continue to grow in importance, are already pervasive enough to support a strong prima facie case for federal and state functional grants to lower levels of government.

The nature of this case for functional grants is examined in the second part of the chapter. Decision-making at the local governmental level, it is shown, will be influenced not only by the presence of benefit spillouts but also by any benefit spillins or cost spillouts that are related to the program under consideration. Satisfactory choices, therefore, are likely to result only if all of these spillovers are absent or if, being present, they are so well balanced that their opposing effects simply cancel out. In the absence of these rather special circumstances, intergovernmental grants are required both to improve the allocation of resources and to achieve interpersonal equity. The ideal kind of grant for this purpose is described in the third section to provide a basis for the subsequent discussion of existing federal grant-in-aid programs. The major criticisms of these programs are then presented and analyzed in the next two sections. Then the wide variety of functions the grant-in-aid programs perform is described, with particular reference to the existence or nonexistence of benefit spillovers. The final section of the chapter stresses the important role that states play as intermediaries for intergovernmental grants and presents a broad statistical picture of the aid they extend to their own local governments.

External Benefits of State and Local Spending Programs

Economists normally distinguish two kinds of benefits that arise from government spending programs: those which flow directly to specific individuals, called private benefits, and those which accrue broadly to the society as a whole, called social benefits. Both of these become external whenever they are enjoyed by persons outside of the government jurisdiction that generated them. When this happens local voters, lacking any financial contribution from outside beneficiaries, are likely to undersupport the programs in question, thereby impairing economic performance by distorting the allocation of resources. The external benefits of state and local expenditures, therefore, should be important elements in any set of policies designed to achieve fiscal equity and efficiency in a federal system.

Public education took 38 percent of state and local general governmental expenditures of $69.3 billion in 1963-64. Education, of course, produces important benefits not only to the individual student and his family throughout his life, but also to many other people who are associated with him in production or consumption or who are simply members of the same economic and political system. It is only the benefits to other people that concern us here, and among them only the ones that accrue outside the school district or state in which the education was received.

Such external educational benefits occur for three reasons. The first is that some of the most important of all educational benefits accrue broadly to everyone in the country. Take the long-recognized relationship between a well-functioning democratic political system and the educational attainments of its citizens. That this relation is a close and important one is generally agreed, and recent empirical research confirms this belief. Voter participation and education are positively related, sometimes to a striking degree. Among males aged less than 34 years and not living in the South, for example, only 60 percent of those with a grade school education voted in the 1952 and 1956 presidential elections, compared to 78 percent of those with a high school, and 88 percent of those with a college, education.[1] More comprehensive measures of citizen participation in political activities, based on work done for political organizations, financial contributions to campaigns, attendance at meetings and so forth, show similar results. Meriting a top rating on these tests were 20 percent of grade school graduates, 30 percent of high school graduates, and 45 percent of college graduates.[2] These mea-

[1] In the South, where restrictions on voting obscure the relationship in which we are interested, comparable figures were 19 percent for grade school, 55 percent for high school, and 81 percent for college educations. See Angus Campbell, Warren Miller, Philip Converse, and Donald Stokes, *The American Voter* (Wiley, 1960), p. 495.

[2] V. O. Key, Jr., *Public Opinion and American Democracy* (Knopf, 1961), pp. 331 and 564-65.

sures, of course, deal only with the quantitative dimension of political action, but we may assume that quality also increases with educational level.

Nor is political participation the only social benefit to be considered. For many people, variety and change, the excitement of new discoveries, the satisfactions from meeting new challenges and from accomplishing undreamed-of things are all part of the good life; and the good life, in this sense, is much more likely to be found in an educated, and particularly a well-educated, society. In general, the more a society is geared to technological advancement and economic growth, the more universal is its need for minimum levels of public education. Those who lack training in the mechanics of learning are often unable to adapt to new conditions of work, and by failing to keep up, these people impede the attainment of the goals society has set for itself. Needless to say, no part of this first class of external educational benefits lends itself to quantitative measurement. It is no less important for that reason, however.

A second group of educational benefits is private in nature, but these accrue to outsiders—people who associate in one way or another with the person who is educated. Knowledge and skills tend to rub off onto fellow workers, and employers can often accomplish more when they are dealing with a trained and literate labor force.[3] Education also has a pervasive effect on the flavor of community life. Families with few, or no, children may support the schools partly to secure a quieter and more responsible neighborhood in which to live and partly in the hope that the cultural and artistic life of the whole community will thereby be improved. One of the attractions of the big city, surely, is the escape it offers from the stultifying atmosphere created by limited intellectual attainments. In the past, there have been so few highly educated and talented people that only the largest cities could contain enough of them to make a difference in community life. In the future, however, more and more of the smaller cities and towns should be able to achieve comparably high cultural and intellectual standards. Education, therefore, may represent an important, long-run solution to the problem of urban congestion (see Chapter V). Finally, we must

[3] Werner Z. Hirsch, Elbert W. Segelhorst, and Morton J. Marcus, *Spillover of Public Education Costs and Benefits,* Institute of Government and Public Affairs, University of California (1964), pp. 335-41.

note the important effect of education on governmental expenditures for police and fire protection and for health and welfare services of all kinds. By spending money now to develop a man's talents and interests so that he can support his family and lead a satisfactory life, society can avoid the future costs that are imposed on it by ineffectual and frustrated people.

Benefits of this second kind, which are attached to the educated person himself, become external, in the geographic sense, whenever that person moves away from the area in which he received his schooling. Migration, then, is the force that creates these spillovers, and there is no need to stress its importance in the postwar U. S. economy. About one-fifth of the nation's population moves each year, and though many of these moves are within the area served by particular local governmental units, a large portion of them undoubtedly are not. The Council of Economic Advisers noted in its last report that ". . . nearly 6.5 million people move across State lines every year,"[4] and a recent study of migration patterns in Clayton, Missouri, a suburb of St. Louis, showed the following results:

Area	Percent of Migrants Moving to Clayton from Area	Percent of Migrants Moving from Clayton to Area
Rest of St. Louis County	$49\frac{1}{2}$	58
Metropolitan St. Louis	18	8
Rest of Missouri	5	$3\frac{1}{2}$
Rest of U. S.	$24\frac{1}{2}$	$28\frac{1}{2}$
Rest of World	3	2

On the basis of these and other data the author of the study concluded: "Mobility of the United States population is such that the vast majority of financial returns from public elementary and secondary schooling are generally realized outside the school districts which provided the child's education."[5] Many of the educational benefits that are external to the student and his family, therefore, will also be external to the government that educated him.

The third and final kind of external educational benefit results from overlapping units of government. Consider a group of people who, having received a certain amount of additional education,

[4] *Economic Report of the President* (January 1966), p. 95.
[5] Burton A. Weisbrod, *External Benefits of Public Education* (Industrial Relations Section, Princeton University, 1964), p. 62.

produce during their lifetimes more goods and services and earn higher personal incomes than they otherwise would have. These additional incomes, so long as they are at least equal to the value of the additional goods and services, will, in the absence of government intervention, enable the educated group to purchase for their own use all of the additional output that they create. Modern methods of taxation, however, divert some of the extra buying power to all three levels of government and, through them, redistribute it to other people in all parts of the country. Whether this redistribution takes the form of lower tax rates or higher levels of governmental services or lower terms of credit because the government competes less vigorously for loans is immaterial for the present study. What does matter is that some of the additional output created by education flows, as a result of governmental operations, into the hands of people who live outside the governmental unit of the educated group. The benefits they receive may consequently be classified as external educational benefits.[6]

Education, then, is one state and local government program that generates large amounts of external benefits and disseminates them broadly throughout the entire country. Other public programs have similar benefits though their importance is sometimes more open to question and their scope is often confined to one region. While this study need not undertake a comprehensive analysis of all of these benefits, there are specific questions that, in my opinion, should be asked about any functional grant-in-aid program that purports to serve the national interest.

The questions are three in number.

1. Does the program generate external benefits of at least one of the three types discussed in the case of education?

2. Exactly what is the nature of the benefits? Research by economic and political scientists has now reached the point where policy makers can demand more than vague generalities in support of a given activity. They can expect to be told in what specific ways a program operated in one area is likely to benefit

[6] This conclusion rests on the assumption, which appears reasonable, that better educated people do not counterbalance the extra taxes they pay by additional demands for government services whose benefits accrue entirely to themselves. Additional demands for public goods that generate only social benefits will, of course, benefit others as well as themselves. *Ibid.,* p. 70.

other areas—by expanding possibilities of production, by raising consumption and living standards, or by improving the operation of the political system.

3. How important are the benefits? Answering this question requires a combination of rough quantitative measurements and subjective political judgments. All external effects of the kinds discussed earlier should be evaluated on their merits, but many others can be excluded—the purely pecuniary spillovers that merely change the values of existing resources and alter the distribution of a given amount of national income. These distributional effects are ordinarily too insignificant and too thinly spread to be worth including in the evaluation of specific public programs.[7]

These three questions are the basis of the evaluation of existing federal grant-in-aid programs given in later sections. As a background for that discussion, Table III-1 presents a classification of a selected group of government services according to the scope and importance of their external benefits. In the local category are placed programs with few spillovers beyond the jurisdiction of the operating government; the intermediate category contains programs that tend to spread significant benefits over an entire region, such as a metropolitan area or a river valley; and the third class includes activities that appear to have sufficient interstate spillovers to qualify them for federal grant assistance.

Several features of the classification, which is admittedly a highly personal one, deserve specific comment at this point.[8]

1. Few, if any, local public services leave outsiders completely unaffected. Poor fire protection along the boundary of one governmental unit may impose extra costs on its neighbors, and good public libraries will attract readers from a whole region and provide educational services of general public significance. The benefits of police protection are probably localized, but in the mobile and technical economy of today they can be realized only with the help of state and federal law enforcement programs.

[7] See Roland N. McKean, *Efficiency in Government Through Systems Analysis* (Wiley, 1958), pp. 134-50.

[8] The division of programs between the local and intermediate classes will be discussed more fully in Chapter V.

TABLE III-1. Classification of Selected Government Services by the Geographical Scope of Their Benefits

1. Local[a]	Fire Protection
	Police Protection
	Parks and Recreation
	Public Libraries
	Water Distribution
	City Streets
2. Intermediate[b]	Air and Water Pollution
	Water Supply
	Parks and Recreation
	Public Libraries
	Sewage and Refuse Disposal
	Mass Transit
	Arterial Streets and Intercity Highways
	Airports
	Urban Planning and Renewal
3. Federal[c]	Education
	Parks and Recreation
	Aid to Low-Income Groups
	Communicable Disease Control
	Research

[a] Services with few important benefit spillovers beyond the local level of government.
[b] Services with significant spillovers beyond the local level but not beyond the regional level.
[c] Services with significant spillovers beyond the regional level.

2. Parks and recreational facilities are difficult to classify because, depending on their nature, they may serve only residents of the immediate neighborhood or they may attract users from much wider areas. The second type of facility need not pose serious financial problems as long as user charges are feasible. Whenever such collections are administratively impracticable, however, free benefits will flow to people living in other local jurisdictions or even in other states. Effective programming probably will require various kinds of cooperative intergovernmental planning and financing arrangements. These may involve all municipalities in a given urban area or all state and local governments in a given interstate river basin, and in each case federal stimulus and aid may be needed as a catalyst.

3. That the benefits of a reduction in air pollution typically overlap local and metropolitan boundaries, and often state lines as well, needs no demonstration. On the other hand, there do not appear to be any spillovers to other parts of the country. It is true

that manufacturers of smog-control devices may find their in-come-earning powers enhanced, and automobile makers may find their profits reduced, but these are pecuniary spillovers and should be excluded from consideration.

4. The justification for placing education in the federal cat-egory has already been given. If included there, it would also carry with it an important group of complementary services, in-cluding health care, public housing, and other types of assistance for low-income families with children, as well as the preschool care and training of disadvantaged children. In the absence of these programs, public education could not realize its full poten-tial, and many of its external benefits would consequently never materialize.

5. Probably the most controversial entry in the table is the placement of intercity highways, the single most important feder-al grant-in-aid program, in the intermediate class. Whether high-speed highways should be there or in the federal class is a moot question. The Advisory Commission on Intergovernmental Rela-tions, for example, attributes "large indirect social benefits" to urban transportation though it does not identify them,[9] but J. M. Buchanan concludes that the spillover effects of interstate high-ways are relatively insignificant.[10] While non-users certainly benefit from the highway system in their own part of the country, many of these benefits come to them through commercial trans-actions—that is, better transportation facilities enable them to obtain a greater variety of goods or to have the same goods at lower prices. This being the case, one may wonder whether their demands would not induce highway users to induce the appropri-ate state or regional authorities to construct the desired highway facilities. When most program services can be financed by user charges and these charges are passed on to non-user beneficiaries through the market place, there should, in other words, be no need for federal intervention in the area. Not all highway benefits, of course, fall in that category. Non-users benefit from

[9] *Performance of Urban Functions: Local and Areawide* (September 1963), p. 263.

[10] "Federal Expenditure and State Functions," in *Federal Expenditure Policy for Economic Growth and Stability,* Joint Economic Committee, 85 Cong. 1 sess. (1957), p. 178.

highway services in their social relations, and an interstate highway system may contribute to the national defense. It is over the importance of these spillovers that disagreement occurs.

Economic analysis of the external benefits of state and local spending programs is still in its infancy. There is no doubt, however, that these benefits exist, and in a number of important areas they appear to be extensive enough to justify the existence of federal, functional grants-in-aid. The case that can be made in support of such grants is discussed in the next section.

Program Spillovers and Determining Local Governmental Spending

The role that benefit and cost spillovers usually play in the choice and extent of local governmental programs may be understood by considering the behavior of a rational voter and then modifying that pattern, insofar as possible, to conform with an imperfect and somewhat irrational world. By "rational voter" I do not mean one who knows all, sees all, and weighs all effects with great care. Information is not a free good; some of it is uncertain and undependable, and the decision-making process takes time and effort. Here the voter is assumed to have adapted himself to this situation by restricting his attention to those program effects that are both important and reasonably certain to occur. He is also assumed to be motivated only by those effects which bear directly on him and on the area in which he lives and works.

The problem, let us suppose, is whether or not a proposed expansion in a local government program should be approved. If there were no spillovers at all, the choice would be simple. The rational voter would compare benefits and costs and reach his decision on the basis of which side outweighed the other. If he included all important social, as well as private, benefits and costs, the choice would be optimal in the economic sense. With spillovers present, however, an optimal choice becomes considerably more difficult. While for society as a whole all incremental gains and losses should be considered,[11] local voters will ignore those which affect

[11] For purposes of this discussion international spillovers may be ignored.

outsiders only. Optimality will be threatened, therefore, whenever important external benefits and costs exist and do not cancel out each other's effects. In other words, the fact that education has significant external benefits does not necessarily mean that the program will be undersupported by rational voters, since there may be opposing effects that neutralize the distorting influence of the benefit spillovers. These offsets can be of two kinds: benefit spillins and cost spillouts.

As noted in the preceding section, some important educational benefits are shifted about the country by migration. The residents of any given area, therefore, lose to the extent that people they have helped to educate move out but gain to the extent that people who were at least as well educated elsewhere move in. A close balance, qualitative as well as quantitative, between these benefit spillouts and spillins does not, however, guarantee the proper amount of support for local education. Among the gains to be realized from better schools rational local voters will wish to include only those benefit spillins that are in fact induced by their own higher school expenditures, but they will exclude from consideration all benefit spillouts. Support for local schools will consequently be based on the proper stream of educational benefits only if the value of the induced spillins exactly equals the value of all spillouts.[12]

Of course, a superior local school system will attract residents from other parts of the same metropolitan area or even induce businesses to locate plants in one city or state rather than in another. Even so, there are good reasons to suppose that in the great majority of cases local choice will be based on an estimate of educational benefits that is too small.

1. Whereas benefit spillouts can be readily related to known population movements out of the locality in question, induced

---

[12] If B = the present value of the future benefits (from a given local project) that can be expected to remain in the district,

  B_o = the present value of project benefits that will be shifted elsewhere by migration (benefit spillouts), and

  B_i = the present value of induced benefit spillins (which will be benefit spillouts to some other locality), then

optimal choice from the national point of view would be based on the total benefit stream of the project in question, which is $B + B_o$, whereas rational choice from the local point of view would be based on $B + B_i$.

spillins can be estimated only by a quantitative analysis of human motivation. Better schools are not the only reason that people move, and moreover, higher educational spending in one community may induce higher expenditures in another, so that together they gain fewer new residents than either could have gained in isolation. Because of these uncertainties, benefit spillins may appear to many voters as a minor justification for higher school expenditures.

2. In addition to inducing some benefit spillins, a better education program is likely to increase the rate of out-migration from the community. This is because the propensity to move tends to increase with education level. The following figures illustrate the relationship:[13]

Amount of Schooling	Probability of Migrating, 1950, People Aged 25 and Over
Less than 5 years	0.036
5-8 years	0.038
12 years	0.053
16 years	0.083

These forces, of course, tend to reduce the benefits that will be considered by local voters.

3. Some educational benefits are external because they accrue automatically to outsiders and do not depend on the existence of migration. Consider, by way of example, the improvement in political decision-making at the federal level that might result from increased spending on the part of one school district in the country. Clearly, the gain would be very small indeed unless the one district's action induced similar behavior on the part of many other districts. This is hardly a likely enough possibility to sway a local voter's sympathies toward better schooling. Therefore, some important educational benefits will not be adequately considered at the local level of government.[14]

[13] Weisbrod, *op. cit.*, p. 48.

[14] Even at the state level, increased spending for higher education may appear to have only a minimal impact on federal political processes. It might, of course, have an important effect on governmental operation within the state, but only to the extent that the better educated people remain there, rather than migrating

To many readers benefit spillins and spillouts may appear too esoteric to be taken seriously as factors motivating the average voter. In response, one may cite recurring complaints about "brain drains"[15] and point to statistical studies whose results are consistent with the hypothesis that spillovers do matter. A recent multivariate analysis of 1957 per capita expenditures for police, fire, sewage, sanitation, and recreation in 478 counties with population densities over 100 per square mile, for example, revealed a statistically significant negative correlation between per capita expenditures and the number of governmental jurisdictions operating in a county.[16] These results, in the author's view, imply that benefit spillouts, which are likely to rise in importance as the number of jurisdictions per county increases, tend to keep governmental expenditures per capita lower than they otherwise would be. Similar results were obtained by Burton A. Weisbrod in his study of state-local noncapital expenditures on elementary and secondary education per student in forty-eight states in 1960.[17] Independent variables measuring each state's net out-migration and net in-migration rates between 1950 and 1958 were included, but only out-migration showed a statistically significant relation to educational expenditures, and it was in the expected negative direction. Because these estimates are based on interstate population movements rather than on those from one school district to another, they provide only a crude answer to the question asked. However, along with some other evidence cited by Weisbrod,[18] they do suggest that local attitudes toward education are influenced by benefit spillouts, that spillins are relatively unimportant, and that local support for schools will consequently be inadequate unless some other offsetting force operates. One remaining possibility is a spillout of educational costs sufficient to balance whatever net spillout of benefits is expected.

---

to other states. It may be noted that migration rates appear to be especially sensitive to the effects of higher education. Whereas the probability that a high school graduate aged 25-29 would migrate was only 0.085 in 1950, the corresponding probability for a college graduate was 0.165. *Ibid.*

[15] *Ibid.*, p. 102.

[16] Robert F. Adams, "On the Variation in the Consumption of Public Services," *Review of Economics and Statistics*, Vol. 47 (November 1965), pp. 400-05.

[17] *Op. cit.*, pp. 107-15.

[18] *Ibid.*, pp. 102-06.

In theory, a local government can, by carefully selecting the taxes it employs, shift some of the burdens of its spending programs onto outsiders. A tax on hotel and motel rooms is thought to burden the tourist and not the innkeeper, and a tax on business property is said to be paid mainly by consumers, many of whom may come from other governmental jurisdictions. Given these possibilities, it is easy to imagine situations in which local self-interest should produce at least as good public service choices as more enlightened national interests would justify. A loss of 20 percent of the benefits from increased school expenditures through out-migration, for example, would be counterbalanced by the use of a method of financing that imposed 20 percent of the total cost on outsiders.[19] The crucial questions then are: how important are these cost spillouts likely to be in specific instances, and how much influence are they likely to have on voter behavior?[20]

To answer the first question one must determine the incidence of taxation, a subject on which many learned treatises have been written. The results, I fear, are much less impressive than the analysis by which they were derived. Economists are not agreed among

[19] If we let

C = the present value of project costs
to be borne by local residents, and
C_o = the present value of project costs
to be borne by outsiders, then

making use of the symbols defined above in footnote 12, we can contrast the decision-making rules that will be dictated by national, as opposed to local, considerations. Under the socially optimum rule new projects should be undertaken if:

$$1) \quad B + B_o \geqq C + C_o.$$

Under a local self-interest rule, on the other hand, new projects would be undertaken if:

$$2) \quad B + B_i \geqq C.$$

Pursuit of local interests, therefore, would lead to optimal choices only if:

$$3) \quad B_o - B_i = C_o.$$ In the absence of this precise balancing of spillover effects local projects would be under- or over-supported according as $B_o - B_i$ exceeds or falls short of C_o.

[20] Cost spillouts from the point of view of one area are, of course, cost spillins from the point of view of another. Spillins are excluded from the analysis in the text on the argument that the inflow of costs from other jurisdictions is mainly, or entirely, independent of the spending decisions made by the local government in question. Induced cost spillins would occur only if spending or taxing decisions in one area motivated some other area to adopt taxes that would be shifted to residents of the first area.

themselves about where the burdens of property, sales, and corporate income taxes lie. Though elaborate empirical measurements of the distribution of these burdens continue to be made,[21] the findings are no less arbitrary than the assumptions about tax incidence upon which they depend.

This widespread disagreement among the experts about the location of tax burdens makes it hard to persuade local officials and voters that certain public spending projects will serve their own interests because part of the costs can be shifted elsewhere. It is possible, of course, that local taxpayers think they have greater powers to shift their burdens onto outsiders than economists believe to be the case. Given the human tendency to underplay one's benefits and to overestimate one's costs, however, the weight of taxpayer opinion is likely to be on the other side. School bond issues, for example, are frequently opposed by businessmen even though the higher property taxes they would have to pay to finance the bonds are supposed by economists to be shifted in large part to the consumer. Similarly, sales and excise taxes are seldom viewed by businessmen with the equanimity one would expect from people who simply collect the tax from the consumer and transmit it to the government.

If this assessment of taxpayer attitudes is realistic, cost spillouts are not likely to play an important role in local evaluations of new government programs. And even if, contrary to the present argument, voters are not very skeptical of the possibilities of tax shifting and do support higher local spending partly because they expect to escape some of its costs,[22] they may at the same time be less than fully rational in their evaluations of project benefits. They may underestimate benefits because, unlike costs, they are frequently intangible and spread well into the distant future.[23] The more important biases of this sort are, the more existing cost spillouts are needed to offset their distorting influence, and the less, therefore, are cost spillouts available to counteract the distorting effects of benefit spill-

[21] See, for example, Hirsch and others, *Spillover of Public Education Costs and Benefits, op. cit.*

[22] It should also be noted that whenever a government uses more than one kind of tax to finance its activities, it is impossible to tell which tax pays for what projects.

[23] See, for example, Anthony Downs, "Why the Government Budget is Too Small in a Democracy," *World Politics*, Vol. 12 (July 1960), p. 541.

outs. That job, it would appear, is best left for federal and state functional grants-in-aid.

Optimizing Grants

Intergovernmental grants designed to minimize the distorting effect of benefit spillouts on the level of state and local spending should have four main qualities. First, they should be categorical or conditional—that is, restricted to state and local programs that do have significant external benefits. Within that group, the size of the grant should increase with the importance of the external benefits of a program. Second, they should be matching grants with both the grantor and the grantee governments sharing in the cost of the supported programs. In principle the grantor's share of program costs should equal the ratio of external benefits to total benefits, but in practice problems of measurement compel the use of only a rough approximation to the ideal. Nevertheless, some reasonable distinctions between programs, and between states under a given program, should be possible. The spillout of benefits from state and local educational programs, for example, is presumably greater for low-income than for high-income areas, since the former typically have the higher rates of out-migration. Such a situation calls for variable matching grants, the grantor government paying a higher share of program costs in the lower-income states and localities. Moreover, rates of return on additional educational expenditures are likely to be higher in low-income areas where, even with above-average tax effort, it is difficult to match the program levels reached by more affluent states.[24] If such a combination of above-average returns on additional schooling and above-average levels of

[24] Weisbrod, for example, found the rate of return on schooling to be higher in the South than elsewhere (*op. cit.,* p. 134). There is also evidence that the productivity of the earlier stages of education exceeds the productivity of later stages. Thus W. Lee Hansen ("Total and Private Rates of Return to Investment in Schooling," *Journal of Political Economy,* Vol. 71 (April 1963), pp. 134-35) estimated the internal rates of return to total resource investment in schooling for U.S. males in 1949 to be 15.0 percent for elementary school, 11.4 percent for high school, and 10.2 percent for college. These computations, moreover, take no account of the value to the student completing a given level of education of the option he thereby acquires to obtain still more education (see Weisbrod, *op. cit.,* pp. 138-43). Inclusion of these values would raise all three rates of return and increase the differences among them.

tax effort is thought to justify above-average financial support from higher levels of government, optimizing grants could readily be designed to take both factors into account.[25]

The remaining two characteristics of optimizing grants are more controversial. The third is that the grantor government, since it is paying for benefits received, is entitled to ask that its funds be used efficiently and to exercise some controls over the grantee's operation of all supported programs. The difficulty, of course, is to specify the kinds of controls that are justifiable and to assess the risk that the grantor will wish to push the controls beyond their limits, once the program has been initiated. These problems about which opinions differ widely, are discussed in the next section.

The fourth and final distinguishing characteristic of optimizing grants is that they should be open- rather than closed-end—that is, the grantor should agree to share whatever program costs the grantee wishes to incur and not limit its support to some fixed amount each year. This is desirable because as programs are expanded, external benefits presumably continue as long as internal benefits continue, though not necessarily in some constant relation to each other. If that relation were correctly reflected in the matching requirements of the grant program, self-interest should keep the grantee from overexpanding its activities, since with each program expansion it would continue to pay the full cost of its own benefits.[26] Difficulties of measurement being what they are, however, governments making open-ended grants can be expected to insist on some program controls, and indeed, the danger of excessive interference from above is presumably greater with open-end than with closed-

[25] Specific methods of doing so are discussed in Chapter IV. For closed-end federal grants, for example, the funds allocated each year to states could vary inversely with per capita personal income and directly with measures of relative tax effort. Variable matching could also be used to make state contributions vary inversely with per capita incomes.

[26] An implicit assumption throughout the discussion in the text has been that for each grant-supported program internal (local or state) benefits are significantly greater than external (state or federal) benefits. Should the reverse relation prevail in a given case, it would provide a strong reason for shifting the administration of the program either from the local to the state government or from the state to the federal government. If this rule were always followed, of course, internal benefits would, by definition, always be more important than external benefits.

end grants. It is appropriate, therefore, that the discussion in the next section deal with an existing federal program of the open-end type. Fortunately, a recent study by the Advisory Commission on Intergovernmental Relations provides some highly germane evidence.[27]

The Problem of Controls

> "What makes me tear my hair in frustration is when you say there are no controls," Mr. Goodell said. "Mr. Goodell, you call it controls, I call it objectives," Mr. Celebrezze replied quietly.—*New York Times* (Saturday, January 23, 1965), p. 9.

This exchange of views between Representative Charles E. Goodell of New York and Anthony J. Celebrezze, Secretary of Health, Education, and Welfare (HEW), illustrates nicely the disagreement that is possible when two people look at the same federal grant program with different theories in mind about the basic role of intergovernmental grants. If the sole purpose is to reduce existing inequalities in the fiscal abilities of different states to support their own programs (see Chapter IV), federal controls are not called for, and to adopt them is to imply, as Mr. Goodell remarked,[28] that the states are not to be trusted to know their own best interests.

The situation is quite the contrary with optimizing grants, however. Since the public benefits to be paid for in this case accrue jointly to the citizens of two different levels of government, the responsibility for the effective operation of the programs should also be shared jointly. Partnership arrangements, to be sure, are not always easy for the participants to live with, but the point is that the modern world is increasingly calling for exactly that kind of approach to the operation of some of the most important governmental activities. With persistence and good will, the difficulties should be surmountable, and the states can, in any case, simply withdraw from any federal grant-in-aid program that they feel interferes unduly with their own freedom to act. If the needs for fiscal equaliza-

---

[27] *Statutory and Administrative Controls Associated With Federal Grants for Public Assistance* (May 1964).

[28] The occasion for his remarks was congressional consideration of President Johnson's 1965 Message on Education.

tion are taken care of by other means, as they should be, no state could plead poverty as a reason for having to accept a grant on terms it didn't like.

This is not to say that the federal government never has, and never will, interfere unduly with state and local activities. It is easy to exaggerate the dangers involved, however. As a result of its study of federal grants for public assistance, for example, the Advisory Commission concluded that "The States have had a much greater voice in shaping their public assistance programs than frequently has been assumed by critics of the Federal role."[29] Their report describes in detail the wide variation that has come to exist in state standards for eligibility and in the amounts of aid provided to each qualified recipient.[30] Table III-2 gives some of the relevant data for our selected group of states. It shows that aid to dependent children in June 1963 ranged from $9 per recipient per month in Mississippi to $47 in New Jersey and Minnesota, and that old-age assistance varied between $35 per recipient per month in Mississippi and $109 in Minnesota.[31] The proportion of aged receiving public assistance, shown in the last column of Table III-2, depends in part, of course, on income levels within each state, but it is also related, as the Commission shows, to three of the requirements that states are free to adopt or not, according to their wishes. States that place liens on the public assistance recipients' property or require recovery from their estates, states that require support of the needy aged by their children and other relatives, and states that require local governmental participation in old-age assistance costs all tend to have low recipient rates, though there are, of course, individual exceptions to this rule.[32]

Open-end grants and detailed federal controls have not, therefore, gone hand in hand in the public assistance field. The states, unfortunately, have not used their freedom to best advantage. In recent years instances of lax administration and bad management began to receive wide publicity. Congressional concern over the op-

[29] *Statutory and Administrative Controls Associated With Federal Grants for Public Assistance*, p. 27.

[30] *Ibid.*, pp. 30-59.

[31] In each case these were the maximum and minimum amounts for all fifty states.

[32] *Ibid.*, pp. 53-56.

TABLE III-2. Average Monthly Public Assistance Payment Per Recipient by Program, and Proportion of People Receiving Old-Age Assistance, Selected States, June 1963

States[a]	Average Monthly Public Assistance Payment, Per Recipient			Persons Aided per 1,000 Population Age 65 and Over
	Families with Dependent Children	Blind	Old-Age	
A. Massachusetts	$43	$137	$ 83	96
B. New York	41	105	87	31
New Jersey	47	86	96	30
Maryland	32	70	72	38
C. Indiana	28	80	76	53
Illinois	44	94	86	62
Wisconsin	44	93	101	74
D. Minnesota	47	115	109	118
Missouri	24	70	66	208
E. Florida	17	67	64	110
Mississippi	9	38	35	383
Tennessee	19	48	48	148
Virginia	24	68	61	42
F. California	44	123	107	170
Colorado	37	101	104	267
Oregon	38	92	84	79

Source: Advisory Commission on Intergovernmental Relations, *Statutory and Administrative Controls Associated with Federal Grants for Public Assistance* (May 1964), pp. 48–53.
[a] Grouped by geographical area.

eration of the program mounted, and in 1962 the Senate Committee on Appropriations directed HEW to make a systematic review of Federal Aid to Families with Dependent Children. This survey, the first to be conducted on a nationwide basis under federal direction and standards, disclosed that "a high percentage of recipients in many States received incorrect payments, and in an even larger number of instances, case records did not indicate that eligibility had ever been properly established."[33] Under these circumstances, it is not surprising that federal requirements that states participate in a system of continuous quality control were tightened. The whole episode provides a good example of the dilemma that is

[33] *Ibid.*, p. 15.

frequently faced by those responsible for federal grant programs. On the one hand, irresponsible state or local behavior virtually requires the imposition of detailed federal controls, but, on the other hand, detailed controls cannot readily be adapted to the great variety of conditions prevailing in the different states. The New York State Commissioner of Social Welfare, for example, argued strongly that the new federal quality control procedures would not accomplish their objectives in his state. He was not, however, successful in persuading HEW to accept his alternative proposals.[34]

Still another problem is that controls that were once justifiable may be continued even though the need for them steadily decreases. An example in the public assistance field is the requirement that the programs be administered by a single state agency. This rule did much to bring order out of chaos in the beginning, but now it may unduly hamper legitimate state efforts to reform their governmental organizations. The Advisory Commission cited the long and fruitless controversy between Oregon and HEW on this subject,[35] and then proceeded to recommend that federal law be changed to waive the single state agency rule whenever this did not sacrifice any of the program objectives of the Social Security Act.[36] The merits of this particular proposal need not be debated here, but it does emphasize the importance of flexibility in the administration of federal grant programs and the desirability of regular Congressional reviews of all statutory provisions that may become outdated.

The most frequent criticism of HEW by the state public assistance directors who were consulted during the course of the Advisory Commission's study dealt with what many would regard as inevitable characteristics of the modern world. Directors complained about the large amounts of paperwork required in the administration of the programs, the lengthy and complicated federal regulations, and the long and involved clearance process through which materials submitted by the states to HEW must go. Whether much can be done to ameliorate these foibles of large-scale organizations is debatable. In any case, HEW is not unaware of the problem, and it did initiate in late 1963 a project, entitled Handbook Simplification

[34] *Ibid.,* pp. 74-75.
[35] *Ibid.,* pp. 76-79.
[36] *Ibid.,* pp. 96-97.

and Clarification, which itself is likely to go through a lengthy and complicated process.

As far as federal controls are concerned, then, designers and managers of functional grant programs face a familiar problem— they cannot live without them, and they find it difficult to live with them. Similar problems have been encountered in other connections, however, and often with very happy results.

Other Criticisms of Federal Grant-in-Aid Programs

Quite apart from the difficult question of centralized controls, federal grants-in-aid have not lacked for critics. To some observers there are too many separate programs imposing excessively complex conditions and using unduly complicated allocation formulas. Others claim that the round trip taken by funds from the states to Washington and back again creates inefficiency and waste and impairs the adaptability of programs to changing conditions. Grants have been criticized for misdirecting state and local expenditures, for rigidifying state budgetary procedures, for curtailing local autonomy, for undermining state and local incentives both to spend their funds wisely and to raise enough of them from local sources, and for shifting too many public responsibilities to Washington so that political power is unduly centralized and citizens are prevented from participating actively in the choice and administration of governmental programs.

This list of complaints is probably less impressive than it appears. It does not constitute a general indictment of grants as an intergovernmental fiscal device, nor does it, for the most part, identify inherent defects which must be balanced against the benefits of individual grant programs. Take, for example, the alleged distortion of the allocation of local funds to different programs. Badly designed grants may do this, but grants that simply finance external benefits will have exactly the opposite effect. Such grants do not shift state and local responsibilities to Washington, but rather lift from local taxpayers the burden of paying for benefits they do not receive. Local funds continue to be raised for local purposes, and local incentives to tax and to spend wisely are in no way weakened. Indeed, when for one reason or another these activities are not well carried out, federal grants-in-aid provide a vehicle for effective fiscal reform. A larger proportion of federal funds may be allocated to states making an average, or above average, effort to tax themselves (see Chapter IV), and the Kestnbaum Commission's *Report* stressed the higher standards in state and local service and administration that have resulted in the past from the leadership and supervision of federal grant-in-aid agencies.[37]

It is true, of course, that federal grants do complicate the planning and administration of the aided programs. To expect complete local autonomy in the management of programs with significant external benefits, however, is to close one's eyes to the requirements of the modern economic world. It is a complicated environment in which to operate, and simple procedures, carried out in isolation, no longer yield satisfactory solutions. These remarks should not be taken to imply that federal administrative operations themselves are above suspicion. Government efficiency has to be worked at constantly, and federal grant programs are no exception to this rule. In his 1957 study of the operation of nine important grant programs, I. M. Labovitz estimated direct administrative expenses to be 1 percent of the amount of grants paid out, with individual programs ranging from one-tenth of 1 percent for public assistance to 11 to 13 percent for low-rent public housing.[38] Interpretation of these figures is difficult in the absence of measures of program output and performance—high administrative expenses may be justified by the high benefits they produce, and low expenses may disguise low productivities—but the Bureau of the Budget has undertaken detailed studies of government productivity which promise future improvements in federal operating efficiencies.[39]

The rapid postwar growth in the number of federal grant programs,[40] each with its own special features, raises obvious ques-

[37] *Message from the President of the United States Transmitting the Final Report of the Commission on Intergovernmental Relations*, H. Doc. 198, 84 Cong. 1 sess. (1955), p. 126.

[38] *Federal Expenditures Associated with the Administration of Programs of Grants-in-Aid to State and Local Governments*, Legislative Reference Service, Library of Congress (April 17, 1957). Inclusion of the prorated costs of tax collection and of the General Accounting Office raised average administrative expenses to 1.6 percent of grants paid out.

[39] U.S. Bureau of the Budget, *Measuring Productivity of Federal Government Organizations* (1964).

[40] Counting the number of different grant programs is a game in which each

tions about the need for some consolidation of separate, but related, programs and for greater uniformity among those that remain.[41] Reaching agreement on what should be done, however, has proved to be a difficult task. While the first Hoover Commission recommended in 1949 a shift to a system of broad, consolidated grants, the Kestnbaum Commission in 1955 found strong reasons for confining most grants to relatively narrow areas of activity.[42] The major difficulty, it would appear, has been the lack of a widely accepted logical basis on which to judge grant programs, and it is hoped that the theory of optimizing grants, presented earlier, can do something to fill that gap. Once the existence of external benefits from a program has been adopted as the basic economic justification for federal functional grants, it is easy to set down the broad policy guidelines that should be used. These are: (1) that no program should be established, or continued, unless the activities it supports do generate significant external benefits; and (2) that two different programs, with different allocation and fund-matching formulas, should be set up only if the benefit spillovers involved are demonstrably more important in the one area than in the other. Under this rule existing programs would be consolidated whenever their contributions to the national welfare appeared to be of the same general order of magnitude. Some applications of this test will be suggested in the next section.

The final criticism, listed at the beginning of this section, that needs to be considered is the argument that federal grants tend to rigidify state and local budgetary procedures. The danger alluded to here is that states will simply match all federal grant funds that are available without close regard to the merits of the various alternative uses to which their own funds might be put. Once again the validity of this criticism can be determined only by considering the

---

player is likely to come up with a different answer. The Advisory Commission on Intergovernmental Relations, though it excluded a number of programs included on the Treasury Department's official list, showed sixty different programs in existence in fiscal 1962, and thirty-seven of these had been enacted since World War II. See their *The Role of Equalization in Federal Grants* (January 1964), pp. 16 and 89-92. The 87th Congress set up eleven new programs, and the 88th Congress, by almost any test, was even more prolific.

[41] For a comprehensive analysis of both of these questions see Selma J. Mushkin, "Barriers to a System of Federal Grants-in-Aid," *National Tax Journal,* Vol. 13 (September 1960), pp. 193-218.

[42] *Op. cit.,* pp. 193-98.

extent to which federal grants do in fact finance internal, as well as external, program benefits. If they cover only the latter, as a set of optimizing grants would do, the price at which internal benefits can be obtained is not altered by the grants, and hence there should be no distortion of state and local budgeting. If the federal grants do finance some of the internal benefits of a given program, however, the cost at which the state or local government can obtain those gains is correspondingly lowered, and if that reduction is large enough, budgetary officials can hardly be blamed for assuming that there are no superior uses for their funds.[43]

Distortions are also likely to be minimized if categorical grants are open- rather than closed-end. With the closed-end type there is a maximum amount of federal money to be obtained, and state officials may be placed under a strong psychological compulsion to qualify for it, even though, to do so, they must divert their own funds from superior uses. Open-end grants, in contrast, set up no artificial goals, and under them there would appear to be less danger that Congress will decide to finance a larger share of total program costs than the relative importance of external benefits justifies. Having decided to limit the amount of its annual contribution, in other words, Congress may then be tempted to be lenient with regard to the matching requirements it imposes on the grantee government. Finally, there is the point, discussed earlier, that whenever marginal external benefits exist, federal contributions should not be limited by a closed-end arrangement if optimal decision-making at the state and local level is to be attained.

Functional grants, it is clear, must be designed with skill and care. The gains to be obtained from such effort, however, are great, and their importance is likely to increase in the future. In a tightly integrated society, where the effects of actions taken in one locality or state radiate widely, a premium is placed on effective fiscal cooperation among all levels of government, and federal conditional grants are an important instrument for that purpose. It is not surprising, therefore, that the postwar period has witnessed a rapid growth in their use. As a result, the country now has an important set of programs, serving a wide variety of purposes. What these

[43] If internal benefits are to be financed, in other words, there is much to be said for the use of completely unconditional grants. See the discussion of these in Chapter IV.

purposes are, how much federal money they currently require, and what specific external program benefits they seem to cover are all considered in the next section.

Federal Grants-in-Aid in 1964

In fiscal 1964 federal grants-in-aid amounted to $10 billion, a figure which was 8 percent of federal, and nearly 20 percent of state and local, cash payments to the public in that year.[44] Though a great variety of programs were included, those for highways and public assistance alone accounted for nearly two-thirds of the total. In this section an attempt is made to group the programs according to the nature and extent of the national interest they serve. This is difficult because of the intangibility of many of the external benefits in question and because of the propensity of federal grant programs to fulfill more than one purpose. The grants, therefore, must be classified according to their major function, and on this score there is certainly room for differences of opinion.

In the table which follows (based on Tables III-3 through III-8) six different groups of federal grant-in-aid expenditures in fiscal 1964 have been used: education and research, aid to low-income families, health, resource development and recreation, transportation, and functions for which the federal government itself has primary responsibility:

Program Group	Amount (Millions)
Education and Research	$ 755
Aid to Low-Income Families	3,677
Health	692
Resource Development and Recreation	326
Transportation	3,672
Primary Federal Responsibility	845
Total	$9,967

The first three of these are closely interrelated because they all contribute to the development of the nation's human resources, and

[44] The grant-in-aid total is from *The Budget of the United States Government, Fiscal Year Ending June 30, 1966,* pp. 467-71, and cash payments to the public are from the *Economic Report of the President* (January 1965), p. 261. State and local cash payments exclude federal grants-in-aid, as well as contributions for social insurance.

it is indicative of current concern over this important source of economic growth that most of the program increases projected for fiscal 1966 fall in those three areas. To highlight these prospects, figures for both fiscal 1964 and 1966 are shown in the detailed tables (III-3 through III-8); existing programs are ranked by their projected 1966 levels; and estimates for the new programs to be proposed to Congress are included at the bottom of each table.[45] Finally, as a background for the discussion in the next chapter, those programs that incorporate an equalizing factor in the formulas used to determine fund allocations and/or state matching requirements are distinguished by an (E) written immediately after the year in which they were enacted.

Education and Research

> Increased Federal support for education is vital because of the crucial role of educated talent in our free society. Each individual must have an opportunity for education to the maximum of his capabilities to fulfill his own potential and to be prepared to work in an increasingly complex economy.—*United States Budget, Fiscal 1966*, p. 123.

Until quite recently well over half of all federal grants-in-aid for education were made under a program—assistance for schools in federally affected areas—whose main purpose was not to expand educational services but rather to reimburse local governments for fiscal burdens placed on them by federal government operations.

[45] The 1967 Budget, which came out after this section was written, projects major increases over the 1966 estimates in three general areas:

1. Educational aids are to rise, mainly because of estimated grant expenditures of $1,200 million for elementary and secondary schools, $204 million for vocational education, $197 million for higher education, and $51 million for libraries.

2. Economic opportunity programs are expected to rise to $1.1 billion in 1967.

3. Grants for housing and community development are projected to rise from $688 million in 1966 to $878 million in 1967.

On the other hand, significant decreases are expected in 1967 grant expenditures for accelerated public works (only $8 million in 1967), schools in federally affected areas ($252 million in 1967), and medical assistance for the aged ($289 million in 1967).

Total federal grants-in-aid, which were $10.7 billion in 1965, are projected to rise to $14.6 billion in 1967. See *Special Analyses of the United States Budget, 1967*, pp. 134-43.

TABLE III-3. Federal Grant-in-Aid Programs for Education and Research, Actual 1964 and Estimated 1966[a]

Program	Year Enacted	Federal Expenditures	
		Actual 1964 (Millions)	Estimated 1966 (Millions)
Schools in Federally Affected Areas	1950	$323	$358
Vocational Education	1917		
	1963 (E)	41	182
Manpower Development and Training	1962	80	125
Vocational Rehabilitation	1920 (E)		
	1954	88	123
Construction of Higher Education Facilities	1963 (E)	—	109
National Defense Education Act	1958 (E)	84	104
Cooperative Agricultural Extension Work	1914	77	83
Agricultural Experiment Stations	1887		
	1963	40	51
Rural Library Services	1956 (E)	7	37
Others[b]		15	29
		———	———
Total		$755	$1,201
New Proposals:			
Elementary and Secondary Education		—	495
Manpower Development and Training		—	67
Others[c]		—	15

Source: *United States Budget, Fiscal 1966.*
[a] (E) Program incorporates equalizing factor to determine allocations and/or matching requirements for states.
[b] Land-grant colleges (1862; 1890), educational television (1962), water resources research (1964), teaching materials for the blind (1879), and special training for teachers of the handicapped (1963).
[c] Vocational rehabilitation, civil rights education, and higher education.

The 88th Congress, however, may have set the stage for an expanding federal role in this area. Called by President Johnson the "Education Congress," it inaugurated grants for the construction of higher education facilities, greatly expanded the vocational education program, and either began or increased federal support for research at agricultural experiment stations, at state institutes for the development of water resources and fisheries, and at local centers for the study of mental retardation. Table III-3 shows that these and other existing educational grants are expected to expand by nearly 60 percent between fiscal 1964 and 1966. In addition, the 89th Congress in its first session both increased federal aid to colleges and broke precedent by authorizing a three-year program of grants to school districts with large numbers of children from low-income families. The benefit spillovers of state and local schools, universities, vocational educational centers, and research institutions have clearly moved more firmly into the center of national attention.

Assistance for Low-Income Families

The Economic Opportunity Act of 1964 launched an unprecedented national effort to combat poverty in the United States. The objective of this effort is to break the vicious circle in which one generation's ignorance, disease, and poverty are transmitted to the next.—*United States Budget, Fiscal 1966,* p. 118.

Federal grant programs to aid low-income families have been established in two concentrated waves, the first in 1933-37 in response to the Great Depression and the second in 1962-64 in response to the persistence of high unemployment rates in the midst of national affluence and to the increasing demands on human capabilities of an automated and technological economy. In fiscal 1964 public welfare grants amounted to nearly $3.7 billion and were expected to increase by one-third, to $4.9 billion in 1966. It should be stressed, however, that these figures do not represent the total amount of federal grant aid going to low-income families. The Manpower Development and Training program, included earlier under Education, and several of the health programs to be considered later also make important contributions.

Federal participation in this area may be justified on ethical and humanitarian grounds—namely, that no family in any part of the country should be allowed to fall below some minimum subsistence level of income. On this basis, the programs are likely to generate more argument about what constitutes an appropriate minimum income level and what the effects on work incentives might be than about whether the federal or the state and local governments should shoulder the main responsibility. The economic justification for anti-poverty programs, on the other hand, tends to reverse the emphasis. Effective development of human abilities and incentives clearly requires expanded and integrated governmental support for education, family welfare, and health. Seen in this light, the gains

TABLE III-4. Federal Grant-in-Aid Programs in Support of Low-Income Families, Actual 1964 and Estimated 1966[a]

Program	Year Enacted	Federal Expenditures	
		Actual 1964 (Millions)	Estimated 1966 (Millions)
Public Assistance:[b]		$2,944	$3,242
Old-Age Assistance	1935 (E)	1,390	1,404
Aid to Families with Dependent Children	1935 (E)	1,011	1,126
Medical Assistance for the Aged	1960 (E)	209	351
Aid to Permanently and Totally Disabled	1950 (E)	280	329
Aid to the Blind	1935 (E)	52	52
Economic Opportunity Act	1964 (E)	—	854
Food Stamp and Donation of Surplus	1961		
Agricultural Commodities	1933	510	497
Low-Rent Public Housing	1937	183	224
Disaster Relief[c]	1950 (E)	29	84
Area Redevelopment Program	1961 (E)	11	11
Low-Rent Rural Housing	1964	—	2
Total		$3,677	$4,914
New Proposals:			
Public Assistance			114
Area Redevelopment			35

Source: *United States Budget and Budget Appendix, Fiscal 1966.*
[a] (E) Program incorporates equalizing factor to determine allocations and/or matching requirements for states.
[b] Figures for the individual programs are for obligations and do not add to the total expenditure figures given at the top of this table and included in the grand total.
[c] Includes special 1964 programs for earthquake and flood assistance to Alaska and California, respectively.

become more concrete, but their geographical distribution is less easily specified. In effect, income-support and health programs operate in conjunction with education and training programs to produce a single set of public benefits, and these are subject to the same spillover effects that were discussed earlier for education. Not all of the public welfare grants listed in Table III-4, however, contribute equally to this set of economic gains. The Economic Opportunity Act of 1964 was, of course, specifically designed for that purpose, but neither Old-Age Assistance nor Medical Assistance for the Aged adds materially to the productivity of the labor force. Those who place economic growth above income redistribution as a national goal would favor fewer federal grants for the aged and

TABLE III-5. Federal Grant-in-Aid Programs for Health, Actual 1964 and Estimated 1966[a]

Program	Year Enacted	Federal Expenditures	
		Actual 1964 (Millions)	Estimated 1966 (Millions)
School Lunch and Special Milk	1946 (E)		
	1954 (E)	$276	$300
Hospital and Medical Facilities Construction	1946 (E)	187	218
Maternal and Child Health and Welfare	1935 (E)	84	139
Community Health	various	60	97
Waste Treatment Works Construction	1956 (E)	66	80
Environmental Health	various	7	14
Others[b]		12	27
Total		$692	$875
New Proposals:			
Maternal and Child Health			25
Community Health			2

Source: *United States Budget, Fiscal 1966.*

[a] (E) Equalizing factor to determine allocations and/or matching requirements for states.

[b] Includes operating and mental health grants of the National Institutes of Health and miscellaneous grants to Indians, Alaska, and Hawaii.

more for the support of families with dependent children and for the development of work-training projects.

Health

> In 1787 Thomas Jefferson wrote that "without health there is no happiness. An attention to health, then, should take the place of every other object."—President Johnson's Special Message to Congress on the National Health Program, *New York Times,* Jan. 8, 1965.

The list of federal grants for health in Table III-5 is deceptively short, for several of the categories shown contain a number of separate programs, each with its own distinctive apportionment formula. Under Community Health, for example, fall programs for the control of tuberculosis, cancer, heart disease, venereal disease; support for health services for the chronically ill and aged; and grants to finance public health activities with the most obvious spillover benefits of all, the control of communicable diseases. Environmental health deals with such modern-day dangers as air and water pollution and radiation sickness and disease.[46] In many of these programs two different types of grant are used. "Formula grants" are allotted to the states, usually on the basis of both need and fiscal capacity, to carry out state plans that have received federal approval. "Project grants" are awarded on the basis of specific applications and are typically used to finance research, training, or demonstrations of new techniques. In several cases technical assistance by federal personnel may be substituted for the more usual cash payment, and project grants are frequently given in health fields, such as diabetes and arthritis control, for which formula grants are not available. In these ways a notable degree of flexibility has been achieved.

Federal grants for public health may be justified on a number of bases. The Kestnbaum Commission *Report* recognized national responsibility for research, the dissemination of information, and the promotion of minimum standards of public health operations.[47] Communicable disease has already been mentioned. Disadvantaged children obviously need to be healthy and to know how to remain that way if they are to benefit from education and become productive workers. Comparing the amounts spent in fiscal 1964 for health and education grants ($1.4 billion) with the amount spent for public welfare ($3.7 billion), tempts one to wonder if more had been done earlier in the first two areas, less would now be needed for the third—which until the passage of the Economic Opportunity Act was largely a holding operation. Be that as it may, increasing attention is being paid to resource development, including some of the more esoteric forms included in the next category of federal grants.

Resource Development and Recreation

> America owes her greatness partly to the large public and private investments made to develop her abundant natural resources. Rapid growth and urbanization require intensified efforts to solve old problems and imaginative approaches to new challenges.—*Economic Report of the President, January 1965*, p. 18.

[46] For a concise description of these programs, as they existed in fiscal 1964, see *Catalog of Federal Aids to State and Local Governments,* prepared by the Legislative Reference Service for the Senate Committee on Government Operations, 88 Cong. 2 sess. (1964), pp. 57-66.

[47] *Op. cit.,* pp. 251-52.

TABLE III-6. Federal Grant-in-Aid Programs for Resource Development and Recreation, Actual 1964 and Estimated 1966

		Federal Expenditures	
Program	Year Enacted	Actual 1964 (Millions)	Estimated 1966 (Millions)
Urban Renewal	1949	$212	$329
Watershed Protection and Flood Prevention	1954	57	62
Recreation Planning and Land Acquisition	1964	—	33
Fish and Wildlife Restoration	1937		
	1950	20	22
Open Space Land	1961	5	17
Urban Planning Assistance	1954	16	17
Forest Protection and Utilization	1911 1940 1956	16	16
Community Development Training	1964	—	6
Total		$326	$502

Source: *United States Budget, Fiscal 1966.*

The conservation of natural resources is a problem that required little attention in this country until quite recently. As Table III-6 indicates, it was not until 1911 that the first federal grant program for this purpose was enacted, to protect the nation's forests by preventing fires, reforesting denuded areas, and encouraging good management of woodlands. Later in this century, however, it became increasingly clear that blight was not a monopoly of the rural areas. Urban slums with their heavy demands on public services, their meager contribution to public revenue, and their obvious waste of valuable resources elicited more and more concern. Though the elimination of slums promised benefits that would accrue mainly to people in each separate metropolitan area, obtaining the necessary funds from that same area was no easy problem. Central cities lacked access to the tax bases of the suburbs and were kept from raising their own tax rates by fear of losing business and residents. Frequently cities found the rural-dominated state legislatures unsympathetic to their plight.

The one remaining source of support was the federal government, and in 1949 the urban renewal program—now rapidly leaving the $250 million a year level of operations behind—was born.

Many people have lamented this direct fiscal relation between national and local governments, but few have done much to solve the political problems that gave rise to it. In its wake have come grants for urban planning (1954), for the preservation of open-space land (1961), for the development of mass transportation plans (1961) and facilities (1964), and for construction of essential water and sewer facilities (1965).

Earlier in this chapter it was noted that benefit spillovers of parks and the other public recreational facilities, when they exist, can frequently be handled effectively by means of user charges. For this reason primary responsibilities in this area remain with the state and local governments, but the federal government does have several important functions. Whenever the facilities to be developed will serve vacationers from many states and user charges are not feasible, the federal government is the only public body with sufficient interest in the results to justify the necessary expenditures. Forest and mountain trails and President Johnson's proposed national wild rivers system[48] are examples of this kind of project. Even when user charges can be employed, federal leadership and coordination is likely to be needed to develop recreation areas that straddle state boundaries. Finally, there is a strong possibility that states, with their continuous preoccupation with short-run financing problems, will undervalue, or even ignore, the future benefits to an ever-growing population of a widespread system of public parks and wilderness areas. From its position of greater fiscal affluence, the federal government is in a better position to judge these matters and to finance the necessary land acquisitions before it is too late.

Transportation

> If the United States is to maintain and advance its productive and defensive strength, which depends so largely upon the efficiency and economy of the transportation system, an acceleration of the rate of highway improvement is needed, particularly with respect to major highways.—Kestnbaum Report, p. 215.

Few government commissions, particularly those dealing with federal-state-local fiscal relations, have seen their recommendations put into effect so rapidly and so massively as the Kestnbaum Com-

[48] See his Message to Congress on Natural Beauty, *New York Times,* Feb. 9, 1965.

TABLE III-7. Federal Grant-in-Aid Programs for Transportation, Actual 1964 and Estimated 1966

Program	Year Enacted	Federal Expenditures	
		Actual 1964 (Millions)	Estimated 1966 (Millions)
Federal-Aid Highway	1916		
	1956	$3,607	$3,822
Airport Construction	1946	65	60
Urban Transportation Assistance	1964	—	40
Total		$3,672	$3,922

Source: United States Budget, Fiscal 1966.

mission's proposals for an acceleration of highway expenditures. When it submitted its report to the President in mid-1955, federal aid authorizations for highways for each of the next two fiscal years stood at $875 million. Little more than a year later construction of the 41,000 mile, $46.8 billion national interstate and defense highway system was approved, and highway grants expanded steadily, reaching $3.6 billion in fiscal 1964 (Table III-7). Among grant programs, the Interstate Highway System is distinguished by the high proportion of costs financed by the federal government (90-95 percent)[49] and by the fact that these costs are met from earmarked taxes on motor fuels, tires and tubes, and other products purchased by highway users. The program consequently is free of the usual appropriation controls, and since it clearly finances a large share of intrastate highway benefits, it is likely to divert state funds from superior uses. Whether the program as a whole is justified is not at issue here, but it does illustrate some of the features which many experts find objectionable about federal grant-in-aid programs. It is one of the fiscal ironies that it was established by an Administration dedicated to a strengthening of state and local government responsibilities.

Other Federal Grants-in-Aid

All of the remaining grant programs deal with such primary national responsibilities as unemployment, civil defense, roads and

[49] Costs of constructing primary, secondary, and urban extension highways, in contrast, are shared equally between the states and the federal government.

TABLE III-8. Federal Grants in Areas of Primary Federal Responsibility, Actual 1964 and Estimated 1966

Program	Federal Expenditures	
	Actual 1964 (Millions)	Estimated 1966 (Millions)
Administration of Employment Security Programs	$405	$502
Public Works Acceleration in Redevelopment and Substantial Unemployment Areas	257	145
District of Columbia	38	52
Forest and Public Lands Highways	37	40
Grants to Territories and Alaska	51	34
Civil Defense	20	27
National Guard and State and Local Planning for National Emergencies	14	9
Bureau of Indian Affairs	9	11
Veterans Administration: Aid to State Homes	8	9
Miscellaneous	6	8
Total	$845	$837

Source: *United States Budget, Fiscal 1966.*

highways on or near federal lands, and aid to territories, new states, Indians, and the District of Columbia. To a large extent, therefore, they represent a decentralization of federal operations in the interest of flexibility and administrative simplicity and need not be discussed here. Table III-8 lists the programs involved.

The States—Intermediaries for Intergovernmental Aid

State governments are both major recipients and major dispensers of intergovernmental fiscal aid. In fiscal 1964, for example, they received $9 billion from the federal government and paid out $13 billion to their own local units.[50] The $13 billion dis-

---

[50] U.S. Bureau of the Census, *Compendium of State Government Finances in 1964*, pp. 6-7. As defined by the Census Bureau, intergovernmental aid includes grants-in-aid, shared taxes, payments in lieu of taxes, and payments for services performed on a reimbursement or cost-sharing basis by the recipient government (*Ibid.*, p. 56). Such aid is measured both as intergovernmental expenditure by the payor and as intergovernmental revenue to the payee, but differences in timing prevent the two from being exactly equal for any given year. A grant made toward the end of the year may not be recorded by the recipient until the next year, and whenever the fiscal years used by the two governments involved do not

TABLE III-9. State Intergovernmental Expenditure, Amounts and Fiscal Importance, Selected Years, 1902–64

Year	Amount (Millions)	Percent of Total State General Expenditure	Percent of Total Local General Revenue
1902	$ 52	28.0	6.1
1913	91	23.5	5.6
1922	312	23.2	8.1
1932	801	29.0	14.1
1942	1,780	39.1	25.0
1948	3,283	34.7	28.9
1953	5,384	36.7	29.3
1958	8,089	34.4	29.2
1963	11,885	34.6	28.8
1964	12,968	34.8	29.2

Sources: U. S. Bureau of the Census, *State Payments to Local Governments*, Census of Governments, 1962, Vol. VI, No. 2, p. 9; *Governmental Finances in 1963*, pp. 22–24; and *Governmental Finances in 1963–64*, pp. 22–23.

pensed by the states is a significant figure—35 percent of all state general expenditures and 29 percent of all local government general revenues. While both of these percentages have been remarkably stable during the last fifteen years, they now stand well above the levels prevailing during the first three decades of the present century (Table III-9). In 1902, for example, state intergovernmental expenditures were only 28 percent of total state general expenditures and 6 percent of total local general revenues.

State aid to local governments has developed partly in response to specific economic emergencies, such as the Great Depression, and partly in response to the long-run forces, discussed earlier, which make for a more mobile and closely integrated economy. With each decade more and more of the benefits from local programs have spread beyond the boundaries of the enacting government, and local tax administration has become increasingly difficult and costly. One possible solution was to move both spending pro-

---

exactly coincide, even grants recorded by both in the same calendar month can be allocated to different fiscal years. In 1963-64, for example, state intergovernmental expenditures to local governments were $12,968 million (the figure used in the text) whereas local intergovernmental revenues from states were reported as $12,873 million. See U.S. Bureau of the Census, *Governmental Finances in 1963-64*, pp. 22-23.

grams and tax collection to the state level, decentralizing state operations whenever this promised administrative economies. The other solution was to leave the programs in local hands, with the hope that this would stimulate greater citizen participation in their operation, but to supplement their financing with state aid. That the latter alternative has been widely adopted is clear from Table III-9.

Though some state aid is unrestricted as to purpose, most of it is earmarked for education, highways, and public welfare, and local expenditures in all three areas are relatively less important now than they were in earlier years. In 1962, for example, state aid covered 37 percent of total local expenditures for education, 36 percent of local expenditures for highways, and 70 percent of local

TABLE III-10. State Intergovernmental Expenditures for Selected Functions as a Percentage of Local General Expenditures for the Same Functions, Selected Years, 1902–62

Functions	1902	1913	1922	1932	1942	1952	1962
Education	19	16	13	20	36	37	37
Highways	1	1	7	25	49	34	36
Public Welfare	—	—	5	8	56	70	70

Source: U. S. Bureau of the Census, *State Payments to Local Governments*, p. 9.

expenditures for public welfare (Table III-10). At the beginning of the century highways and welfare received almost no state support, and local schools were less than 20 percent state financed. In regard to the structure of state aid itself, several changes are worth noting. As Table III-11 shows, highway assistance increased rapidly in relative importance after the introduction of the automobile, as did public welfare grants during the Great Depression, and education recovered some of its former predominance after World War II, probably in response to the rapid increase in the school population. Unrestricted state aid, in contrast, began and ended the period covered in roughly the same relative position, about 10 percent of state intergovernmental expenditures in both 1902 and 1962.

The fiscal effects of state aid to local governments may be classified into six basic patterns. Taking first the reactions at each level of government separately, there are the following possibilities:

Local taxes lower, local expenditures (including state unchanged;

Local taxes unchanged, local expenditures higher;

L3   Both local taxes and local expenditures higher;

S1   State taxes higher, state nongrant expenditures unchanged;

S2   State taxes unchanged, state nongrant expenditures lower.

These possibilities, in turn, may be combined into the six basic patterns:

L1S1   *Tax Substitution.* State taxes have been substituted for local taxes with no change in state or local spending programs.

L2S2   *Expenditure Substitution.* Tax programs are unchanged but local spending has been substituted for state spending.

L1S2   *Expenditure Reduction.* Both local taxes and state nongrant expenditures are lower, while state taxes and local spending programs remain the same.

L2S1   *Expenditure Expansion.* Higher local expenditures are financed by higher state taxes, local taxes and state nongrant expenditures remaining unchanged.

L3S1 and L3S2   *Increased Local Tax Effort.* Here state grants induce an increase in locally financed governmental activities.[51]

TABLE III-11. State Intergovernmental Expenditures, by Function, Selected Years, 1902–62

Functions	Percentage Distribution by Years						
	1902	1913	1922	1932	1942	1952	1962
General Local Government							
Support	10	6	11	17	13	11	8
Education	86	90	65	50	44	50	59
Highways	4	4	22	29	19	14	12
Public Welfare	—	—	1	3	22	19	16
Other	—	—	—	1	2	5	4

Source: U. S. Bureau of the Census, *State Payments to Local Governments*, p. 9.

In practice, of course, elements from several of these patterns are likely to be combined, the precise outcome depending, among numerous other factors, on the type of state aid given. Though empirical research in this area is still in its infancy, two recent studies

[51] For simplicity these patterns assume that local nontax revenues, such as licenses, fees, and user charges, are not affected by state-local grant programs.

do illuminate some important parts of this complex fiscal picture. The first, which involved a multivariate, linear regression analysis of state and local expenditures in 1960, showed state aid to be positively correlated with these expenditures and yielded the following estimates of the additional amounts of per capita state-local expenditures of various kinds that were associated, on the average, with an extra dollar of per capita state aid:

Total direct general expenditures	$0.90–$1.34
Highways	$0.67
Welfare	$0.20
Health and Hospitals	$2.53–$2.78
Local Schools	$0.52.[52]

In all categories, therefore, elements of the *expenditure expansion* pattern (L2S1) appear to be present, but in some cases they were presumably combined with tax or expenditure substitution[53] and in other cases, with higher levels of local tax effort.

The second study, which dealt with the influence of state aid on school expenditures in some 1,400 New England towns and cities in 1961-62,[54] found that the relationship varied significantly between small and large urban areas. While in the former, an additional dollar of state aid per pupil was associated with an increase in expenditures per pupil of between 40 and 80 cents, in the latter, state aid had no discernible impact on school expenditures.[55] As far as state-wide averages were concerned, lower local tax burdens emerged as the main fiscal effect.[56] In part this result may be attrib-

[52] Seymour Sacks and Robert Harris, "The Determinants of State and Local Government Expenditures and Intergovernmental Flows of Funds," *National Tax Journal,* Vol. 17 (March 1964), p. 83. Only the net regression coefficients that were statistically significant at the .05 level have been given in the text.

[53] It should be stressed that a regression coefficient of less than $1 for a specific grant-aided program may underestimate the total amount of induced local expenditure expansion, since the local funds released by the grant may be used to increase expenditures on some other program, rather than to reduce tax rates.

[54] George A. Bishop, "Stimulative Versus Substitutive Effects of State School Aid in New England," *National Tax Journal,* Vol. 17 (June 1964), pp. 133-43.

[55] *Ibid.,* p. 139. To identify large urban areas the census definition of a Standard Metropolitan Statistical Area was used.

[56] Bishop interprets this to mean a substitution of state for local taxes (pattern L1S1). Since his study dealt only with local expenditures, however, he was able to distinguish only between lower local taxes (L1) and higher local spending (L2), and his results are consequently consistent with both the *tax substitution* (L1S1) and the *expenditure reduction* (L1S2) patterns.

utable to the relative importance, among New England school aids, of state support for a minimum, or foundation, educational program. Once a school district has achieved that level of operation, state foundation aid provides no direct incentive for it to go further, since all additional costs must be borne locally.[57] As Bishop notes, school aid in New York State is relatively more important, and is granted in more stimulative forms than it is in New England, and a recent study of New York state aid showed it to be highly effective in raising school expenditures.[58]

Another fiscal distinction of some importance is that between shared taxes and grants-in-aid. The former provide most of the unrestricted aid given to local governments, and shared-tax aid, by its very nature, has some automatic sensitivity both to short-run economic fluctuations and to long-run economic growth. This can vary substantially depending upon the type of tax involved. Netzer's estimates of the long-term GNP elasticity of different tax bases, for example, range from 0.50 for alcoholic beverage excises to 1.70 for the personal income tax.[59] Individual states also differ greatly in the extent to which they engage in tax sharing with local governments. In 1962, for example, New Jersey distributed only $2 million that way, out of total state intergovernmental expenditures of $198 million, whereas in Wisconsin shared taxes were 44 percent of total state aid of $335 million.[60] Wisconsin also illustrates well the variety of sharing arrangements that are used: $67 million from high-elasticity corporate and individual income taxes were returned in 1962 to the local governments of origin; $6 million from the low-elasticity alcoholic beverage sales tax were allocated on the basis of population for general local purposes; and $36 million of highway-

[57] Foundation aid does, however, raise the fiscal well-being of each school district, and this change may itself stimulate higher school expenditures.

[58] *Ibid.*, p. 133, and Seymour Sacks, Robert Harris, and John J. Carroll, *The State and Local Government . . . The Role of State Aid*, New York State Comptroller's Studies in Local Finance, No. 3 (1963). Their estimate was that an additional dollar of state aid per capita tended to raise per capita school expenditures by 90 cents.

[59] Dick Netzer, "Financial Needs and Resources over the Next Decade: State and Local Governments," *Public Finances: Needs, Sources and Utilization* (National Bureau of Economic Research, 1961), p. 30. The estimates are for the period 1957-70.

[60] U.S. Bureau of the Census, *State Payments to Local Governments,* pp. 70-71 and 105-07.

TABLE III-12. Range of Per Capita State Intergovernmental Expenditures, by Selected Programs, 1962

Function	Average for all Fifty States	Highest Amount	Lowest Amount or Number of States not Providing
Total State Aid	$59	California—$97	New Hampshire—$11
General Support of Local Government	5	Hawaii—$27	6 states
Education	35	New Mexico—$79	Hawaii[a]
Highways	7	Wisconsin—$17	3 states
Public Welfare	10	Colorado—$39	17 states

Source: U. S. Bureau of the Census, *State Payments to Local Governments*, p. 12.
[a] Less than $0.5.

user revenues were transferred to towns, cities, and counties for road construction. Both shared taxes and state grants in Wisconsin tend to be related to population density, though in opposite ways. According to a 1957 study by Alan H. Smith, shared taxes favored the large cities and were important enough to offset roughly the biased allocation of grants to rural areas.[61] Similar distributional patterns in other states, however, would not be likely to produce such a balanced outcome.

As noted earlier, in the country as a whole state aid now goes mainly for education, highways, and public welfare, but there are significant differences among the states. As Table III-12 shows, highway aid ranges from none at all in three states to a high of $17 per capita in Wisconsin, and though seventeen states distributed no public welfare grants, Colorado provided $39 per capita, nearly four times the national average. School grants, which were provided by all states in 1962, showed the widest range of all, from 3 cents per capita in Hawaii to $79 in New Mexico. A low level of state aid for a given function, however, does not necessarily imply a low level of state financial support for that activity, as Table III-13 shows. Both Hawaii and New Hampshire make few education grants, but the centralized Hawaiian school system is largely state financed. New Mexico and New Hampshire provide a quite different picture. School expenditures were made almost entirely at

[61] "State Payments to Local Governments in Wisconsin," *National Tax Journal*, Vol. 15 (September 1962), pp. 297-307. The study was based on data made available in the 1957 Census of Governments.

TABLE III-13. State Grants and State Support of Local Schools, 1962

State	State Grants for Education (Millions)	Noncapital Expenditures for Local Schools		Expenditures for Local Schools Per $1,000 of State Personal Income	
		State	Local	Amounts	Ranking of State
		(Millions)			
Hawaii	$ 0	$45	$ 6	$41	29
New Hampshire	4	—	38	34	49
New Mexico	80	1	89	58	1

Source: U. S. Bureau of the Census, *Compendium of Government Finances* (1962), pp. 73–74, 87, 105, 107.

the local level in each, but New Hampshire provided little state aid and ranked 49th among the states in the amount of its school expenditures per $1,000 of state personal income, and New Mexico ranked first both in the amount of state school aid per capita and in the amount it spent for local schools in relation to its income.

There are some more important public programs with benefit spillovers extending beyond the boundaries of most local governments that have not been discussed so far. Some of these activities receive well-above-average support in one or at most a few states. Table III-14 illustrates this proposition for health and hospital grants. Other activities, the most important of which are shown in Table III-15, receive aid directly from the federal government. In one way or the other, then, most local programs with significant regional or interstate benefit flows do receive some assistance from

TABLE III-14. Five Largest Per Capita State Grants for Health and Hospitals in 1962

Health		Hospitals	
State	Amount	State	Amount
New York	$2.77	Hawaii	$3.64
California	0.87	Wisconsin	2.84
Kentucky	0.72	Georgia	1.95
Georgia	0.67	Mississippi	1.94
Pennsylvania	0.65	Arkansas	1.51
U. S. Average	0.50		0.52

Source: U. S. Bureau of the Census, *State Payments to Local Governments*, p. 12.

TABLE III-15. Federal Grants-in-Aid Made Directly to Local Governments in 1962[a]

Programs	Amounts (Millions)
Construction and Operation of Schools in Federally Affected Areas	$256
Urban Renewal	160
Low Rent Public Housing	149
Construction of Waste Treatment Facilities	42
Construction of Airports	33
Urban Planning Assistance	6
Indian Education and Welfare	1
Construction of Health Research Facilities	1

Source: Advisory Commission on Intergovernmental Relations, *The Role of Equalization in Federal Grants*, p. 26.
[a] Excludes grants made to communities for demonstration purposes, research grants made to individuals employed in local public agencies, and grant program of less than $1 million.

higher governmental units, but it is difficult to judge, in the absence of a systematic study of the question, whether the differing amounts of aid provided realistically reflect interprogram variation in the spillover of benefits.

Summary

The basic economic justification for federal functional grants-in-aid is provided by the widespread, and ever-increasing, spillover of benefits from some of the most important state and local expenditure programs.[62] Under these circumstances, complete local autonomy is impossible, and effective program operation requires the development of fiscal partnerships so that all interested governmental units can participate. The appropriate means would be a set of optimizing intergovernmental grants based squarely on external benefit flows and varying with changes in the relative importance of these flows from one state and local program to another. Such grants would rationalize decision-making at all levels of govern-

[62] For an evaluation of federal grants that emphasize political considerations see Phillip Monypenny, "Federal Grants-in-Aid to State Governments: a Political Analysis," *National Tax Journal*, Vol. 13 (March 1960), pp. 1-16, and for a concise presentation of the economic case for federal grants, based primarily on the existence of benefit spillovers, see Kenneth G. Ainsworth, "A Comment on Professor Monypenny's Political Analysis of Federal Grants-in-Aid," *National Tax Journal*, Vol. 13 (September 1960), pp. 282-84.

ment, improve the allocation of resources both within the public sector and between it and the private sector, and raise the general level of fiscal equity. Judged in terms of this ideal, some existing federal grants would be discontinued because the external benefits they deal with are not national in scope, others would be consolidated into a single broad program because the external benefits of the different components are all approximately the same, and still others would be expanded so as to bring them more in line with the importance of their benefit spillovers. In addition, greater use of open-ended grants would be made so that state and local decisions to expand or contract aided programs could be based on more realistic comparisons of internal benefits and costs.

Federal functional grants may also serve as catalysts in situations where coordinated regional action is called for but where, for one reason or another, the counties, cities, and states concerned have been unable to get together. Particularly useful for this purpose are planning and demonstration loans and grants. Since the programs dealt with are not national in scope, however, primary responsibility for them should remain at the state and local level where it may be met, at least in part, by means of state grants-in-aid. One potential difficulty with this solution, of course, is that state fiscal capacities may not be equal to the task. If widespread fiscal deficiencies of this sort do exist, unconditional federal grants-in-aid, to be discussed in the next chapter, may become an important means of strengthening the federal system.

CHAPTER IV

Unconditional Grants-in-Aid

FROM ITS SECLUDED EXISTENCE in the world of fiscal theory the suggestion that the federal government should offer unrestricted grants-in-aid to the states burst suddenly into the public arena during the fall of 1964. Sponsored in different forms by Presidential candidate Goldwater and by a task force appointed by President Johnson, the proposal enjoyed a brief period under the klieg lights and then retired, somewhat battered, into the quieter regions from which it had come.[1] Clearly, the plan possessed both merits and weaknesses that attracted widespread attention, and the purpose of this chapter is to appraise those qualities and to compare unconditional grants with other ways of achieving the same goals. This will involve, among other things, an analysis of the equalization powers of existing federal grant-in-aid programs.

[1] The original idea came from Walter W. Heller, who recommended unrestricted federal grants to the states as a method of reducing the "fiscal drag" generated by rising federal receipts under conditions of rapid and sustained economic growth. (See *U.S. News and World Report*, June 29, 1964, p. 59.) The task force submitted its report in November 1964, but details of the report have never been released. The views of Joseph A. Pechman, who served as chairman of the task force, are given in "Financing State and Local Government," *Proceedings of a Symposium on Federal Taxation* (American Bankers Association, 1965; Brookings Institution Reprint 103, 1965). For Professor Heller's detailed views, see his *New Dimensions of Political Economy* (Harvard University Press, 1966), Chapter III.

107

Balancing Grants

Unrestricted intergovernmental grants are ideally suited to off-setting, or balancing, any general fiscal deficiencies to which state or local governments may be subject. These deficiencies can arise for two reasons. The first is that a high concentration of low-income families tends to make the cost of providing even an ordinary level of public services prohibitive, to say nothing of the additional services that such families typically require from government. One can easily visualize the problem that would face a locality made up entirely of families which received, say, only $2,000 a year—a figure which might represent the minimum cost of an acceptable level of private consumption alone. If this were the case, the community would have no ability whatsoever to support government services, such as public schools or fire protection, which, being indispensable, would have to be financed somehow. While functional grants, made to finance education, vocational training, relocation of economic activity, and the like, would be the obvious solution, they could not exert their effects quickly. In the short run, therefore, the community would need large amounts of outside general assistance with its fiscal affairs. Nor does past experience indicate that the short run would necessarily be very short. Even with vigorous state and federal anti-poverty programs, it might be a generation before the community could afford on its own what is currently regarded as the standard set of local government services, and by that time the nation might well have adjusted its standards still higher.

The second type of fiscal deficiency arises from what many regard as a fundamental gap between state-local spending responsibilities and their revenue-raising abilities. Even the richest states, it is argued, cannot levy enough taxes to finance the program expansions that are justified by the benefits that could be obtained from them. One's view of this matter obviously depends both on the importance one attaches to state and local programs such as education, urban renewal, environmental health and on the extent to which one believes that state and local taxes are held down by fears of interstate competition for business and wealthy residents rather than by a lack of initiative in developing new and better tax bases.

These complex issues have been discussed at length in earlier chapters. Suffice it to note that if this second kind of fiscal deficiency were the only one to be dealt with—that is, if each state government's resources were adequate for its fiscal needs but not fully exploitable—the appropriate solution would not be grants-in-aid at all but some form of tax sharing whereby revenues were returned to the jurisdictions of origin. Either centralized tax administration or tax credits would accomplish the purpose desired. (See Chapter II.) Given the presence of both kinds of fiscal deficiency, however, a single program of unconditional grants would provide one effective means of dealing with both difficulties at once. Such a solution would also have the great political appeal of granting assistance to every state, or to every local government within a state, whereas a pure set of equalizing grants would go only to the poorest jurisdictions.

The function of unconditional intergovernmental grants-in-aid, then, is to offset whatever fiscal deficiencies exist at the state and local level. Of the two kinds of deficiencies that can be balanced in this way, the more basic is the one that arises from geographical concentrations of low-income families and individuals, since without it there would be no justification for unconditional grants. The next section, accordingly, considers the interstate differentials that currently exist in fiscal needs and resources.

Interstate Differences in Fiscal Capacity

Since 1929 there has been a dramatic reduction in per capita income inequality among the states. As Table IV-1 shows, per capita personal income in the country's richest region fell from 138 percent of the national average in 1929, when that region was the Mideast, to 118 percent in 1963, when the Far West had taken over top place; while during the same period per capita income in the poorest region, the Southeast, rose from 52 to 74 percent of the national average. There was, in other words, more than a 40-point reduction in the maximum regional income differential. Most of the change, however, occurred during World War II and the immediate reconversion period. This can be seen both in Figure IV-1, where the trends in relative regional per capita income are shown, and in

TABLE IV-1. Regional Per Capita Personal Income in 1929, 1948, 1957 and 1963

Region[a]	Per Capita Personal Income as a Percentage of the National Average			
	1929	1948	1957	1963
Mideast	138	116	117	115
Far West	129	120	117	118
New England	125	106	112	113
Great Lakes	114	112	110	107
Rocky Mountain	85	98	92	92
Plains	81	100	91	95
Southwest	67	83	87	83
Southeast	52	68	71	74
United States	100	100	100	100

Source: Robert E. Graham, Jr., "Factors Underlying Changes in the Geographic Distribution of Income," *Survey of Current Business* (April 1964), p. 21.
[a] Ranked by their 1929 order.

the following tabulation of changes in the coefficient of variation for state per capita income:

1929	32	1948	18
1940	29	1953	19
1944	20	1957	18
1946	18	1963	16[2]

Particularly notable is the 9-point drop in this measure of income inequality between 1940 and 1944 and its virtual stability from 1946 to 1957.

Two aspects of postwar regional income trends are particularly important for our purposes. The first is that whereas the industrial structure that existed in 1948 would, by itself, have acted to widen interregional income differentials, these industry mix effects were typically swamped by the more important and opposing effects of interregional changes in industry shares. The regional impact of these two sets of forces is summarized in Table IV-2. This table shows that the industry-mix effects, which show the extent to which the industries existing in a given region in 1948 grew more or

[2] Robert E. Graham, Jr., "Factors Underlying Changes in the Geographic Distribution of Income," *Survey of Current Business* (April 1964), p. 30. The coefficient of variation is the mean difference between per capita income in each state and in the nation as a whole, these differences being taken without regard to sign, weighted by population, and their average then expressed as a percent of U.S. per capita income.

FIGURE IV-1. Relative Regional Differences in Per Capita Personal Income, 1929–63

Regional Differences in Average Income Levels Narrowed Sharply During World War II and Reconversion; Since Then Convergence Has Been Small

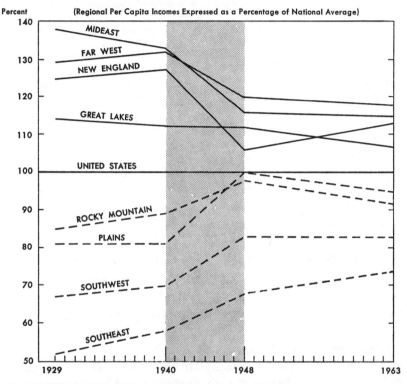

Source: U. S. Office of Business Economics, *Survey of Current Business* (April 1964), p. 25.

less than the average for the country as a whole thereafter, are all positive for the four regions with above-average per capita income and all negative for the other four regions.[3] Three of the four regions that gained a greater share of total industrial activity between 1948 and 1962, in contrast, fell at the bottom of the income scale, and in each case these regional-share effects were more important than the opposing industry-mix effects. It would appear, therefore, that changes in the location of industrial production, at

[3] Agriculture, which is highly concentrated geographically and which had a negative rate of growth during the period, dominated the industry-mix effects. *Ibid.*, p. 23.

TABLE IV-2. Industry-Mix and Regional-Share Effects on Income from Participation in Current Production, by Region, 1948–62

(Billions of dollars)

Region[a]	Changes in Total Participation Income[b] Due to		
	Industry-Mix Effects	Regional-Share Effects	Net Effect[c]
Far West	1.8	8.0	9.8
Mideast	5.4	−9.8	−4.4
Great Lakes	1.5	−8.1	−6.6
New England	1.1	−1.7	−0.6
Plains	−4.4	−0.3	−4.7
Rocky Mountain	−0.7	1.3	0.6
Southwest	−0.7	3.5	2.8
Southeast	−3.9	7.2	3.2

Source: Robert E. Graham, Jr., "Factors Underlying Changes in the Geographic Distribution of Income," *Survey of Current Business* (April 1964), p. 24.
[a] Ranked by per capita income in 1948.
[b] Consists of wages and salaries, supplementary labor income, and earnings of self-employed persons. On the average it constitutes 80 percent of total personal income.
[c] Sum of the preceding two columns. Figures are rounded and may not add to totals.

least in the broad sense of the differential regional growth rates exhibited by given industries, favored the low-income states during this period. Since unconditional federal grants-in-aid, if enacted, would presumably do the same thing, their probable impact on industrial location would be to accentuate trends already under way.

The second notable postwar development is the extent to which population growth and income growth have been matched geographically, thereby producing a high degree of stability in per capita interstate income differentials. Two states provided a vivid illustration of these trends. Between 1948 and 1963 California gained 7.5 million people and tripled its total state income. Over the same period West Virginia lost 121,000 residents and suffered a one-third decline in its share of the country's total income. Yet California's per capita income was virtually the same percentage of the national average in 1963 as it was in 1948 (122 percent compared to 123 percent in 1948), and West Virginia's position had declined only from 81 percent of the national average in 1948 to 77 percent in 1963. One population movement that did affect state per capita income, however, was the migration of Negroes with their below-average income from the South to the North and West, and primarily from the five states of North and South Carolina, Georgia, Ala-

TABLE IV-3. State Per Capita Personal Income as a Percentage of the National Average in 1963

District of Columbia	139	Iowa	93
Nevada	138	Montana	92
Delaware	133	Kansas	91
Connecticut	129	Utah	87
New York	123	Arizona	87
California	122	Florida	86
Illinois	121	Vermont	86
New Jersey	119	Virginia	85
Massachusetts	117	Texas	84
Alaska	115	North Dakota	83
Maryland	114	Maine	82
Michigan	103	Oklahoma	80
Oregon	103	Idaho	79
Missouri	103	South Dakota	79
Washington	103	New Mexico	77
Ohio	102	West Virginia	77
Hawaii	101	Georgia	76
Indiana	101	North Carolina	74
Pennsylvania	100	Kentucky	73
Wyoming	99	Tennessee	73
Rhode Island	98	Louisiana	72
Colorado	98	Alabama	68
Wisconsin	97	Arkansas	65
Minnesota	95	South Carolina	65
New Hampshire	94	Mississippi	56
Nebraska	94		

Source: Robert E. Graham, Jr., "Factors Underlying Changes in the Geographic Distribution of Income," *Survey of Current Business* (April 1964), p. 21.

bama, and Mississippi to New York, Illinois, and California, and in somewhat lesser numbers to New Jersey, Michigan, Ohio, and the District of Columbia. The result was a spillover of the costs of inadequate public education that should whet the appetite of the in-migration states for federal grant assistance, not only to themselves to help with the immediate problems of poverty but especially to the South, where any long-run solution to the problem must be found.

Though the interstate distribution of per capita income is clearly less unequal now than it was in earlier years, it still shows a very wide dispersion that implies major differences in state fiscal capacities. In 1963, for example, Mississippi's per capita income of $1,379 was only 56 percent of the national average ($2,443) and barely 40 percent of the $3,398 and $3,372 averages enjoyed by the residents of the District of Columbia and of Nevada, respective-

TABLE IV-4. Four Measures of State Fiscal Capacity and Actual Tax Collections, by States, 1959 and 1960

(Per capita as a percent of the U. S. average)

State and Region	Personal Income 1959	Income of Above-Minimum Families 1959	Income Produced 1959	Yield of Representative Tax System 1960	Actual Tax Collections 1960
New England	111	110	101	97	109
Maine	83	81	72	78	99
New Hampshire	92	97	83	98	93
Vermont	83	81	78	85	110
Massachusetts	113	112	105	96	116
Rhode Island	100	98	89	87	98
Connecticut	129	130	115	112	105
Mideast	116	115	114	100	115
New York	125	122	128	105	143
New Jersey	120	125	111	105	102
Pennsylvania	102	100	97	91	87
Delaware	136	114	97	112	98
Maryland	108	110	94	93	99
District of Columbia	133	129	159	126	107
Great Lakes	107	108	109	105	100
Michigan	104	105	101	99	109
Ohio	106	106	106	103	94
Indiana	97	99	102	101	89
Illinois	119	119	126	116	102
Wisconsin	98	100	96	97	107
Plains	92	90	96	107	96
Minnesota	91	93	97	103	108
Iowa	91	88	96	114	103
Missouri	100	93	103	99	75
North Dakota	72	72	80	108	99
South Dakota	70	69	81	107	99
Nebraska	91	87	100	119	86
Kansas	92	95	87	113	108
Southeast	72	71	73	76	71
Virginia	83	85	85	81	68
West Virginia	76	71	81	74	75
Kentucky	70	69	74	74	59
Tennessee	70	68	69	71	67
North Carolina	69	66	76	72	69
South Carolina	62	59	60	60	64
Georgia	72	71	74	69	70
Florida	91	94	83	101	91
Alabama	66	65	65	66	60
Mississippi	53	48	48	57	64
Louisiana	74	72	81	88	93
Arkansas	61	55	56	69	62
Southwest	87	88	95	113	84
Oklahoma	83	85	89	94	88
Texas	88	87	96	120	80
New Mexico	84	87	92	102	86
Arizona	89	98	96	99	103
Rocky Mountain	94	97	97	116	108
Montana	92	91	96	129	111
Idaho	83	87	84	108	96
Wyoming	104	103	108	161	118
Colorado	101	103	101	114	114
Utah	86	93	96	101	100
Far West	118	123	116	119	133
Washington	104	111	102	102	100
Oregon	102	105	94	103	116
Nevada	126	130	142	146	136
California	124	128	121	126	138
Alaska	117	126	117	69	80
Hawaii	96	103	96	76	117

Source: ACIR, *Measures of State and Local Fiscal Capacity and Tax Effort* (October 1962), pp. 54–55.

114

ly. Table IV-3 fills out this picture by ranking the states by their 1963 per capita income. One must, of course, be cautious about inferring fiscal capacities from per capita income figures alone. Two states that are equal in per capita income may have very different distributions of family income and therefore different abilities to raise revenue by either progressive or regressive taxation. In addition, interstate income may be taxed more frequently by the state of origin than by the state of residence, and some of the most important state and local taxes are levied on bases that differ in relation to income from one state to another.

To illustrate some of these differences, Table IV-4 gives four alternative measures of state fiscal capacities that were developed recently by the Advisory Commission on Intergovernmental Relations (ACIR). In the first column is the series based on Department of Commerce estimates of state per capita personal income, and in the second is a series that uses Bureau of the Census data on above-minimum family and individual incomes. By excluding income received by families with less than $2,000, and by individuals with less than $1,000, a year, the latter measure concentrates more precisely on personal abilities to pay taxes,[4] but in order to do so it has to use statistical data that, being derived from personal interviews, are probably less accurate than the Department of Commerce personal income estimates.[5] The second column in the table, in other words, is not necessarily superior to the first as a measure of state

[4] A still more precise measure would be one based on an index of family welfare that expressed total household resources as a percentage of the cost of basic household needs, which would be a function, among other things, of family size, family composition, and the prices of necessities in different parts of the country. For a discussion of such an index and a demonstration that it differs significantly from per capita disposable income as a measure of family welfare, see Martin David, "Welfare, Income, and Budget Needs," *Review of Economics and Statistics*, Vol. 41 (November 1959), pp. 393-99.

The fiscal capacity of a given state would be a function of the per capita income received by all families residing in it that had a welfare index greater than unity, and a measure of special needs for public services (or subsidies) could be derived by estimating the additional amount of income needed to bring all families with indexes below unity up to that level.

[5] The large difference between the two income relatives for Delaware (136 versus 114), for example, probably reflects the well-known difficulties involved in obtaining accurate information about high family incomes by means of interview surveys.

fiscal capacities. In any case, it may be noted that the differences
between the two are not great.[6]

Income produced is of interest as a potential allocator of federal
equalization grants because state and local systems tend to tax income flows at their origin rather than at their destination.[7] To use it
in this way would, as Table IV-4 shows, favor most of the New England and Mideast states as well as Florida, Mississippi, Kansas, and
Oregon. Most of the Plains, Southwestern, and Rocky Mountain
states, in contrast, show lower fiscal capacities when the measure of
these is Personal Income than when it is Income Produced.[8] As allocators of federal grants, then, the two series would clearly give different results, so it is important to decide to what extent they should be
used. On theoretical grounds each has a strong claim, but pragmatic considerations, at least for the immediate future, give the choice
overwhelmingly to Personal Income because estimates are more
available and reliable.[9]

All three of the measures discussed so far deal with state fiscal
capacities in the abstract—that is, with the economic bases that are
theoretically available to state and local governments for tax purposes. For political and other reasons, however, tax practice may de-
part significantly from economic principle. The policy-maker may
wish an index of fiscal capacity that takes these differences into account. Such a measure is provided by the Advisory Commission's
estimates of the yield of the Representative State and Local Tax System in 1960, given in the fourth column of Table IV-4. To derive
the series the Commission first selected all those taxes which in

---

[6] Only twelve states exhibit differences as large as five points between the two
measures. If Bureau of the Census data for all families are compared with those
given in column 2 of Table IV-4, thereby isolating the effect of excluding low-
income families and individuals, only Arkansas, Mississippi, and Tennessee show
differences as great as three points. See ACIR, *Measures of State and Local Fiscal
Capacity and Tax Effort* (October 1962), p. 54.

[7] This is especially true of corporate profits levies, but it also applies, in varying degrees, to property, sales, and other business taxes, and even state individual
income taxes tend to favor the state of origin by giving credits for taxes paid
elsewhere more frequently to residents than to nonresidents.

[8] North Carolina, Louisiana, and Nevada also fall in this category.

[9] Allocating national income produced to the different states, in which the
National Planning Association has pioneered, is subject to all of the difficulties,
both theoretical and statistical, noted in Chapter II. The series given in the third
column of Table IV-4, which is derived from NPA estimates, should be regarded
only as a first approximation to the measure desired. ACIR, *Measures of State and
Local Fiscal Capacity and Tax Effort*, p. 25.

1960 either were used by states with more than half the total population of the country, or were used by states accounting for more
than half of the nationwide potential tax base.[10] It then applied to
each of the selected tax bases in each state an average tax rate equal
to the rate prevailing in the country as a whole in 1960. This
means, for example, that in the Representative Tax System each
state is assumed to levy a general retail sales tax at a uniform tax
rate (2.9 percent) sufficient to produce for all 51 states (including
the District of Columbia) the same 1960 sales tax revenues as were
received in that year by the 37 states that actually did impose general sales taxes.[11] Similar procedures were followed for each of the
other taxes included in the Representative System. The result is a
measure of fiscal capacity that differs considerably from either Personal Income or Income Produced. In general, the Representative
System approach attributes greater taxpaying abilities to the Plains,
Southwestern, and Rocky Mountain states, and lower abilities to
the Mideastern and some of the New England states, than either of
the income series.

The Advisory Commission suggests several reasons for these
differences, but the most important appears to be the well-known
tendency, arising from variations in the rate of return on different
types of wealth, for the burdens of a tax on property—which plays
a dominant role in the Representative System—to be distributed
differently from the burdens of a tax on income. In the present in-
stance, it is the relatively low postwar rate of return on farm property
that has given the predominately agricultural states in the West and
Southwest a greater ability to raise taxes on the basis of wealth than
on the basis of income.[12]

It is important to note that population, used as a divisor in each
of the measures of fiscal capacity so far discussed, performs a dual
function. Not only does it convert aggregate income into a meaning-
ful index by which each state can assess the ability of its inhabitants
to pay taxes, but it also serves as a rough measure of their need for
public services. To allocate federal grants according to the reciprocal of state per capita income, for example, would be to distribute

[10] Both severance taxes on gas and oil and stock-transfer taxes meet the
second test but not the first.

[11] For further details concerning the derivation of the Representative Tax
System see ACIR, *Measures of State and Local Fiscal Capacity and Tax Effort*,
pp. 31-51, 107-21.

[12] *Ibid.*, pp. 56-71.

the funds simultaneously on two different bases—directly in relation to need and inversely in relation to fiscal capacity. The great advantage of using population in this way lies in the simplicity and ready availability of estimates rather than in any inherent superiority.

Numerous refinements in per capita income figures can be conceived of, but for one reason or another only a few could be used to good effect at the present time. Consider, for example, four different characteristics of a state's population that are all positively related to its need for most kinds of public services: the ratio of young and old people to those of working age, the percentage of the population with very low incomes, the density of its geographical distribution, and its rate of growth in the recent past. Measures of the first two "needs" factors appear to be rather closely related to state per capita income (Table IV-5); their addition to the grant allocation formula would probably not change its operation materially. The ten states with the highest percentages of dependent and low-income people in 1959-60, for example, also had very high average rankings (41 and 46, respectively) in the state distribution of per capita income (using 1 for the highest income state and 51 for the lowest), whereas the corresponding ranks for the ten low-need states were only 8 and 9.

Rapid population growth, on the other hand, has characterized some high income (Delaware, Nevada, and California) as well as some low income (New Mexico and Utah) states, but it does not appear to have a consistently important effect on the level of all kinds of state and local expenditures.[13] Population density, however, is a major determinant of city expenditures that is not closely correlated with per capita income.[14]

[13] Glenn W. Fisher, for example, found population increase during the 1950's to be significantly related to 1960 per capita state and local expenditures for local schools, police, general control, and interest payments (positively) and highways (negatively), but not to higher education, public welfare, health and hospitals, fire, or sanitation. See "Interstate Variation in State and Local Government Expenditures," *National Tax Journal*, Vol. 17 (March 1964), pp. 57-74.

Harvey E. Brazer, on the other hand, found population growth during the 1940's to be significantly related only to 1951 city expenditures for fire and for general operating purposes, and in both cases the correlation was negative. See *City Expenditures in the United States*, Occasional Paper 66 (National Bureau of Economic Research, 1959), p. 25.

[14] *Ibid.*, pp. 67 and 76.

TABLE IV-5. Ratios of Dependent Population to Working Age Population and of Low-Income Families to All Families, Ten Highest and Ten Lowest States, 1959–60

State[a]		Percentage of Dependent to Working Age Population[b]	State[a]		Percentage of Low-Income to Total Families and Individuals[c]
Ten Highest States					
Mississippi	(51)	122	Mississippi	(51)	42
Utah	(33)	118	Arkansas	(50)	38
North Dakota	(44)	114	South Carolina	(49)	32
South Carolina	(49)	114	Alabama	(48)	31
South Dakota	(40)	113	Kentucky	(46)	31
New Mexico	(39)	112	Tennessee	(47)	30
Arkansas	(50)	110	North Carolina	(45)	29
Montana	(29)	109	Louisiana	(42)	28
Vermont	(36)	109	Georgia	(43)	27
Louisiana	(42)	109	West Virginia	(41)	27
Ten Lowest States					
District of Columbia	(2)	74	Connecticut	(3)	11
Nevada	(4)	82	New Jersey	(8)	12
New York	(5)	83	Nevada	(4)	12
New Jersey	(8)	84	Hawaii	(19)	12
Connecticut	(3)	88	Alaska	(7)	12
Pennsylvania	(17)	90	California	(6)	13
California	(6)	90	Wyoming	(15)	13
Illinois	(9)	90	Massachusetts	(10)	13
Rhode Island	(20)	91	New York	(5)	14
Alaska	(7)	92	Washington	(14)	14

Source: ACIR, *Measures of State and Local Fiscal Capacity and Tax Effort*, pp. 24, 99.
[a] Number in parenthesis is the rank of the state in per capita personal income in 1959–61 (high to low).
[b] Population under 21 years of age and 65 and over as a percent of the population 21 through 64 years of age in 1960.
[c] Families with incomes below $2,000 and unrelated individuals with incomes under $1,000 in 1959 as a percent of total number of families and unrelated individuals.

By any measure used (and state per capita personal income seems to be the best single choice currently available) interstate differences in both fiscal capacity and the need for public services are clearly very wide. A marked lessening in inequality did occur during World War II, but it has proceeded at a much slower pace since then and gives no sign of accelerating in the near future. Many people would consequently regard the existing degree of interstate inequality as sufficiently great to establish a strong prima facie case for a comprehensive program of federal equalization grants. Some elements of such a program already exist, but as will be seen in the next section, they are still haphazard and relatively unimportant.

The Equalization Powers of Existing Federal Grants

Taken as a whole, federal grants-in-aid tend to be concentrated neither in the wealthy nor in the poor states. In 1961-62, for example, the correlation coefficient between per capita federal grants and per capita state income was slightly negative (—0.04) but not statistically significant.[15] As will be seen below, however, this rough proportionality to income resulted not from a homogeneous set of grant programs but rather from the combination of a minority with significant equalizing effects and a majority of the opposite nature.

It is often argued that federal grants have significant redistributional effects because they are financed by progressive federal taxes. Measurements of these effects are then made by allocating federal taxes among the states on the basis of standard assumptions as to tax incidence.[16] In my view, however, such measurements are likely to be more misleading than helpful. In the first place, they assume unjustifiably that fewer federal grants would mean lower federal tax receipts rather than higher federal expenditures of other kinds. Which of these two results is the more realistic cannot be determined, but the possibility of grant-expenditure substitutions seems far too important to be eliminated from considera-

[15] ACIR, *The Role of Equalization in Federal Grants* (January 1964), p. 63.
Somewhat larger negative coefficients were obtained for 1952 and 1959 (— 0.09 and — 0.26, respectively) by M. A. Haskell, but he went on to show that the negative association disappeared entirely when population density was introduced into the analysis. In his three-variable model, federal grants were inversely related to population density (mainly because of the highway program), population density was positively related to state income, and these relationships alone were strong enough to produce a negative, zero-order correlation coefficient between grants and state income. With population density held constant, grants in 1959 showed a nonsignificant positive correlation with income (0.05). See "Federal Grants and the Income-Density Effect," *National Tax Journal*, Vol. 15 (March 1962), pp. 105-08.

[16] For a recent attempt to measure the redistributional effects both of federal grants themselves and of the taxes that finance them see James A. Maxwell, *Financing State and Local Governments* (Brookings Institution, 1965), pp. 61-66.

tion. Second, even if new grants do induce higher federal taxes, the nature of these taxes is usually unknown; they could be either considerably more or considerably less progressive than the federal tax system as a whole. To assume that any additions to the federal tax system will exactly reproduce the redistributional effects of the system may well be the only way to derive a quantitative measure of the equalizing effects of grant-financing taxes, but it hardly contributes to one's confidence in the usefulness of that measure.

Finally, lack of knowledge about the true incidence patterns of both corporate income taxes and excise taxes means that even measurements of the interstate burdens imposed by the whole tax system have some highly arbitrary characteristics. All things considered, it seems best to concentrate, as is done in the rest of this section, on the redistributional powers of federal grants taken by themselves alone.

Introducing explicit equalizing formulas into federal grant programs is largely a postwar phenomenon (Table IV-6). The use of these formulas appears to be increasing,[17] but in 1962 less than 19 percent of the $7.0 billion granted to state and local governments was distributed on the basis of formulas that either allocated a higher proportion of the available funds to low-income states or increased the federal share of total program costs in states with low per capita income.[18] Moreover, as Table IV-6 shows, public assistance programs were a major segment (73 percent) of the total equalization group, and under them measures of state fiscal capacity were used only in setting the matching requirements. To qualify for a larger share of federal funds, therefore, low-income states had to put up money of their own. Under the grant programs listed in the top part of Table IV-6, in contrast, equalization applied to the

[17] Statistical measures of the relation between grants and state per capita income confirm this trend. Haskell's net correlation coefficients (population density held constant), for example, declined from 0.24 in 1932, to 0.13 in 1952, and then to 0.05 in 1959 (*op. cit.*, p. 106).

James A. Maxwell obtained similar results from rank correlation analysis, his gross coefficients being 0.31 in 1940-41, —0.18 in 1951-52, and —0.59 in 1952-53. See his "The Equalizing Effect of Federal Grants," *Journal of Finance*, Vol. 9 (May 1954), p. 209

[18] Not only were equalization formulas used in programs that distributed only a small portion of total grant funds ($2.9 billion of the $7.0 billion total), but in many of these programs equalization applied only to part of the funds available (Table IV-6).

TABLE IV-6. Federal Grants-In-Aid Distributed on the Basis of a Fiscal Capacity Index, by Program,[a] 1962

Program	Year Equalization Provision Introduced	Type of Equalization Provision[b]	Distributions Based on Fiscal Capacity Index	
			Amount (Millions)	Percentage of Total Funds Distributed Under Program

Programs Using Fiscal Capacity Index in Apportionment Formula

Program				
Maternal and Child Health	1935	N/Y	$ 9	37
Crippled Children's Services	1935	N/Y	10	41
General Health	1935	N/Y	14	95
Tuberculosis Control	1944	N/Y	1	18
Mental Health	1946	N/Y	2	30
Hospital and Medical Construction	1946	HB	61	100
School Lunch	1946	N/Y	89	100
Cancer Control	1948	N/Y	2	60
Heart Disease Control	1948	N/Y	3	63
Basic Rehabilitation Services	1954	HB	63	100
Water Pollution Control	1956	N/Y	3	58
Waste Treatment Works Construction	1956	N/Y	19	46
Child Welfare Services	1958	HB	16	86
National Defense Education Act	1958	HB	45	70
Community Health Services	1961	N/Y	5	100
Total			$339	80

Programs Using Fiscal Capacity Index in Matching Formula Only

Program				
Library Services in Rural Areas	1956	A	$ 8	100
Water Pollution Control	1956	A	2	42
Old-Age Assistance	1958	F	538	44
Aid to Dependent Children	1958	F	213	26
Aid to the Blind	1958	F	17	37
Aid to the Disabled	1958	F	70	36
Child Welfare Services	1958	HB	3	14
Medical Aid for the Aged	1960	F	111	94
Total			$ 962	39
All Programs			$1,301	46

Source: ACIR, *The Role of Equalization in Federal Grants* (January 1964), p. 43.

[a] Excludes the disaster relief and special milk programs which allocated their funds, to a limited extent, according to state fiscal capacities.

[b] N/Y = allocation by indexes of program need and inversely by per capita income.

HB = Hill-Burton formula.

A = variable matching on the basis of the Hill-Burton Allotment Percentage.

F = variable matching on the basis of the Federal Percentage.

apportionment formulas so that low-income states automatically qualified for a higher portion of funds distributed. The superior equalizing power of the latter arrangement is indicated by the fact that while the correlation coefficient between equalized public assistance grants and state per capita income in 1962 was only −0.213, the correlation between the rest of the grants listed in Table IV-6 and state income was −0.601.[19]

In general, federal grant programs make use of three different kinds of equalization arrangements. The first is the Hill-Burton formula, which in its basic form defines the grant to be made to a given state as:

$$G_i = \frac{P_i A_i^2}{\sum P_i A_i^2} F; \qquad A_i = 100 - 50 \frac{Y_i}{Y}$$

where:

G_i = amount of grant to be made to the i-th state,
P_i = population in the i-th state,
A_i = allotment percentage for the i-th state,
Y_i = per capita personal income in the i-th state,
Y = per capita personal income in the United States,
F = total funds appropriated for distribution in a given year.[20]

In effect, Hill-Burton grants are distributed on the basis of weighted population, and the weights used increase rapidly as per capita state income declines. The extent of the variation in the weights may be seen in the following tabulation, which covers approximately the range in state per capita income that currently prevails:

Y_i	A_i	A_i^2
$Y_i = 1.4Y$	30	900
$Y_i = Y$	50	2,500
$Y_i = 0.5Y$	75	5,625

---

[19] ACIR, *The Role of Equalization in Federal Grants*, p. 64.

[20] The grant amounts derived from this formula are frequently adjusted so that no state's allotment falls below a stated dollar minimum and the allotment percentages used do not fall outside a fixed range.

According to calculations made by I. M. Labovitz, if $1 billion were to be distributed to the states by the Hill-Burton formula, using 1960 population data and average state per capita incomes in 1957-59, and giving no state less than $4 million, the highest-income state (Delaware) would receive only $238 per capita, while the lowest-income state (Mississippi) would receive $1,176 per capita.[21] Of the four Hill-Burton programs listed in Table IV-6, two use the basic formula and two replace total population with subgroups that are more closely related to the purpose of the grants.[22]

The second kind of equalization formula, used in 1962 for nine health-grant programs listed in Table IV-6, is determined administratively within general statutory guidelines that specify allocation on the basis of program need and state fiscal capacity. There is, consequently, considerable diversity among the programs, as can be seen from the following greatly abbreviated tabulation based on 1963 laws:

Program	Percentage of Funds Allocated on the Basis of P_i/Y_i	Other Measures Used as Allocators
General Health	95%	Reciprocal of population density
Community Health	40	Population 65 and over; $1/Y_i$
Tuberculosis Control	20	Morbidity and mortality
Cancer Control	60	Mortality and reciprocal of population density
Mental Health	30	Total population
Heart Disease Control	63 (in 1962)	First 100,000 of state population
Water Pollution Control	67	Population density and the number of waste-producing businesses
Radiological Health Control	35	Number of radiation sources; $1/Y_i$
Crippled Children's Services	0	Population under 21 (double weight in rural areas) and state per capita income
Maternal and Child Health Services	0	Live births (double weight in rural areas) and state per capita income

[21] *Federal Grants to States: Comparison of Selected Hypothetical Distribution Formulas and Matching Requirements,* Library of Congress, Legislative Reference Service (March 1961). In the computations no allotment percentage was allowed to exceed 75 percent or to fall below 33⅓ percent.

[22] Child welfare grants are based on the population under 21 years of age, and NDEA grants for the acquisition of special school equipment use school-age population both for P_i and in the computation of Y_i.

It will be noted that under all programs a portion of the funds is distributed inversely in relation to state per capita income (Y_i). Matching provisions are typically on a 50/50 basis, and all but the first program guarantee the states a fixed minimum grant.[23] Two other programs listed in Table IV-6 (School Lunch and Waste Treatment Works Construction) also distribute their funds on the basis of program need and state per capita income, but the formulas used are set by statute rather than by administrative discretion.

The third type of equalization applies to public assistance grants and works so as to reduce matching requirements for low-income states that support program levels above a stated minimum. This is accomplished by defining a federal percentage, F, so that

$$F = 100 - Y_i^2/Y^2 \quad \text{and} \quad 50 \leq F \leq 65$$
$$\text{or} \quad 50 \leq F' \leq 80,$$

and using F and F' in the second and third stages, respectively, of a three-stage grant formula:

A. Each state receives a fixed percentage of the first $\$x$ of its average monthly payment per assistance recipient.

B. Each state receives a variable percentage, F, of the next $\$y$ of its average monthly payment per assistance recipient. It will be noted that F (or F') is 50 percent for all states with average or above-average per capita income.

C. Every state receives an additional grant, under the old-age, blind, and disabled assistance programs, equal to the larger of:

(1) A fixed percentage of the first $\$m$ of payments made to vendors of medical or remedial care for the aged, blind, and disabled and

(2) A variable percentage, F', of the smaller of:
    (a) total vendor payments for medical or remedial care, or
    (b) the next $\$z$ of all average monthly payments per adult assistance recipient that exceed $\$x + \$y$.

It will be noted that the equalization provisions of Stage C will apply only to states with below-average per capita income that

[23] For further details see ACIR, *The Role of Equalization in Federal Grants*, pp. 159-63, 171-86, 192.

make above-scale—that is, greater than $x + $y—average monthly assistance payments.[24]

Some equalization under the Kerr-Mills program, which assists the states to provide medical assistance for individuals aged 65 or over who do not receive old-age assistance but who are unable to meet the costs of necessary medical services, is also achieved by making the federal grant equal to F' times the total amount spent by each state for such medical assistance. This meant that in 1962, for example, West Virginia was able to spend $6.1 million at a cost to itself of only $2.0 million, whereas all of the states with above-average per capita income had to match federal funds equally. Apart from West Virginia, however, the ten lowest-income states participated so little in the program that their average per capita grant for medical assistance to the aged was only 37 cents in 1962, compared to an average grant of 84 cents per capita in the ten highest-income states.[25]

Given the variety of equalization formulas used in 1962 and their uneven application to different programs, it is not surprising to find that a classification of federal grants by broad program groups produces few areas in which average per capita grants are systematically related to state per capita income. When the states are divided into quintiles[26] on the basis of per capita personal income (Table IV-7), for example, neither health grants nor grants for assistance to low-income families show any pronounced tendency to rise as average state income falls until the two lowest quintiles are reached. Grants for federally affected schools and for transportation, neither of which are distributed on an equalization basis, exhibit remarkably similar patterns, rising steadily in average amount from the first to the fourth quintile and then dropping abruptly when the group of lowest-income states is reached. Urban development grants, as would be expected, are concentrated in the weal-

[24] For further details see *Catalog of Federal Aids to State and Local Governments,* prepared by the Legislative Reference Service of the Library of Congress for the Senate Committee on Government Operations, 88 Cong. 2 sess. (1964), pp. 85-98. In 1963, $x = 35 for aid to the aged, blind, and disabled and $17 for aid to dependent children; $y = 35 for the first three programs and $13 for the last; and $m = $15 = z$.

[25] See ACIR, *The Role of Equalization in Federal Grants,* p. 158.

[26] Alaska was omitted because its geographical characteristics make it a special case.

TABLE IV-7. Federal Grant-in-Aid Expenditures in 1962, by Selected Program Group:[a] Average Per Capita Amounts for States by Quintiles Based on State Per Capita Personal Income[b]

	Program Group						
	Education		Low-Income Assistance	Health	Transportation	Resource Development	
Quintile	Federally Affected Schools	Other				Urban	Other
Highest	$1.77	$1.35	$11.10	$0.93	$17.30	$3.25	$1.15
2	2.14	1.75	11.68	0.84	20.60	2.10	1.37
3	2.32	1.92	12.04	0.88	22.50	0.70	1.45
4	2.78	2.42	15.66	1.24	27.30	0.48	1.96
Lowest	0.95	2.54	19.46	1.62	15.30	1.57	1.79

Source: Computed from data on per capita grants given in ACIR, *The Role of Equalization in Federal Grants'* (January 1964), pp. 110ff.

[a] With the exceptions noted below the program groupings are the same as those used in Chapter III, Tables III-3 through III-7. Since the emphasis here is on equalization rather than on benefit spillovers, a few of the multi-purpose programs have been reclassified: low-rent public housing being moved from low-income assistance to urban resource development; grants for crippled children, maternal and child health, and child welfare being shifted from health to low-income assistance; and the school lunch and special milk programs being shifted from health to nonurban resource development. Finally, grants-in-kind, such as those made under the food stamp and surplus agricultural commodity programs, have been omitted.

[b] Quintiles are based on 1962 per capita income, but the state rankings are exactly the same as those given n Table IV-3.

thiest states, except for the lowest quintile which outranks the middle-income states by a wide margin.

Though they have been increasingly exploited in this country in recent years, the equalization powers of functional federal grants are strictly limited. Basically, the reason is that the grants themselves have a restricted role to play in the federal fiscal system— namely, to raise interpersonal equity and increase economic efficiency by paying for the external benefits generated by the spending programs of state and local governments. Properly used, therefore, functional grants cannot help to equalize the abilities of those governments to support activities of purely local interest. To employ them for that purpose would be to interfere unjustifiably with state and local prerogatives to manage their own fiscal affairs. When equalization is the goal, it is unconditional grants-in-aid that should be the center of attention.

The Distributional Effects of Unconditional Federal Grants-in-Aid

The specific function of unconditional federal grants-in-aid would be to increase the income of all state and local governments, and to do so by favoring those with relatively high ratios of needs to resources. As noted earlier, these ratios can be defined with varying degrees of complexity. At our present stage of discussion, however, there is much to be said for simplicity. Economic analysis has yet to produce the ideal measures of fiscal capacity and of basic public needs, and new governmental programs are difficult enough to evaluate even when presented in their simplest feasible form. Allocation formulas must also, of course, be based on data that are obtainable at regular intervals, perhaps annually, at reasonable cost to the government. In this section six specific formulas, each meeting the twin tests of simplicity and availability, will be used to show the wide variety of distributional effects that could be generated by means of federal balancing grants.

The calculations presented below are based on the assumption that $1 billion is to be distributed unconditionally to the states. This sum was selected because it is large enough to make some difference and because the individual state shares derived from it can readily be adjusted to show the effects of larger or smaller grant programs. The six allocators to be considered are:

1. Federal individual income tax collections in 1962 (the latest available year). This was chosen to show the effects of a tax-sharing arrangement that returned income tax revenues to the jurisdictions of source.

2. State personal income in 1963. By itself, a set of proportional grants would be distributionally neutral, though if they were financed by a progressive tax, the entire program would have an equalizing effect. That effect, however, should be attributed to the tax and not to the grants, and the latter are included here as a benchmark series that involves no interstate redistribution of personal income.

3. Population in mid-1963. This is the simplest and most readily available measure of the general need for public services.

4. Population weighted by the reciprocal of state per capita personal income in 1963—$P_i \cdot Y/Y_i$, in terms of the symbols used earlier in the chapter. This formula, now used in several functional grant programs, gives greater assistance to low-income states than straight per capita grants.

5. Population weighted by the reciprocal of per capita income and by an index of state and local tax effort—$P_i \cdot Y/Y_i \cdot E_i/E$, where $E_i = T_i/Y_i$ P_i is the ratio of tax collections to total personal income in the i-th state, and $E = T/YP$ is a similar measure for the country as a whole. The addition of tax effort to the allocation is primarily intended to minimize the danger that unconditional federal grants would be used by some of their recipients to shift legitimate fiscal responsibilities onto others. In addition, it would have the presumably unobjectionable effect of favoring states whose residents have a relatively strong liking for public services. The series used for this purpose is one of several developed from 1959-60 data by the ACIR.[27] All of these series will be discussed below.

6. The Hill-Burton Formula—$P_i A_i^2$, where $A_i = 100-50Y_i/Y$—using computations made by I. M. Labovitz from 1957-60 data.[28] Like the fourth allocator, this formula is in current use (see Table IV-6) and gives relatively large amounts of assistance to the low-income states.

These six allocation formulas will now be used to illustrate the broad variations in distributional effects that could be achieved with a $1 billion program of unconditional federal grants-in-aid.[29] Though perfectly adequate for this purpose, the allocators do use data from slightly different periods of time and hence do not show the precise results that would be produced by a perfectly homogeneous set of formulas.

To highlight the potential equalization and fiscal effects of federal balancing grants, the fifty states and the District of Columbia

---

[27] *Measures of State and Local Fiscal Capacity and Tax Effort,* Chapter 5. Readers may obtain a rough picture of the differences among the Commission's measures of tax effort by comparing the last column of Table IV-4 with each of the preceding four columns. See also Appendix Table A-6.

[28] *Op. cit.*

[29] The basic data needed for each of the allocators are given in Appendix Table A-1.

TABLE IV-8. Distribution of Unconditional Federal Grants, Allocated by Six Alternative Methods, Among Quintiles of States

(Percentage distributions)

	Grant Allocator					
Quintile	Federal Individual Income Taxes 1962 (1)	State Personal Income 1963 (2)	Mid-1963 Population (3)	$P_i \cdot \dfrac{Y}{Y_i}$ (4)	$P_i \cdot \dfrac{Y}{Y_i} \cdot \dfrac{E_i}{E}$ (5)	Hill-Burton[a] (6)
Highest[b]	45	42	35	27	28	21
2	25	25	24	23	21	22
3	9	10	11	11	12	12
4	11	12	14	17	16	17
Lowest	9	12	16	22	23	28

Source: Appendix Table A-2.

[a] The allotment percentage, A_i, was kept within the limits of 33-1/3 and 75 percent, and no state received less than 4/10 percent of the total sum to be distributed.

[b] Includes Alaska whose maximum share was 4/10 percent under the Hill-Burton formula. All other shares were under 2/10 percent.

have been divided into quintiles based on their 1963 per capita personal income.[30] Table IV-8 then shows the proportion of grants that would be received by each group of states under each of the six distribution formulas. As expected, Hill-Burton grants would be the most equalizing, providing 28 percent of all funds distributed to the bottom quintile of states, compared to 16 percent for straight per capita grants and only 9 percent for a return-to-the-source sharing of the federal individual income tax. Comparing the fourth and fifth columns of the table, one may note that the addition of a tax effort index has little effect on the distribution of grants among the five groups, though, as will be seen later, some states would experience significant changes in their individual shares. Column (2) shows both the allocation pattern of a set of proportional grants and the degree to which personal income is distributed unequally among the states. Federal individual income taxes, of course, are even more unequally distributed.

In 1963 a new $1 billion program of federal grants would have

[30] See Table IV-3. The first quintile contains ten states and the District of Columbia. Since Alaska, which also falls in the first quintile, has some very special characteristics, it is either excluded entirely or included but shown separately.

TABLE IV-9. Summary of Four Alternative Methods of Distributing $1 Billion Among the States

Allocators and Grant Ratios	Quintile Averages[a]				
	Highest	2	3	4	Lowest
Distribution by Federal Income Tax Receipts					
Average Percentage of Grant to:					
1. Personal Income	.24	.21	.19	.18	.17
2. State-Local Taxes	2.66	2.29	1.86	1.81	1.91
3. State-Local "Own" Expenditures[b]	2.13	1.78	1.45	1.36	1.39
Per Capita Distribution					
Average Percentage of Grant to:					
1. Personal Income	.18	.22	.24	.27	.31
2. State-Local Taxes	1.95	2.30	2.23	2.65	3.33
3. State-Local "Own" Expenditures[b]	1.57	1.79	1.74	1.99	2.52
Per Capita with Income (Y/Y_i) Weight					
Average Percentage of Grant to:					
1. Personal Income	.14	.20	.24	.31	.44
2. State-Local Taxes	1.51	2.17	2.32	3.11	4.66
3. State-Local "Own" Expenditures[b]	1.22	1.69	1.81	2.33	3.51
Per Capita with Income (Y/Y_i) and Tax Effort (E_i/E) Weights					
Average Percentage of Grant to:					
1. Personal Income	.13	.21	.27	.35	.46
2. State-Local Taxes	1.39	2.16	2.59	3.45	4.72
3. State-Local "Own" Expenditures[b]	1.19	1.67	2.02	2.60	3.56

Source: Appendix Tables A-3, A-4, and A-5.
[a] Alaska excluded. The state-local tax and expenditures series are for 1963.
[b] Total state-local expenditures minus intergovernmental revenue received from federal government.

been equivalent to a 2.25 percent increase in the tax receipts of all state and local governments and would have financed a 1.75 percent increase in all of the direct general expenditures that they paid for from their own funds.[31] These percentages, of course, would have varied considerably from one group of states to another, depending upon the method used to allocate the $1 billion among them. As Table IV-9 shows, tax sharing would have financed a 2.1 percent increase in state-local "own" expenditures for the top quin-

[31] In 1963 total state and local taxes were $44.3 billion, total direct general expenditures were $64.8 billion, and intergovernmental revenue received from the federal government was $8.7 billion. State and local expenditures from their own funds, therefore, were $56.1 billion. See U.S. Bureau of the Census, *Governmental Finances in 1963* (November 1964), pp. 31 and 34.

tile of states but only a 1.4 rise for the bottom quintile. A per capita distribution weighted by both income and tax effort would have paid for only a 1.2 percent increase in spending by the highest-income group and for more than a 3.5 percent increase by the lowest quintile. The redistributive effects of the four allocators used in Table IV-9 may be seen by comparing the grant distributions they produce, relative to state personal income (given in the top row of figures for each allocator), with the flat .22 percent of personal income which a $1 billion set of proportional grants would provide in each state. By this standard, tax sharing would be mildly regressive, a straight per capita allocation would have important equalizing effects, and these effects could be increased by the addition of weights based inversely on state per capita income. Once again, use of the tax effort index would not affect the quintile averages materially.

No program of federal grants-in-aid can be evaluated without careful attention to its effect on individual states. Full details for the six allocators already discussed are given in Appendix Tables A-2 to A-5, but Table IV-10 presents a condensation of these results for a selected group of states. While some states, such as Colorado and Oregon, would not be much affected by the choice of distribution formula (at least among those shown in Table IV-10), others would clearly have much larger grants under some programs than under others. Perhaps the most striking contrast is between Delaware and Mississippi, each of which would receive $4 million if the $1 billion total were distributed on the basis of federal individual income tax revenues. Because Delaware is a high-income, low-effort state, however, it would receive little more than $1 million under the fourth allocator, whereas low-income, high-effort Mississippi would receive $25 million. Among the states that would be significantly affected by the use of a tax effort index are California, New York, South Dakota, and Wisconsin, all of which would gain, and Illinois, Missouri, New Jersey, and Virginia, all of which would lose. It is important, therefore, to consider the basic determinants of tax effort and the problems involved in using some measure of it as one of the allocators of unconditional intergovernmental grants.

The degree of tax effort that is made in different jurisdictions is clearly a function of both fiscal capacity and the need for public services. Of two states with equal needs, the wealthier will have to

TABLE IV-10. Grant Amounts Allocated to Selected States by Five Alternative Methods of Distributing $1 Billion

(In millions of dollars)

State[a]		Federal Income Taxes (1)	Population (2)	Population Weighted by per Capita Income (3)	Population Weighted by per Capita Income and Tax Effort (4)	Hill-Burton Formula[b] (5)
A. Massachusetts	(9)	$ 32.8	$27.7	$22.8	$23.5	$20.6
B. New York	(5)	127.1	93.8	73.5	83.1	50.0
New Jersey	(8)	44.6	34.3	27.8	23.6	20.1
Delaware	(3)	4.0	2.5	1.8	1.3	4.0[b]
Maryland	(11)	21.3	17.4	14.8	13.6	13.9
C. Illinois	(7)	72.7	54.0	43.1	36.6	32.5
Indiana	(18)	24.4	24.9	23.6	21.7	25.7
Wisconsin	(23)	19.7	21.5	21.3	23.0	22.2
D. Minnesota	(24)	15.6	18.6	18.7	22.3	21.1
Missouri	(14)	21.6	22.9	21.5	16.1	24.3
South Dakota	(40)	2.1	3.9	4.8	6.7	5.6
E. Virginia	(34)	17.9	23.0	26.1	21.4	28.3
Tennessee	(46)	13.5	19.6	25.9	24.6	32.4
Alabama	(48)	9.6	17.7	25.2	22.9	31.5
Mississippi	(51)	4.2	12.1	20.8	25.0	25.6
F. Colorado	(22)	10.0	10.4	10.2	11.6	9.9
California	(6)	116.2	93.2	73.5	83.8	52.0
Oregon	(13)	9.2	9.7	9.0	10.2	9.8

Source: Appendix Table A-2.
[a] Grouped geographically. Numbers in parentheses are the 1963 rankings by per capita income (high to low).
[b] The allotment percentage, A_i, is kept within the limits of 33-1/3 percent and 75 percent, and no state receives less than $4 million.

strain less to meet them, and of two states with equal incomes, the one with greater needs will be able to satisfy them only by greater fiscal efforts. In addition, a strong taste for public goods will, other things being equal, make for a higher tax effort, and vice versa. The Advisory Commission's indexes of tax effort all relate actual state and local tax collections in 1960 to its basic 1959-60 need-capacity measures—per capita personal income, per capita above-minimum family income, per capita income produced, and the per capita yield of the representative tax system. Since these four measures, as noted earlier, differ significantly among themselves, the tax effort indexes derived from them behave in a similar fashion. Some states, therefore, cannot be classified by tax effort unless one is willing to make a choice among the alternative indexes. This same difficulty, of course, must be faced if grants are to be allocated inversely by state fiscal capacities, and if personal income is selected for this purpose, it should also be used in any tax effort index that is to be added to the grant allocation formula.

There does not appear to be any strong, systematic relationship between tax effort and state per capita income levels, though a definitive answer to this question must await a multivariate, statistical analysis of all of the determinants of tax effort.[32] In the meantime, Table IV-11 shows that while some high-income states show high tax effort (New York, California, and Massachusetts), others exert relatively low efforts (Delaware, Connecticut, Illinois, and New Jersey). A similar contrast prevails among the low-income states: Louisiana and Mississippi are in the high-effort category, and Kentucky, Tennessee, Alabama, and Arkansas are in the low-effort class. Table IV-11 also shows that of the seven high-income states making a below-average effort according to the personal income index, only Illinois fails to show a significantly higher effort by the representative tax system test. This suggests that the base of the representative system rises less than proportionately to income as income rises. Furthermore, it suggests that states are reluctant to push their own tax rates much above those prevailing elsewhere, with the result that affluent states often fail to exploit their full fiscal capacities. If these suggestions are true, the economic and political measures of tax capacity, and therefore of actual tax effort, will diverge, and the policy-maker may feel obliged to adopt some compromise between them as an allocator of federal grants.

Another aspect of the tax effort index that is chosen is the frequency with which its values will be changed as time passes. If this is to be done annually, and there is much to be said for keeping the

[32] Among the variables that it would be interesting to include in such a study would be federal grants-in-aid, which by lowering needs for public services might tend to lower state tax efforts, and a measure of the extent to which different states rely on "exportable" taxes. If legislators and voters really believe that such taxes can be shifted largely to outsiders, states making extensive use of them should, other things equal, show high degrees of tax effort. By way of intriguing possibilities—of the three states that made extensive use in 1962 of severance taxes, which are presumably among the most "exportable" of taxes, Louisiana was a high tax-effort state, Texas was a low-effort state, and New Mexico was about average. For the tax effort indexes of these states see Appendix Table A-6.

TABLE IV-11. Tax Effort Indexes for the Top and Bottom Quintiles of States Ranked by 1963 Per Capita Personal Income[a]

	Tax Effort Indexes (E_i/E) Based on	
	Personal Income	Representative Tax System
Top Quintile		
District of Columbia	79	85
Nevada	109	93
Delaware	73	87
Connecticut	82	94
New York	113	136
California	114	109
Illinois	85	88
New Jersey	85	97
Massachusetts	103	121
Alaska	71	116
Maryland	92	106
Bottom Quintile		
West Virginia	97	101
Georgia	97	102
North Carolina	99	96
Kentucky	83	80
Tennessee	95	93
Louisiana	126	106
Alabama	91	91
Arkansas	100	90
South Carolina	103	106
Mississippi	120	113

Source: Appendix Table A-6.
[a] E_i =(1960 state and local tax collections in the *i*-th state) ÷(1959 personal income or 1960 yield of the representative tax system in the *i*-th state)
E =similar ratios for the country as a whole.

index as current as possible, some readily available base such as state personal income will be preferable to measures such as the representative tax system which are more difficult to construct. The very decision to keep the tax effort index up-to-date will, of course, affect the interstate distribution of grants, since some states at least can be expected to react by exerting more tax effort in order to qualify for additional federal money. While the first year's allocation of $1 billion might, for example, be that shown in column (4) of Table IV-10, in subsequent years the low-effort states might well succeed in increasing their shares.

Finally, it should be stressed again that all existing tax effort indexes are but crude approximations of ideal measures. Before ideal measures can be derived, however, much more will need to be discovered about such things as: the effects of urbanization on fiscal capacities and fiscal needs; the extent to which user charges, fees, and licenses should be incorporated into measures of fiscal effort; the extent to which such measures are distorted by tourism unless adjustments are made for taxes thought to be borne by vacationers rather than local residents; and the extent of the adjustments needed for interstate differences in the prices of public services of the same quality.

This section has dealt with some of the simpler allocation formulas that might be used to distribute a given sum of money among the states in the form of unconditional federal grants. Even on this restricted basis, however, a wide range of distributional effects could be generated. Still different results could be achieved in various ways—by applying different weights to the factors discussed above; by working with a broader, and more complex, set of fiscal measures; or by segregating part of the total funds to be distributed and allocating this part entirely to the lowest-income states. Joseph A. Pechman, for example, has noted that, "Even if as little as 10 percent of the total were divided among the poorest third of the states (say, in proportion to population weighted by the reciprocal of per capita personal income), the grant to the poorest state would be almost double the amount it would obtain on a straight per capita basis."[33] Federal balancing grants, it is clear, could achieve whatever pattern of distributional effects is desired, and moreover, they could do this by the use of relatively simple and efficient apportionment formulas.

The Allocational Effects of Unconditional Federal Grants-in-Aid

The changes in the allocation of resources that a program of unconditional federal grants would bring about are extremely difficult to specify, except in the broadest terms. They constitute, therefore, a highly controversial aspect of the whole problem, and

[33] "Financing State and Local Government," *op. cit.*, p. 82.

one on which the critics of unconditional federal grants have concentrated their attention. Among the questions that they have asked, and that will be discussed in this section, are the following:

—Will the states spend the money wisely and efficiently for the right programs?

—Will local governments, particularly those in urban areas, receive a large enough share of the funds?

—Will the states use the grants to expand expenditures rather than to hold tax rates below levels that otherwise would have prevailed?

—Will the grants impede or accelerate the movement of workers from resource-poor areas to regions where suitable employment opportunities are available or can be developed?

The Structure of State and Local Spending

No one, so far as I know, has yet developed a reliable method of predicting how legislators and administrators, when presented with a certain sum of money, would allocate the proceeds among different government programs. And, all things considered, perhaps this is just as well. Lacking such a forecasting model, one must turn to past actions as the best available guide to future behavior. Between 1953 and 1963, as shown in Table IV-12, state and local governments devoted 40 percent of the decade's increase in general expenditures to education, 17 percent to highways, 7 percent to public welfare, 6 percent to health and hospitals, and the rest to a long list of less costly functions. Among the most rapidly growing areas were higher education, interest on general debt, and public welfare expenditures not assisted by functional federal grants. Support for local schools did outpace state and local expenditures in general, but not by much. Nevertheless, one may infer from these data that a major share of any unconditional federal grants made to the states would be spent on education.

Of course, each state is likely to react differently, and that very diversity is one of the strongest arguments in favor of assisting states, insofar as they need help with their internal fiscal affairs, by means of unconditional grants. Table IV-13 illustrates this point for the group of states selected for special attention in this study. For

TABLE IV-12. State and Local Direct General Expenditures, by Major Function, Fiscal Years 1953 and 1963ª

(Dollar amounts in billions)

Function	Amounts		Increases 1953–63		
	1953	*1963*	*Amount*	*Percentage Distribution*	*Percentage Increase*
Total General Expenditures	$27.9	$64.8	$36.9	100	132
Education	9.4	24.0	14.6	40	156
Local Schools	7.8	18.8	11.0	30	141
Higher Education	1.4	4.7	3.3	9	246
Other	0.2	0.5	0.3	1	150
Highways	5.0	11.1	6.1	17	123
Public Welfare	2.9	5.5	2.6	7	88
Functional Cash Assistance	2.2	3.4	1.2	3	57
Other	0.8	2.1	1.3	4	179
Health and Hospitals	2.3	4.7	2.4	6	104
Police and Fire	1.6	3.5	1.8	5	112
Sewerage and Sanitation	0.9	2.2	1.3	3	141
Natural Resources	0.7	1.6	0.9	2	125
Housing and Urban Renewal	0.6	1.2	0.6	2	98
General Control and Financial Administration	1.3	2.5	1.2	3	96
Interest on General Debt	0.6	2.2	1.6	4	258
Other	2.6	6.3	3.8	10	147

Sources: U. S. Bureau of the Census, *Governmental Finances in 1963* (November 1964), and *Historical Statistics on Governmental Finances and Employment*, Census of Governments, 1962, Vol. VI, No. 4.
ª Excludes insurance trust, liquor store, and public utility expenditures. Includes federal grants-in-aid.

each of the five categories of general expenditure shown, 1957-62 increases in spending varied considerably in relative importance from one state to another. Increased spending on local schools, for example, accounted for 44 percent of the total rise in spending in Massachusetts but for only 22 percent in Tennessee; health and hospitals attracted 9.5 percent of the 1957-62 expenditure rise in Mississippi, compared to 4 percent in Virginia and Wisconsin. If some of the increases shown are considered to be too small in terms of the national welfare, the appropriate solution would be an expansion in functional federal grants-in-aid. Once benefit spillovers have been taken care of in this fashion, however, there is much to be said for allowing each state to determine its own mix of public services.

TABLE IV-13. Increases in State and Local General Expenditures, by Major Function, Selected States, 1957–62

State[a]	Percentage of 1957–62 Increase in Total General Expenditures Devoted to					Amount of Increase in Total General Expenditures (In millions)
	Local Schools	Higher Education	Highways	Public Welfare	Health and Hospitals	
A. Massachusetts	44	5	−12	13	5	$ 377
B. New York	27	5	13	8	7	2,228
New Jersey	35	8	8	7	5	637
Maryland	40	8	0	7	8	332
C. Illinois	31	8.5	8.5	11	5	1,059
Indiana	43	12	13.5	3	6	451
Wisconsin	31	10	19	7	4	494
D. Missouri	33	7	21	6	8	355
E. Virginia	32	8	19	7	4	380
Tennessee	22	6	29	5	6	331
Mississippi	26	12	16	9.5	9.5	243
F. Colorado	37.5	16.5	3	10	9	216
California	28	14	9.5	8	6	2,964
Oregon	29	12	13	6.5	6.5	228

Source: U. S. Bureau of the Census, *Historical Statistics on Governmental Finances and Employment,* Census of Governments, 1962, Vol. VI, No. 4.
[a] Grouped geographically.

The Principle of Financial Responsibility and Governmental Efficiency

A common criticism of unconditional grants is that they infringe the principle of financial responsibility which asserts that public funds will be well spent only when they are raised and spent by the same governmental unit. The argument is that voters will scrutinize the use of public funds more carefully when they themselves provide them than when the money comes from outsiders. From this it follows that any set of fiscal gifts will increase, at least to some extent, waste and inefficiency in governmental operations.

In the categorical form just stated, the principle of financial responsibility must be rejected. Although unconditional grants may engender carelessness in an affluent recipient, or in almost anyone if they are made in very generous proportions, under different circumstances they are likely to have exactly the opposite effect. A government that is forever feverishly seeking funds with which to meet its next payroll will have little time, and less inclination, for effective fiscal planning. Under such conditions, problems will typically be met on an ad hoc basis, with much waste in the process. With some unconditional grants in hand, however, the government would be free to lift its eyes from its immediate concerns and to plan how best to meet its future responsibilities.

Even governments that are better off financially cannot deal effectively with the complex problems of the modern world without administrators and programmers who are highly trained and strongly motivated. To obtain such people state and local governments must have not only the money to pay their salaries but also enough general resources to support a broad range of important public programs. Opinions differ as to how many states, if any, have already reached this level of fiscal affluence, but until most of them do, many talented people are likely to find Washington a more exciting place to work than the state capitals. This drift of brain-power to the federal level of government cannot be lessened by an expansion of functional federal grants-in-aid but it might be by a new program of unconditional grants or some other form of intergovernmental fiscal assistance that leaves most of the initiative for spending decisions in state and local hands.

Fiscal efficiency requires both that state and local governments be able to afford the very best and that they care enough to use it effectively when they have it. Unconditional grants are one important way of dealing with the first problem, and if they do not become too large compared to local revenues, they should not involve any serious sacrifice of incentives toward efficiency. The most critical stage, presumably, would occur at the very beginning, when a new program of unconditional grants—even of fairly modest dimensions—would constitute a significant portion of the additional revenues accruing automatically to state and local governments. Between 1962 and 1963, for example, general revenues to state and local governments from their own sources increased by $3.8 billion, and of this amount perhaps $2.5 billion resulted directly from the growth in GNP during that period.[34] If these revenues are

[34] "General revenue from own sources," as the term is used by the Bureau of the Census, includes taxes, fees, charges, and miscellaneous receipts but excludes both intergovernmental revenue from the federal government and revenue from

projected to 1966 at the same annual rate of growth (7.5 percent), a level of $67 billion is obtained, implying a built-in 1966-67 rise of some $3.3 billion. If a $1 billion program of unconditional federal grants were started at this point, it would represent nearly a third of the additional revenues that state and local governments could expect to enjoy without having to raise tax rates. Depending upon the allocation formula used, the low-income states would enjoy an even greater jump in their available funds (see Table IV-9).

Though an initial fiscal effect of this size may seem impressive, its threat to state and local financial responsibility is minimized by the shortness of its duration. Once the $1 billion program was in full operation, it would constitute a very small proportion of total state and local general revenues from their own sources (1.5 percent in 1966). Moreover, if the grants were made a fixed proportion of the federal individual income tax base—a possibility that will be discussed in the next section—their built-in annual increase of approximately $70 million would be slightly over 2 percent of the built-in increase in state-local "own" general revenues.[35]

The size of this relative effect could presumably be increased substantially without endangering state and local financial responsibility. If some concern is felt over this problem, particularly at the beginning of the program, the first year's grant might be made contingent upon the approval—by an appropriate federal or joint state-federal body—of each state's budget, including the dispositions planned for both the new unconditional federal grants and all other general funds available.[36] Thereafter, when the grant program would be a much less important element in state and local fiscal planning, there might simply be a periodic review by the same body

---

utilities, liquor stores, and insurance trust funds. Between 1962 and 1963 it rose from $50.4 to $54.2 billion. See U. S. Bureau of the Census, *Governmental Finances in 1963,* p. 20. The $2.5 billion estimate in the text was made by assuming a built-in GNP elasticity of unity, so that general revenues from state and local sources should rise by approximately 5 percent a year.

[35] Based on the assumption that the federal individual income tax base will be $260 billion in 1966 and that it will then be increasing at about $18 billion a year. (See the discussion in the next section.) If begun in 1966, therefore, the grants could be set at 0.4 percent of the federal tax base.

[36] Plans for the unconditional grants alone would be meaningless because of the intermingling of money from different sources in the general fund.

of past state and local expenditures. A similar proposal, made recently by Joseph A. Pechman, would require

the governors to file statements showing the plan for the use of the funds in detail. As guidance for the development of such plans, the Congress might indicate the general areas which it regarded as most urgent, including the need for making funds available for local government services. To be sure that the plan represented a broad spectrum of opinion in the state, the governor might be directed to consult with local officials and representatives of citizens organizations before incorporating the plan in his budget. A detailed audited report on the actual use of the funds might also be required, as well as a certification by appropriate state and local officials that all applicable federal laws, such as the Civil Rights Act, have been complied with in the state and local activities financed by these grants.[37]

Such controls do, of course, have their objectionable features. An alternative procedure would be to introduce the new federal program in gradual stages so as to give all competing state-local political groups full opportunity to make their wishes known. In this way, perhaps with the assistance of federal technical experts, alternative expenditure patterns would be debated and weighed, and hopefully one chosen that would best reflect local tastes and public needs.

The Urban-Rural Allocation of Grant Funds

Conditioned by an ingrained belief in the traditional rural bias of state legislatures, many city officials may hesitate to support unconditional federal grants and may advocate instead the expansion of direct federal aid to urban areas. Unless such aid is justifiable by benefit spillovers that extend beyond state lines, however, it weakens the federal system because it bypasses the proper political lines of authority. The solution, which now appears much more attainable than it did only a few years ago, is to reapportion those state legislatures in which urban voters have been seriously underrepresented. Such reforms should broaden the appeal of unconditional federal grants and make them one of the important ways of al-

[37] *Op. cit.*, pp. 83-84.

leviating, through intergovernmental aid, the difficult fiscal problems of metropolitan areas.

The Budgetary Effects of Unconditional Grants

The basic rationale for balancing grants-in-aid implies that the wealthiest recipients would use them only to expand their expenditures and that some of the poorer grantees, having previously pushed their tax rates to excessively high levels in an attempt to maintain quite ordinary levels of public service, might choose to use some of the money to lower those rates, or at least to stabilize them. Since no state is made up exclusively of affluent areas, some substitution of federal unconditional grant funds for state and local tax receipts could well occur in each of them. How important this type of budgetary effect might be is a matter for conjecture and debate, since past experience provides little or no basis for forecasting future behavior. Something is known, to be sure, about the effects on per capita state and local expenditures of existing federal and state grant programs,[38] but all of these grants differ in important ways from unconditional federal grants. The closest match is provided by the unrestricted state grants, but they are a small minority among state grant programs and, unlike federal grants, they cannot add to state fiscal capacities.

Paradoxically, one can say more about the probable composition than the magnitude of any reduction in state and local tax burdens brought about by unconditional federal grants. The following tabulation shows that in recent years property and sales taxes have been the principal source of additional state-local tax revenue; therefore, it is reasonable to suppose that the tax-reducing effects of federal unrestricted grants would be concentrated on them.[39]

[38] The effects of state grants-in-aid are discussed in Chapter III. Similar estimates have been derived for federal grants, but their significance is more difficult to determine because many federal grants are extended only on a matching basis. See the discussion of this question by Glenn W. Fisher, "Interstate Variation in State and Local Government Expenditure," *National Tax Journal,* Vol. 17 (March 1964), pp. 71-72.

[39] U.S. Bureau of the Census, *Governmental Finances in 1963-64* (May 1965), and *Census of Governments: 1962,* Vol. VI, No. 4, *Historical Statistics on Governmental Finances and Employment.*

Composition of Recent Increases in State and Local Tax Revenues

Tax	Percentage Increase in Total Tax Revenue	
	1953-63	1961-64
Property	46%	36%
Sales and gross receipts	32	37
Individual income	9.5	16
Corporate income	2.5	5
All Taxes	100	100

Opponents of property and sales taxes are more likely to favor a new program of balancing grants than those who regard sales and property taxes as perfectly acceptable components of the fiscal system. In any case, it is important to note that the grants will undoubtedly not shift as many resources from the private to the public sector of the economy as the amounts of money tied up in the program would indicate.

Regional Resource Allocation in the Private Sector

One of the liveliest debates in fiscal economics took place a few years ago over the question of whether equalization grants distorted or improved the allocation of resources among different parts of the country.[40] The answer, as with most questions worthy of debate, is that it all depends upon the circumstances. In this case the relevant circumstances are:

1.   The factors accounting for the poverty of certain sections of the country and, in particular, whether or not a significant out-migration of labor is the best solution to the problem;

2.   The extent to which economic adversity can be counted on to induce the kinds of out-migration from depressed areas that will help allocate workers to their most productive occupations; and

3.   The uses to which the grant funds are put, and in particular whether these uses raise or lower the interregional mobility of labor.

The following paragraphs will discuss each point in turn.

[40] James M. Buchanan, "Federalism and Fiscal Equity," *American Economic Review,* Vol. 40 (September 1950), pp. 583-99; A. D. Scott, "A Note on Grants in Federal Countries," *Economica,* Vol. 17 (November 1950), pp. 416-22; James M. Buchanan, "Federal Grants and Resource Allocation," *Journal of Political Economy,* Vol. 60 (June 1952), pp. 208-17, followed by further comments by Scott and Buchanan in the same journal (December 1952), pp. 534-38.

The extent to which regional poverty can be alleviated by the movement of labor out of the area depends, essentially, on the quality of its basic endowments. Opponents of equalization grants are usually skeptical of finding many well-endowed, low-income areas where labor is not in excess supply compared to potential future demand for its services. Admittedly, lack of natural resources is a sufficient cause of poor regional economic prospects. It is not, however, a necessary one. Both technological change and population growth alter the value of different kinds of natural resources, and a given area may be poor because it has not had an opportunity to exploit its newly acquired economic advantages. In addition, there is the well-known tendency for poverty, once it has taken a firm hold on a community, to perpetuate and accentuate itself quite independently of underlying economic potential. A recent study of geographic mobility, made for the Area Redevelopment Administration by the Survey Research Center of the University of Michigan, concluded that "depressed areas tend to lose through out-migration the more productive groups in the labor force: the young, the better educated, the businessman and the professional. The areas retain a disproportionate number of older people, those who have only a grammar school education, those not in the labor force, and blue-collar workers."[41] Finally, high population densities impose some important social costs that will be discussed in the next chapter. When these aspects are taken into account, the movement of people from thinly populated stagnating areas to thickly populated booming ones will frequently appear much less attractive than simple comparisons of per capita private income would indicate. The war against regional poverty, in short, must employ a wide variety of labor force policies. Some depressed areas need mainly to gain skilled and educated workers; some need a combination of in- and out-movements of different kinds of labor; and some need to accelerate outward movements already under way.

To advocates of the last type of policy, intergovernmental equalization grants appear especially dangerous. These grants, they say, would worsen the situation by weakening the incentives of residents to move elsewhere. Once again, one cannot simply answer yes or no. Some economic adversity is clearly a powerful stimulant to

[41] U.S. Department of Commerce, Area Redevelopment Administration, *Migration Into and Out of Depressed Areas* (September 1964), p. 21.

TABLE IV-14. Migration Patterns and Unemployment Levels, 1955–60 and 1957–62

Group	Migration in 1955–60 of Employed Men 14 Years Old and Over	
	Percentage of 1960 Employment	
	Ten Areas[a] of High Unemployment	Ten Areas[a] of Low Unemployment
Out-migrants	9.0	11.6
In-migrants	6.5	15.8
Net migrants	−2.5	4.3

Out-Migration in 1957–62 by Unemployment Level of Counties of Origin	
Unemployment Group	Percentage Moving Out
Little or no unemployment, 1955–62	19
Substantial unemployment for less than 24 months, 1955–62	15
Substantial unemployment for 24 months or more, 1955–62	11

Sources: 1955–60: U. S. Department of Labor, *A Report on Manpower Requirements, Resources, Utilization, and Training* (March 1965), p. 152; 1957–62—U. S. Department of Commerce, Area Redevelopment Administration, *Migration Into and Out of Depressed Areas*, p. 10.
[a] Standard Metropolitan Statistical Areas of 250,000 or more.

labor mobility, but large doses of it may have exactly the opposite effect. The poorest families are typically not well informed about opportunities elsewhere, and they cannot afford to take advantage of the ones they do know about. The mobility study cited above, for example, noted that, "Contrary to expectations, the mobility of people who have been subject to unemployment is barely higher than the mobility of people without unemployment experience."[42] Nor, as Tables IV-14 and IV-15 show, do out-migration rates tend to be highest either from areas with the highest unemployment or from counties with the lowest average family incomes. Of course, equalization grants cannot always be made with impunity to labor-surplus areas, but they may, depending upon the uses to which they are put, provide a stronger stimulus to out-migration than economic adversity alone.

Among the probable uses of unconditional federal grants, education stands first by a wide margin, and there is ample evidence, illustrated in Table IV-16, that geographic mobility is positively and strongly correlated with the average number of years of school-

[42] *Ibid.*, p. 18.

TABLE IV-15. Percentage of Families Moving Between 1957 and 1962 by Median 1960 Family Income in Counties of Origin

South		Other Regions	
Median County Income	Percentage Moving	Median County Income	Percentage Moving
Metropolitan Areas			
$5,950 or more	14	$6,950 or more	15
$4,950–$5,949	14	$5,950–$6,949	12
$4,949 or less	12	$5,949 or less	11
Nonmetropolitan Areas			
$3,950 or more	20	$4,950 or more	23
$2,950–$3,949	25	$3,950–$4,949	11
$2,949 or less	14	$3,949 or less	13

Source: U. S. Department of Commerce, Area Redevelopment Administration, *Migration Into and Out of Depressed Areas* (September 1964), p. 9.

ing completed. Grant funds used for public health programs and welfare grants to low-income families with children may be equally, if not even more, effective in raising average educational levels and hence in stimulating, sooner or later, the movement of workers out of depressed areas. Welfare grants, it is true, might lower mobility in the short run, but if they are combined with assistance to all able-bodied recipients to develop their skills and with incentives to

TABLE IV-16. 1955–60 Migration Rates of Men in Selected Age Groups, by Educational Attainment

Years of School Completed	Age Group	
	25–29 Years	25 Years and Over
No school years completed	13.3	7.5
Elementary: 1–4 years	17.5	9.1
5–8 years	23.2	10.8
High School: 1–3 years	25.6	14.7
4 years	28.6	17.5
College: 1–3 years	38.2	22.4
4 years or more	55.4	31.6
Total	31.8	15.7

Source: U. S. Department of Labor, *Report on Manpower Requirements, Resources, Utilization, and Training* (March 1965), p. 155.

encourage job- rather than subsidy-taking, these dangers should be minimized.

Equalization grants devoted to health, education, and welfare programs then should have favorable allocation effects even when they are allocated to regions that would benefit from a significant out-migration of labor. Such areas, however, may be inferior choices for the initiation of public works or highway construction, and if so, grant funds should not be used for these purposes. Intrastate fund allocations, in other words, should take regional growth prospects into account. Close-working liaisons should be developed between state-local planning and budgetary officials and those federal agencies, such as the Economic Development Administration and the Office of Economic Opportunity, that are concerned with regional welfare and development. Indeed, there is undoubtedly a need for more intergovernmental programming coordination of all kinds, and a program of unconditional federal grants to the states should provide an excellent opportunity to promote it.

If any general conclusion is warranted by the preceding discussion, it would be that unconditional federal grants are more likely to improve than to distort interregional resource allocation. Either result is, of course, possible in specific instances, but if they are established with some of the safeguards noted earlier, balancing grants should not threaten an efficient geographic allocation of resources. As noted earlier in the chapter, low-income regions in this country have experienced a more rapid rate of economic growth during the postwar period than have the high-income regions. Equalization grants, therefore, should mainly accelerate trends already under way.

Evaluation of Unconditional Grants and Their Major Alternatives

No government program, including federal grants-in-aid, is perfect. The final step in evaluating unconditional federal equalization grants, therefore, is to compare them with the major alternatives for expanding high-priority state and local spending programs, and by doing so, to assess the relative merits and weaknesses of each. The most appropriate context for this discussion appears to be the one in which unconditional grants were initially discussed —namely, a budgetary situation in which, at full employment levels of income, federal tax receipts are expanding more rapidly than federal expenditures. The federal revenue dividend resulting, which might run as high as $5 to $7 billion a year, could be used in a number of different ways that would benefit state and local governments. This section considers the main possibilities.

Federal Debt Retirement

To some, the obvious solution would be to use the revenue dividend to retire part of the public debt. Under the right conditions such a policy would further the achievement of national economic goals and give some assistance to state and local governments. If private and government demands for new output were buoyant enough to create inflationary pressures, some combination of fiscal and monetary restraint would be called for. Using surplus tax revenues to purchase outstanding federal securities would be one possibility. Compared to tighter monetary controls, such a policy would benefit state and local governments by enabling them to borrow on more favorable credit terms, and therefore to continue their capital expenditures at high levels while other types of spending were being curtailed in the interest of price stability. Some indication of the quantitative importance of such a policy choice may be obtained from the behavior of municipal investment under the tight monetary conditions of 1955-57. Charlotte De Monte Phelps has estimated that during that period tightening credit led to the postponement or cutback of between $200 and $300 million of municipal capital expenditures a year, or some 4 to 7 percent of the total volume then being made.[43] Federal debt retirement, then, is capable of giving some assistance to state and local governments, though its amount is uncertain and its incidence would be concentrated on capital, rather than current, expenditures.

Economic conditions, however, do not always favor the accumulation of federal budgetary surpluses for purposes of debt retirement. Whenever private demands are relatively weak, such a

[43] "The Impact of Monetary Policy on State and Local Government Expenditures in the United States," in Commission on Money and Credit, *Impacts of Monetary Policy* (Prentice-Hall, 1963), pp. 646-47.

fiscal policy would, unless combined with sufficiently expansionary
monetary policies, tend to keep the economy operating below full
capacity levels. Valuable output would thus be sacrificed, and it
would include various state and local governmental services for
which financing could not be found. Since state-local tax systems
have a GNP elasticity that is close to unity (See Chapter I), those
governments currently tend to lose about half a billion dollars in
revenue for every 6.5 billion that GNP falls below its full employment level. In 1964, for example, when the Council of Economic
Advisers estimated that GNP was $27 billion below its economic
potential,[44] more vigorous expansionary fiscal policies could presumably have raised state and local tax receipts by nearly $2 bil-
lion. There is no need to emphasize the importance of such a sum to
hard-pressed governors and city officials.

Skillfully handled under favorable conditions, then, a deliberate
program of federal debt retirement could assist state and local governments in expanding their capital expenditures. In practice, however, these gains might not materialize, and the economy might be
kept instead at relatively low, undercapacity levels of income that
would curtail state-local expenditures by reducing the tax revenues
these governments would have at their disposal.

Federal Tax Reduction

In considering the case for using federal tax reduction as a
means of avoiding any excess fiscal drag, it is tempting to include the increased state-local tax revenues that would be generated
by the movement of GNP closer to its full employment level.
Rough calculations, for example, show that state and local taxes
would tend to rise automatically by 16 to 24 percent of any reduction that was made in federal individual income tax receipts.[45]
Similar expansions, however, would also accompany the establishment of a program of unconditional federal grants-in-aid, and

[44] *Economic Report of the President* (January 1965), p. 83. The 1964 level of
GNP was $622 billion.

[45] Based on the assumption that a $1 billion cut in individual income taxes
would increase GNP by $2 to $3 billion, and that state and local taxes, which
were 8 percent of GNP in 1963, would expand proportionately, that is, by $160
to $240 million.

therefore they should not be counted as a distinguishing characteristic of either fiscal policy.

What is needed, instead, is to compare tax reduction and unconditional grants as alternative means of attaining some given level of GNP. In this context, the distinctive characteristic of federal tax reduction is that it increases the margin—GNP minus federal tax revenues—from which state and local governments draw their own tax receipts. Whether they would react to these broadened opportunities by raising their tax rates is debatable. To predict the outcome one must decide whether present state-local tax rates are held down primarily by intergovernmental competition for business and industry or primarily by the extent to which the federal government has preempted the tax field.[46] If the tax competition hypothesis is accepted, and the discussion in Chapter I indicated that there is much to be said in its favor,[47] federal tax reduction would clearly not be an effective means of assisting state and local governments. Accepting the second hypothesis makes the evaluation process more complicated, but it would not necessarily change the outcome. If states and municipalities can be counted on to absorb a significant portion of any fiscal slack that is left by federal tax reduction, they are very likely to do so by expanding property and sales, rather than income, taxes. Since future federal tax cuts are likely to apply almost exclusively to the individual and corporate income taxes,[48] the end result, in the eyes of many, would be a less equitable tax system. It might also be a less efficient one, unless significant progress were made in solving some of the tax coordination problems discussed in Chapter II. Finally, the stabilization powers of the federal government would be weakened, and it is highly doubtful that fifty independently acting state governments would prove a reliable substitute.

[46] For purposes of discussion it is assumed throughout this section that state and local tax rates are not held down simply by lack of voters' desire for more state-local services.

[47] See pp. 23-24.

[48] After the tax reductions made by the Excise Tax Act of 1965, as amended in 1966, federal excises with a high priority for later reduction or repeal will have an annual yield of less than $2.5 billion. This assumes that the various benefit-oriented excises, together with tobacco and liquor taxes, will continue to be regarded as permanent parts of the U.S. revenue system.

As a means of assisting state and local governments, then, federal tax reduction suffers from two major weaknesses: it may not succeed in raising their self-financing powers by very much, and if it does, the nation may end up with what many would regard as an inferior tax system. Its chief merit is that it does foster state-local fiscal independence and responsibility, and some of its defects could be minimized by increased use of the tax coordination devices discussed in Chapter II. Among the different means of assisting the states both federal tax reduction and tax coordination deserve serious attention.

Tax Credits and Source-Oriented Tax Sharing

Two effective means of circumventing the debilitating effects of interstate tax competition would be federal credits for specified state and local taxes or a return to the jurisdictions of origin of part of the yield of some federal taxes.[49] Federal adoption of a fractional credit against state and local individual income tax liabilities, for example, might stimulate states without income taxes to adopt the levy and income-tax states to expand their use of it. If so, this would be a way of reducing federal taxes without greatly diminishing the relative importance of personal income taxation in the country's total tax structure. Duplicate, or even triplicate, income tax administrations would be maintained, but with extensive use of the coordination devices discussed in Chapter II, compliance costs could probably be kept to a minimum.

A major difficulty with fractional tax credits is the great uncertainty that exists concerning their fiscal effects. For this reason they can be opposed both by Congressmen who fear the loss of federal revenues that would result from vigorous state reactions to the credits and by proponents of higher state-local spending who fear that credits would fail to stimulate much additional state and local tax effort. An alternative that would meet these objections is some form of tax sharing. If x percent of the federal individual income tax base, for example, were returned to the states of origin each year, state revenues would be raised in a relatively predictable way; and this plan, unlike one that involved sharing a fixed percentage of federal tax revenues, would insulate state and local governments

---

[49] Both of these tax coordination devices are discussed in detail in Chapter II.

from the effects of countercyclical changes in federal individual income tax rates. These gains, however, would be accompanied by a centralization of tax powers that could be avoided under a tax credit plan.

Both tax credits and source-oriented tax sharing have one important weakness—neither is capable of reducing existing inequalities in state and local fiscal capacities. For this purpose one must rely either on federal grants-in-aid of some kind or on direct federal income maintenance programs (including negative tax credits).

Conditional and Unconditional Federal Grants-in-Aid

In principle, conditional and unconditional federal grants serve two separate and distinct purposes. Conditional grants are needed to optimize the allocation of resources to state-local spending programs with significant external benefits; and unconditional grants are needed to balance whatever basic fiscal deficiencies prevent the states from financing internal program benefits at reasonable tax rates. In practice, these distinctions are blurred by the lack of precise measures of the relative importance of external and internal benefits, but there is still much to be said for a federal system that includes both kinds of grants.

Consider, by way of illustration, a state spending program that generates external benefits whose importance is indeterminate within a wide range, say between 10 percent and 40 percent of total social and private benefits. According to the theory presented in Chapter III, functional, open-end federal grants, covering 10 percent of total costs, would expand that program and move its operation closer to the levels justified by its total benefit-cost ratio. To stop federal aid at that point, however, would not guarantee optimal results. Even if external benefits were only 10 percent of total benefits, some states might be unable to finance their own 90 percent shares, and if external benefits were more important than that, even states with ample funds would lack incentives to give the program as much support as it should have.

One solution, of course, would be to increase the federal share under its functional grant program. If the open-end feature of the grants were maintained, however, the danger of distorting state budgeting by paying for internal benefits of a specific type would increase. Moreover, the higher the federal share, the greater would appear the need for detailed federal controls and safeguards. Beyond some unknown point, in short, the federal government could reasonably be accused of unwarranted interference in purely local affairs.

Nor would a shift to closed-end functional grants be likely to improve matters much. There might, it is true, be somewhat less pressure for federal controls because each year's total appropriation could be fully determined in Washington, but at the same time Congress might be induced to raise the federal share beyond justifiable levels. Under the circumstances assumed, for example, a 50-50 shared-cost program would produce an unpredictable mixture of nonoptimal budgetary decisions. Because external benefits are no more than 40 percent of total benefits, each state would have a strong incentive to expand operations so as to qualify for the maximum federal grant. However, incentives for expansion would be deficient beyond that point, because external benefits would be at least 10 percent of the total benefits. Only by pure chance would any one state program end up close to its optimal operational level.

Another solution would be to restrict the open-end, functional federal grants to a 90-10, state-federal, matching basis and to initiate a program of unconditional grants. Greater aid could then be given to the low-income states, and all states would be helped while they were left free to determine for themselves the specific internal program benefits they wished to enjoy. The maintenance of functional grants at minimum levels, however, would risk a serious overexpansion of unconditional grants. As these "costless" funds were increased, states would be more and more tempted to spend them carelessly and wastefully, and in any case, they would not be induced to give sufficient support to programs with above-minimum benefit spillouts.

While it seems clear that both functional and unconditional federal grants are needed, it is not easy to say in what relative amounts. Uncertainty about economic effects creates a need for flexibility, for compromise solutions that minimize the risks of serious distortions, and for trial-and-error, or hopefully, trial-and-success procedures. If one were starting out anew one might begin with a set of minimum-level functional grants and a modest-sized program of unconditional equalization grants. When the state and local governments had adjusted to these, rate of return tests could be used to provide a partial answer[50] to the question of what should be done next by way of intergovernmental assistance. If external-benefit programs, for example, came out better than programs that generated internal benefits primarily, further expansions of functional grants would be called for. If internal-benefit programs also showed superior rates of return, compared to the relevant private rates, more unconditional grants would be indicated, provided that state and local governments were, by and large, making as much tax effort as could reasonably be expected of them. As is already done in this country, functional grants could also be used to finance experimental and demonstration projects that would provide some of the data needed for the rate-of-return tests. Finally, fiscal research could be directed at measurements of the effects of federal grants on different types of state and local expenditures so that Congress could choose more confidently and accurately the best means of achieving desired levels of public services. By these means, and with good luck, one might gradually but steadily approach that mythical goal—the ideal federal grant-in-aid system that an all-knowing superbeing could have set up in the first place.

In this country, of course, we are presently very far from beginning anew. Functional federal grants have been growing rapidly and are likely to continue to do so. Not the least of the merits of a new program of unconditional grants would be the insurance it would provide against excessive use of the functional approach—against budgetary distortion at the state and local level and more control from Washington than is warranted by interstate and national benefit flows. People worry whether unconditional moneys would be well spent, and they are seldom put to much trouble to find evidence to justify their concern. One of the dangers of generous functional federal assistance, however, is that it is likely to keep states in a dependent and inferior role and to prevent them

---

[50] Partial because benefit-cost analysis can deal only with those benefits that can be quantified. For an illuminating discussion of the problems involved here, see Robert Dorfman (ed.), *Measuring Benefits of Government Investments* (Brookings Institution, 1965).

On the other hand, computations of rates of return are much more manageable than estimations of external or internal benefit ratios, because the latter require knowledge of not only all program benefits but also their geographical incidence.

from showing how well they could do on their own. With unconditional grants in their treasuries, states could take a fresh look at the programs that seem best to serve their own individual needs and tastes. The results might be surprisingly good, even from the point of view of outsiders.

If unconditional federal grants are initiated, they should be responsive to economic growth and to rising price levels, since state-local fiscal deficiencies are likely to increase with both. One way of doing this, and of helping states to plan by enabling them to forecast their future grant receipts with reasonable accuracy, would be to distribute each year x percent of the federal individual income tax base, that is, x percent of the total taxable income reported on federal individual tax returns. Between 1955 and 1963, while its statutory definition remained unchanged, the base grew by 64 percent, compared to an increase of only 47 percent in GNP. If this relationship continues to hold and GNP grows at 5 percent per annum, taxable income should rise from nearly $245 billion in 1965 to $340 billion in 1970:

	Federal Individual Income Tax Base	
Year	Amount (Billions)	Percentage of GNP
1955	$128	32
1963	209	36
1965	244	37
1970	340	40

Grants that were proportional to the individual income tax base, then, would have a significant built-in growth component. Some automatic fall-offs during recessions could be expected, but for short economic declines the loss of grant funds is not likely to be great, and in more severe recessions Congress could, if it wished, provide supplementary allocations.[51] To relate the grants to taxable income instead of income tax liabilities would enable the federal government to vary its tax rates countercyclically without creating thereby procyclical fluctuations in its grant distributions.

[51] During the 1953-54 recession, for example, taxable income fell off by only 14 percent of the decline in GNP, and in 1957-58 it moved countercyclically. See Richard Goode, *The Individual Income Tax* (Brookings Institution, 1965), p. 347, and Wilfred Lewis, Jr., *Federal Fiscal Policy in the Postwar Recessions* (Brookings Institution, 1962), pp. 43-44.

Consolidated Grants-in-Aid

Federal grant assistance, allocated by broad program areas with few or no controls, is an intermediate solution to intergovernmental fiscal problems, lying between open-end, matching, functional grants on the one hand, and unrestricted general grants on the other. As noted in Chapter III, some consolidation of existing federal grants may well be justified by the lack of any important differences between the external-internal benefit ratios of the separate programs. Most advocates of consolidated grants, however, go well beyond this in their proposals.[52] Federal assistance, in their view, should be given for education, health, public welfare, and other similar, broad program areas. Since the amount of money allocated to each program would presumably reflect its relative importance from a national point of view and since the use of the money within each program area would be left entirely to state and local governments, the plan would combine some attention to national priorities with a high degree of fiscal decentralization.

Simply to substitute consolidated grants for all existing programs, however, would result in suboptimal support for all state-local programs with important benefit spillouts.[53] This deficiency could be eliminated either by retaining enough functional programs or by distributing consolidated grant funds in a way that stimulates state-local expansions of external-benefit activities. Title I of the 1965 federal school aid bill provides a good illustration of the latter method. The maximum basic grant depended on two variables: the number of school-age children from poor families in the state and average per-pupil state education expenditures. By expanding the latter a state can qualify for a larger basic grant. In addition, special incentive grants based on the amount by which the growth in local school expenditures between 1964 and 1965 exceeds 5 percent were authorized for fiscal 1967.

[52] See, for example, George C. S. Benson and Harold F. McClelland, *Consolidated Grants: A Means of Maintaining Fiscal Responsibility* (American Enterprise Association, December 1961).

[53] The same criticism applies to Senator Goldwater's proposal, made during the 1964 presidential campaign, that present programmatic grants be replaced by completely unrestricted lump-sum cash grants. See, for example, *Congressional Quarterly*, Oct. 23, 1964, p. 2527, and Milton Friedman, "The Goldwater View of Economics," *New York Times Magazine*, Oct. 11, 1964, pp. 136-37.

Basic Title I grants take into account both state-local tax effort and the incidence of poverty. Their redistributive effects are shown by the $1 billion allocation that is expected to be made in fiscal 1966:

Quintiles of States Based on 1963 per Capita Income	Percentage of Basic Grants
Highest	27
2	19
3	9
4	17
Lowest	28

Compared to the distributions given earlier in Table IV-8, this one apportions relatively large amounts to the bottom quintile and relatively few funds to the second and third quintiles. Use of the funds is subject to few federal restrictions;[54] consequently the program exemplifies an interesting compromise between the more specialized and closely controlled grant programs discussed in Chapter III and completely uncontrolled federal aid.

Minimum-Program, Equalization Grants

Achieving, with the assistance of federal grants, a nationwide minimum level of specific public services commands wide support.[55] Such a policy is justifiable either on welfare grounds or by benefit spillouts, but the welfare case is much the stronger. Minimum-program grants, therefore, cannot be regarded as an acceptable substitute for optimizing functional grants, but they might serve as a substitute for unconditional grants or as a factor to be used in designing them.

If it could be shown that the external benefits of state-local

[54] PL 89-10, signed by the President on April 11, 1965, simply states that Title I funds are intended primarily for programs to assist educationally deprived children from low-income families. Within these general guidelines, local school districts are given broad spending discretion, though their plans must be approved by state and federal educational agencies and periodic progress reports must be made to the same authorities.

[55] In his comprehensive survey of federal grant programs Paul Studenski, for example, included it among the four basic purposes that those grants had been set up to serve. See his "Federal Grants-in-Aid," *National Tax Journal*, Vol. 2 (September 1949), pp. 198-99.

spending programs were significant up to some readily identifiable level of operations and then fell off abruptly beyond that point, federal matching aid would be called for in large amounts only up to that point. Beyond it, benefit spillouts might not be considered important enough to cause serious distortions in state-local budget choices, and the result would consequently be a set of fixed federal grants that helped finance a foundation, or minimum, program in each state. The nature of the external benefits discussed in Chapter III, however, leads one to doubt that they do behave in this way. Instead it is more likely that external benefits maintain their importance as program levels are expanded. If this is so, minimum-program grants would risk perpetuating suboptimal service levels in the affected areas.

The other justification for minimum-program grants rests on straight ethical, or welfare, grounds. Every citizen, it may be urged, is entitled to enjoy some minimum level of public services without having to pay excessively high taxes. In general, this could be accomplished by designing a program of federal grants so that:

$G_i = N_i - R_i$, where

G_i = the foundation grant to be made to the i-th state,

N_i = the cost of the minimum programs in the i-th state, and

R_i = the revenue that can be raised by reasonable levels of taxation in the i-th state.

The total grant could either be apportioned by program before being distributed to each state, or it could be given unconditionally so that each state would be free to do its own apportioning. The first method is a demanding one. In principle, it would require a rigorous specification of the minimum beneficial services sought in each area of governmental operations and then an objective measurement of the costs of obtaining those services in different parts of the country. There is no need to stress the difficulties involved in either procedure. Widespread agreement about minimum service levels is unlikely, and governmental input-output relations cannot be measured with a high degree of accuracy.[56] In addition, exten-

---

[56] In Japan these problems are given explicit recognition by including in the grant formula only 75-80 percent of the recipient's standard tax revenues (R_i), the remainder being regarded as a contingency fund for the grantee to fall back on whenever the N_i are underestimated.

sive federal controls would presumably be required to ensure the effective use of the grant funds in each program area.

Trying to guarantee each citizen a specific minimum-sized basket of public goods, therefore, is likely to prove an expensive and controversial undertaking. The second, and simpler, method would be to guarantee only the means needed to purchase the minimum basket, leaving it up to each grantee to decide whether it wanted that basket or some alternative one. In effect, this approach leads to a set of unconditional federal equalization grants, the amounts of which are determined, at least in part, by reference to the costs of minimum public service levels in the different states and to the revenues which each could contribute on its own if it taxed its residents at, say, average tax rates for the country as a whole.[57] Having determined the grants in this way the federal government might then wish to make the maintenance of those standard tax rates either a prerequisite for the receipt of any federal money or a factor in determining what proportion of its total entitlement each state qualifies for.

Income Maintenance Programs

The United States has at present a complex set of income maintenance programs which involve all three levels of government and

[57] The tax rates actually imposed in states of average income and wealth seem as good a determinant of the R_i as any. One alternative, which would derive the standard tax rates from the specification of minimum program levels, would be to proceed as follows:

Given that C_i = measure of the fiscal capacity of state i,
(1) Set $R_i/C_i = k$ for all i, and make
(2) $\Sigma G_i = \frac{1}{2}\Sigma N_i = \Sigma R_i = k\Sigma C_i$, then
$$G_i = N_i - R_i$$
$$= N_i - kC_i \text{ from (1)}$$
$$= N_i - \frac{1}{2}\Sigma N_i/\Sigma C_i \cdot C_i \text{ from (2)}.$$

Under such a program the federal and state governments would share minimum-program costs equally and each state would contribute equally, relative to its own fiscal capacity. The standard tax rate, k, would be one-half of the ratio of total costs to total national fiscal capacity:

$$k = \frac{1}{2}\Sigma N_i/\Sigma C_i.$$

Grants with these characteristics were designed as the basic kind of federal equalization grant by the Advisory Commission on Intergovernmental Relations in their *The Role of Equalization in Federal Grants*, p. 49. See also Selma J. Mushkin, "Barriers to a System of Federal Grants-in-Aid," *National Tax Journal*, Vol. 13 (September 1960), pp. 215-17.

transfer income to rich and poor, old and young, sick and healthy. That these programs are not sharply focused on the poor has long been known, at least to those who cared to look. But only with the recent greatly increased interest in the problems of poverty have some of the quantitative dimensions of the situation been clarified. In fiscal 1965, for example, "an estimated $20 billion of the $40 billion total spent on these public transfer payment programs went to persons who were, or would otherwise have been below the poverty-income line; these payments helped to raise some 3 million households out of poverty, but about 12 million units still received insufficient income to meet the minimal living levels now used to define poverty."[58] In addition, half of the poor, or some 17 million persons, received no public transfer income at all. According to official estimates, "to eliminate completely the poverty-income gap —the amount by which total money income falls short of meeting the poverty-income standard—would require that almost $12 billion be added to the income of the poor."[59]

These deficiencies have stimulated considerable interest in the development of new federal income maintenance progams. One possibility would be to expand the scope and size of existing general assistance payments, now entirely financed by state and local governments, by establishing a new program of matching federal grants for this purpose. Another possibility would be for the federal government to adopt what has come to be called a negative income tax. There are several variants of this proposal,[60] but all would make use of the existing federal individual income tax administrative apparatus to make annual money payments to the poor that would be a positive function of the gap between family income and the poverty-income standard established as appropriate for that family. Thus the federal government might pay 20 percent of the first $500 of

[58] *Economic Report of the President* (January 1966), p. 114.

[59] *Ibid.*, p. 112. The poverty-income standard was defined by the Social Security Administration in response to the passage of The Economic Opportunity Act of 1964 and takes account of differing family sizes and composition and differences between living costs in urban and rural areas. In 1964, for example, the poverty-income line for four-person nonfarm families was set at $3,130, and for farm families of the same size at $2,190.

[60] See, for example, James Tobin, "On Improving the Economic Status of the Negro," *Daedalus*, Vol. 94 (Fall 1965), pp. 891-94; "Income Tax That Pays the Poor," *Business Week* (Nov. 13, 1965), pp. 105-06; and Christopher Green, *Negative Taxes and the Poverty Problem* (Brookings Institution, forthcoming 1967).

deficient family income, 30 percent of the next $500, and 50 percent of any additional deficiency.

The important question for this study is the extent to which these federal income maintenance programs would be substitutes for a new program of unconditional federal grants. Though no specific answer can be given until the nature of the new income maintenance programs is known, the general prognosis seems to be that only a limited amount of substitution would occur. Federal matching grants for general public assistance, for example, might well increase the volume of state-local expenditures for this purpose, thereby intensifying the fiscal pressures on other spending programs. Any additional income support for the poor would, of course, raise incomes and expenditures, and hence state-local tax receipts, especially in the low-income states. However, a set of unconditional equalization grants would, as they were spent by the recipient governments, have many of the same feedback effects. What expanded federal income maintenance programs would accomplish is the reduction, or even the elimination, of one of the important deficiencies in existing state-local expenditure programs. Other deficiencies, it is true, could also be reduced if federal income subsidies were made generous enough to raise both the consuming and the taxpaying abilities of the poor by substantial amounts. This, however, seems an unlikely contingency in the near future. In the meantime, the other state-local spending deficiencies will remain, and, depending upon how serious they are adjudged, will call for the use of unconditional federal grants or some of the other federal aids discussed earlier.

Summary

In this section it has been assumed that current state-local fiscal efforts, and hence state-local expenditure levels, are below the amounts desired by most people, and the major means of eliminating these deficiencies have been compared and evaluated. The range of choice is a broad one, and no one way is likely to prove sufficient to the purpose at hand. The degree to which each method should be used depends upon the strength of the different factors that make for inadequate state-local tax efforts; therefore those factors are listed below, along with the federal fiscal policies that would appear to be most effective in dealing with them.

Reason for Inadequate State-Local Spending Levels	*Appropriate Federal Fiscal Policies*
1. State-local inertia and inefficiency	Federal technical assistance with both expenditure and tax programs
	Tax coordination (Chapter II)
2. Federal preemption of the tax field	Federal tax reduction combined with tax coordination policies designed to maintain the efficiency, equity, and stabilizing powers of the national tax system
	Tax credits
3. Benefit spillouts from state-local expenditure programs	Functional, open-end, matching grants (Chapter III)
	Consolidated grants
4. Interstate competition for business	Tax credits
	Source-oriented tax sharing
	Consolidated grants
	Unconditional grants
5. Inadequate fiscal capacities	Unconditional equalization grants
	Consolidated equalization grants
	Federal income maintenance programs
6. Inadequate rate of growth of full-capacity output (including investment by state and local governments)	Budget surpluses; federal debt retirement; easy monetary policy

This listing includes all of the alternatives considered except minimum-program equalization grants which, for reasons given earlier in the section dealing with them, are not regarded as effective means of dealing with either external benefit flows or inadequate state fiscal capacities. Minimum-program computations, however, might prove helpful in determining both the total amount and the interstate distribution of any unconditional federal grants that are inaugurated.

If, as many believe, both interstate tax competition and inadequate fiscal capacities are important deterrents to the achievement of optimal state-local spending levels, only unconditional or consolidated equalization grants would help to solve both problems at once. Lacking these grants, the federal government would need to combine two or more policies, such as tax credits to deal with interstate competition and equalization grants made only to the poor states to deal with inadequate fiscal capacity.

Unconditional State Grants

Whenever states wish to offset the fiscal deficiencies of their local governments with unconditional grants, they are likely to enjoy one advantage that the federal government lacks—the recipients, being more homogeneous than the individual states, can be grouped on the basis of need into a limited number of classes. Members of each class can then be offered assistance that will enable them to maintain either minimum program levels at average tax rates or, if greater equalization is desired, average program levels at minimum tax rates. An interesting example of the latter plan is the grant program recently proposed for Canada by John F. Graham.[61] Under it, local governments would be grouped according to the factors, other than income and wealth, that determine per capita local government expenditures, and for each separate class, j, the average amount spent per person on all internal-benefit programs, $\bar{E}_j$, would be estimated. The standard local expenditure for any government, i, in class j would then be:

$E_{ij} = P_i \bar{E}_j$, where P_i is the population in jurisdiction i.

For each class of municipality a set of standard tax rates would be derived by comparing standard expenditures with local fiscal capacities:

$k_{ij} = E_{ij}/B_{ij}$, where B is the tax base used in all municipalities, or if more than one tax is used, some appropriate measure of local fiscal capacities.

From these rates the smallest one would be selected to serve as the uniform tax rate in the grant allocation formula:

$$k_{oj} \leq k_{ij}.$$

[61] John F. Graham, "Fiscal Adjustment in a Federal Country," *Inter-Government Fiscal Relationships*, Canadian Tax Papers, No. 40 (Canadian Tax Foundation, December 1964), p. 23.

The unconditional grants to be made to each local government would then be:

$$G_{ij} = P_i \overline{E}_j - k_{oj} B_{ij}.$$

In effect, this type of grant program would guarantee each local government's ability to purchase average service levels at minimum tax rates for its particular class, and within each group grants would be made to all but the richest jurisdictions.[62]

[62] The plan can be readily shifted to one for minimum-program grants by substituting F_{ij}, the cost of some specific foundation program, j, in each government unit, i, for E_{ij}.

CHAPTER V

Metropolitan Fiscal Problems

THE UNITED STATES IS FAST BECOMING a metropolitan country. At the beginning of the century less than one-third of the United States population lived in urban areas; by 1960 that ratio had almost doubled, and official estimates indicate that it will approach three-quarters by the year 2000. Table V-1 shows this population growth in Standard Metropolitan Statistical Areas (SMSA's).[1] In 1960 there were four states with over 85 percent of their population in Standard Metropolitan Statistical Areas and nine more had between 70 and 85 percent (Table V-2). The number of large cities with a million or more people is expected to increase from 24 in 1960, with 34 percent of the nation's population, to 48 in 2000, with 50 percent of the population.[2]

Most people are all too familiar with the ugliness and frustrations of modern urban life—the smog and noise, the stop and start of commuter traffic, polluted rivers and blighted districts, juvenile crime and official corruption, overcrowded slums and the struggles

[1] The Census Bureau defines a Standard Metropolitan Statistical Area as a county or group of contiguous counties containing at least one city of 50,000 or "twin cities" with a combined population of at least 50,000. Contiguous counties must be metropolitan in character and socially and economically integrated with the central city. For convenience the terms "city" and "SMSA" will be used interchangeably in this chapter.

[2] Committee for Economic Development, *Developing Metropolitan Transportation Policies: a Guide for Local Leadership* (April 1965), p. 18.

166

TABLE V-1. Population Growth in Standard Metropolitan Statistical Areas, 1900–2000

Year	Number (In millions)	Percentage of Total U. S. Population
1900	24	32
1910	35	38
1920	46	44
1930	61	50
1940	67	51
1950	85	56
1960	113	63
2000	235	74

Source: Committee for Economic Development, *Developing Metropolitan Transportation Policies: a Guide for Local Leadership* (April 1965), p. 18.

of the poor for better education and broadened economic opportunities. There may be disagreement about the basic causes of these difficulties. Some critics, for example, have traced much of the problem to the automobile,[3] while others have diagnosed the fundamental illness as "economic unity fractured by political multiplicity."[4] But there can be no doubt about the need for public finance

TABLE V-2. Frequency Distribution of States by Percent of Population in Standard Metropolitan Statistical Areas, 1960

Percent	Number of States[a]
85–100	4[b]
70– 84	9
55– 69	9
40– 54	9
25– 39	8
10– 24	6
0– 9	5[c]

Source: Advisory Commission on Intergovernmental Relations (ACIR), *Governmental Structure, Organization, and Planning in Metropolitan Areas* (July 1961), p. 6.
[a] Excludes the District of Columbia which is entirely metropolitan.
[b] California, New York, Massachusetts, and Rhode Island.
[c] Mississippi with 9 percent; Alaska, Idaho, Vermont, and Wyoming with none.

[3] See Mitchell Gordon's discussion of "autosclerosis," an increasingly debilitating urban disease brought on by prolonged exposure to the automobile, in his *Sick Cities* (Penguin Books, 1965), pp. 27-85.

[4] Donald J. Curran, S.J., "The Metropolitan Problem: Solution from Within?" *National Tax Journal*, Vol. 16 (September 1963), p. 213.

specialists to join with other experts in the increasingly important urban reform movement. Upon the success of their efforts may depend the quality of life in this country for many years to come.

Numerous improvements in that quality, fortunately, are already under way, some of them stimulated by the federal urban renewal program.[5] Philadelphia, for example, has eliminated some of its sickest areas by combining the restoration of Georgian houses with the construction of modern tower apartments along the Delaware River. Chicago is experimenting with high-rise buildings designed to achieve a more efficient integration of shopping and residential facilities, and the San Francisco Bay Area is defying the traditions of the most automobile-oriented state in the Union by embarking upon an ambitious mass transit system. Beauty is more and more sharing the stage with utility as a concern of both public and private enterprise. In St. Louis Eero Saarinen's 630-foot-high Gateway Arch is rising beside the Mississippi to symbolize the expansive spirit of the area, and in New York the willingness of at least one giant U. S. corporation to spend money for beauty and other intangible urban benefits has been publicized by a series of mundane tax cases.[6] The crucial question, of course, is whether these encourag-

---

[5] Authorized by the Housing Act of 1949, the program got off to a slow start, particularly before the creation of the Urban Renewal Administration in late 1954. Administrative budget expenditures did not exceed $50 million until fiscal 1958, a year before the annual increase in outstanding guaranteed loans first passed the $100 million mark. For fiscal 1966, however, budget expenditures were projected at $356 million and the increase in guaranteed loans outstanding, representing economic effects not reflected in budget expenditures, was expected to be $368 million. *The Budget of the United States Government, Fiscal Year Ending June 30, 1966*, pp. 303 and 408. For a discussion of the economic effects of guaranteed loan operations see George F. Break, *The Economic Impact of Federal Loan Insurance* (National Planning Association, 1961).

[6] Constructed at a cost of $36 million, the Seagram Building was assessed for tax purposes in the next year at only $20.5 million. Though assessed valuations in New York City are known to be close to 100 percent of full market value, Seagram & Sons challenged the city's assessment, arguing that, when capitalized at a reasonable rate (8 percent), its commercial rentals from the facilities, including an imputed value on the quarters it occupied for its own activities, produced a present value of only $17.8 million for the building. It would appear, therefore, that hard-headed business calculations of profit from the building alone justified only half of the sum actually spent to construct it. Whether there were intangible benefits worth an additional $18 million, and whether these would be reflected in

ing beginnings can be accelerated and expanded in scope. The problems involved—and only the major ones can be discussed here —may be grouped under three heads:

1. *Organization.* Metropolitan areas in this country are typically complex "aggregations of uncoordinated governmental units,"[7] that produce economic benefit and cost spillovers in their most intense form. The challenge, in this case, is to combine economic performance, interpersonal equity, and political responsibility. The effort has only begun.

2. *Systems Analysis and Program Evaluation.* Even the most talented and conscientious urban reformers sometimes find that their plans produce unintended and unwelcome results. New freeways, for example, may not reduce traffic congestion, and slum clearance may only force the poor to live under similar conditions elsewhere. Good initial planning, which is now much more feasible because of the development of modern systems analysis, is particularly important in urban areas for two reasons. The first is that many metropolitan projects involve heavy capital investments which may be wasted unless their future effects are clearly foreseen. The second is that urban programs frequently require the close cooperation of a number of independent metropolitan governments, and this can be obtained only on the basis of systematic, reasonably objective, geographical allocations of program benefits and costs.

3. *Financing.* While both tax coordination and intergovernmental grants-in-aid provide helpful solutions to metropolitan fiscal needs, there is much that cities can do on their own account. Existing taxes can be reformed, new ones can be added, and public services can be priced, either explicitly or by means of user taxes, so as to assess beneficiaries with their fair shares of program costs.

After a brief discussion in the next section of the fiscal charac-

---

higher profits from the increased sale of company products to a beauty-appreciating public are questions that, fortunately, need not be discussed here. For the legal arguments in the case see *Joseph E. Seagram & Sons, Inc. v. Tax Commission of the City of New York*, 238 N.Y.S. 2d 228 (March 5, 1963) and 251 N.Y.S. 2d 460 (June 10, 1964).

[7] Harvey E. Brazer, "Some Fiscal Implications of Metropolitanism," in *Metropolitan Issues: Social, Governmental, Fiscal*, Guthrie S. Birkhead (ed.), Maxwell Graduate School of Citizenship and Public Affairs, Syracuse University (February 1962), p. 79 (Brookings Institution Reprint No. 61, 1962).

)f metropolitan areas, these three groups of problems will
up in turn.

A Fiscal Profile of Metropolitan Areas

Like other local governments, those in metropolitan areas spend
most of their money for education and obtain most of it from property taxes and intergovernmental grants-in-aid. In 1962, for example, SMSA direct general expenditures were divided as follows:[8]

Education	42%	Interest on Debt	4%
Highways	8	Administration	4
Public Welfare	7	Housing and Urban Renewal	4
Sanitation	6	Fire Protection	3
Health and Hospitals	6	Parks and Recreation	3
Police	5	Miscellaneous	9

General revenues in the same year came from the following
sources:

Property taxes	50%	Nonproperty taxes	8%
State grants-in-aid	25	Current charges	11
Federal grants-in-aid	2	Miscellaneous	4

There are, however, some important differences between metropolitan and nonmetropolitan units which are illustrated in Table V-
3. Per capita city expenditures were notably higher for public welfare, health and hospitals, police and fire protection, sewage and
sanitation, parks and recreation, and housing and urban renewal.
All together these functions required $69 per capita in metropolitan
areas in 1962, compared to only $35 elsewhere. Being big spenders
in general, cities had to raise relatively large amounts of revenue,
both from property taxes ($112 per capita compared to $76 elsewhere) and from local sales and income taxes ($14 per capita ver-
sus $2 elsewhere). Their need to do this was intensified by their
smaller share of state grants-in-aid ($55 per capita compared to
$64 in nonmetropolitan areas), a deficiency that in 1962 was only
partly offset by federal grant programs.

[8] U.S. Bureau of the Census, *Census of Governments: 1962*, Vol. 5, *Local Government in Metropolitan Areas*, p. 10

TABLE V-3. Per Capita Government Expenditures and Revenues, Within and Outside Standard Metropolitan Statistical Areas, by Type, 1962

Category	Amounts	
	Within SMSA's	Outside SMSA's
Direct General Expenditures	$233.58	$179.79
Local Schools	94.52	94.13
Capital Expenditures	16.76	13.92
Other Expenditures	77.75	80.12
Higher Education	2.78	1.16
Transportation	22.57	23.57
Public Welfare	16.13	9.78
Health and Hospitals	12.93	9.60
Police	12.59	5.28
Fire	7.79	2.91
Sewerage and Sanitation	13.35	5.48
Parks and Recreation	6.43	1.77
Housing and Urban Renewal	8.69	1.61
Natural Resources	1.97	2.45
Correction	2.03	0.67
Libraries	2.05	1.13
Parking Facilities	0.51	0.34
Administration and Control	8.88	7.74
Public Buildings	2.87	1.96
Interest on General Debt	8.92	4.69
Intergovernmental Revenue	60.26	66.95
Federal	4.91	2.67
State	55.35	64.29
General Revenue from Own Sources	163.52	108.10
Taxes	130.19	82.04
Property	111.78	76.30
General Sales	7.48	0.98
Selective Sales	3.66	0.92
Income	2.41	0.32
Motor Vehicle Licenses	0.63	0.71
Current Charges	23.48	19.18
Miscellaneous	9.86	6.88

Source: U. S. Bureau of the Census, *Census of Governments: 1962*, Vol. 5, *Local Government in Metropolitan Areas*, pp. 184–85.

Public spending varies greatly from one city to another. In 1957, for example, per capita expenditures of all local governments in the twenty-four largest SMSA's in the country ranged from lows of $132 to $134 in Atlanta and St. Louis to highs of $254 and

$257 in Los Angeles and New York, respectively.[9] Such wide variations raise intriguing questions about the causal factors at work. Though no definitive study is yet available, there are several quantitative analyses that deal with particular kinds of expenditures and with special groups of cities.

1.   Brazer's study of 462 cities in 1951 showed population density, median family income, and per capita intergovernmental revenue to be significant determinants of per capita city expenditures.[10] The first of these three findings is especially interesting because it indicates that urban governments do have a special need for public services which, except for highways, is greater on a per capita basis than needs in rural areas. One of the major difficulties encountered by any nationwide analysis of city expenditures is the fact that the allocation of functions between state and city governments varies considerably from one state to another. To the extent that assignment to the city is accompanied by state grants-in-aid, however, this factor is incorporated in Brazer's intergovernmental revenue variable and hence is kept from distorting the influence of the other variables in the study.[11] A second problem, which could not be dealt with for the sample of 462 cities, was the variation from city to city in the allocation of functions to counties, school districts, special districts, and other overlying governmental units.

2.   To handle this difficulty Brazer made a special study of the 1953 expenditures of all local governments operating in forty large metropolitan areas (with 1950 populations over 250,000).[12] Per capita intergovernmental revenue continued to be an important determinant of expenditures, as did population density for spending on police, fire and sanitation (positive regression coefficients) and highways (negative coefficient). Median family income, however,

[9] Seymour Sacks, "Metropolitan Area Finances," National Tax Association, *1963 Proceedings of the Fifty-Sixth Annual Conference on Taxation*, p. 420 (Brookings Institution Reprint No. 84, 1964). For an analysis of expenditure variations in a larger group of cities (462) in 1951 see Harvey E. Brazer, *City Expenditures in the United States*, Occasional Paper 66 (National Bureau of Economic Research, 1959), pp. 2-13.

[10] *Ibid.*, pp. 16-35. All regression coefficients were positive except the one relating highway spending to population density, as would be expected.

[11] *Ibid.*, p. 22.

[12] *Ibid.*, pp. 47ff.

was statistically significant only as a determinant of education and recreation expenditures. Other variables were also tested, the most interesting and most successful being the ratio of city population to the population of the entire metropolitan area. By showing a negative relation with per capita expenditures (except for recreation, highways, and sanitation), this variable strongly suggested that suburbanites do exert financial pressures on central cities.[13] If true, this lends support to financing arrangements, to be discussed later, by which commuters and shoppers make some financial contribution to central city services.

3. One of the most interesting of the empirical studies of specific public programs is Hirsch's analysis of expenditures per pupil in twenty-seven St. Louis school districts in the early 1950's.[14] Assessed property valuations, an index measuring the quality of public education, and the ratio of high school pupils to all pupils in average daily attendance were all found to be positively related to education expenditures; but size of district, a measure of pupil density, and the rate of increase in public school enrollments between 1951 and 1956 were not significant determinants. Hirsch also computed the income elasticity of education expenditures, finding it to be relatively low (0.5 to 0.6) in general and particularly low for instruction costs (0.4). As family incomes rise, it would appear, people would rather spend their school funds on auxiliary services (elasticity of 1.1) and on plant operation and maintenance (0.6) than on teacher salaries.

4. A more recent study took pupil achievement, measured by several standard statewide tests, as the dependent variable and found that in 249 California school districts in 1960-61 it was positively and closely related both to the economic and social status of district families, as measured by median household incomes and

---

[13] *Ibid.*, p. 52. Similar results were obtained by Amos H. Hawley, "Metropolitan Population and Municipal Government Expenditures in Central Cities," *Journal of Social Issues*, Vol. 7 (1951), pp. 100-08, and by Julius Margolis, "Metropolitan Finance Problems: Territories, Functions, and Growth," *Public Finances: Needs, Sources, and Utilization*, A Conference of the Universities, National Bureau Committee for Economic Research (Princeton University Press, 1961), pp. 256-61. Margolis, however, concluded that the evidence was not comprehensive enough to support any definitive conclusions.

[14] Werner Z. Hirsch, "Determinants of Public Education Expenditures," *National Tax Journal*, Vol. 13 (March 1960), pp. 29-40.

median education of adults, and to the quality of instruction, as measured by the percentage of district teachers in the upper salary quartile and instructional expenditures per pupil in average daily attendance.[15] Though numerous other independent variables were tested, none was consistently important in all districts.

The Organization of Metropolitan Governments

Few problems of political economy rival in complexity that of determining the best way to organize public affairs in the modern city. Sometimes there seems to be no one at all in effective charge, and matters drift on rather aimlessly. At other times independent and powerful government agencies determinedly pursue their own ends, regardless of the effects on other agencies or on other parts of the metropolitan area. To describe the situation as "chaos loosely organized" is only a slight overstatement. In any case, the situation offers ample opportunities for private profit—one reason it has survived as long as it has—but only slight promise for rapid progress in the governmental sphere. Many U.S. cities, it would appear, could benefit from a systematic reorganization of their public sectors. Of course, needs in this respect differ greatly from one place to another, but there are enough common threads in the urban fabric to warrant a brief discussion of problems and prospects.

The Allocation of Public Programs among Metropolitan Governments

The first problem concerns the level of government that should handle each public function or subfunction. Five criteria, of varying degrees of importance in specific instances, are usually thought to provide the basis for rational choice on this question. They are external benefits and costs, economies of scale, variety of consumer choice, political participation, and interprogram evaluations. The first three are primarily economic in nature, and the last two mainly political.

EXTERNAL BENEFITS AND COSTS. In many respects metropolitan areas constitute a single economic entity but are serviced by a mul-

<hr>

[15] Charles S. Benson and others, Report of the California Senate Fact Finding Committee on Revenue and Taxation, *State and Local Fiscal Relationships in Public Education in California* (March 1965), pp. 38-58.

tiplicity of smaller governmental units. Therefore, the spillover problem with the inefficiencies and inequities that result (see Chapter III) appears in its most intense form in city finance. One solution is to expand the geographical scope of governmental units so as to convert external benefits and costs into internal ones. Another solution, which avoids some of the disadvantages of highly centralized and unified government operations, is to make increased use of intergovernmental fiscal aids. Both are discussed in detail later.

ECONOMIES OF SCALE. If education costs fall by $27 per pupil as the size of the school district is increased from 1,500 to 50,000 pupils in average daily attendance but increase by $10 per pupil if the size is extended to 80,000, as has recently been estimated by Nels W. Hanson,[16] the advantages of keeping school districts close to the 50,000 level are obvious. On the other hand, as already noted, Hirsch found economies of scale to be statistically insignificant in his 1951-55 study of St. Louis school districts ranging in size from 600 to 84,000 students.[17] Though his study had much less geographical scope than Hanson's, it did attempt to allow for quality variations in school services which must be held constant if economies and diseconomies of scale are to be measured accurately. Given the well-known difficulties involved in measuring educational quality, however, the question of what constitutes the optimal size of school district is likely to remain unresolved for some time. Nonetheless, since 26 percent of metropolitan school districts still enroll fewer than 300 pupils,[18] much can still be done to increase school efficiency.

For other municipal services the problem of measuring quality seems less intractable, and various economic analyses can be drawn on to apply the economy-of-scale criterion. Though unit costs and size show little interrelationship for police and fire protection and for refuse collection,[19] significant scale economies appear to character-

[16] "Economy of Scale as a Cost Factor in Financing Public Schools," *National Tax Journal,* Vol. 17 (March 1964), pp. 92-95.

[17] *Op. cit.,* p. 36.

[18] Advisory Commission on Intergovernmental Relations (ACIR), *Metropolitan Social and Economic Disparities: Implications for Intergovernmental Relations in Central Cities and Suburbs* (January 1965), p. 47.

[19] Werner Z. Hirsch, "Expenditure Implications of Metropolitan Growth and Consolidation," *Review of Economics and Statistics,* Vol. 41 (August 1959), pp. 232-41, and "Cost Functions of an Urban Government Service: Refuse Collection," *ibid.,* Vol. 47 (February 1965), pp. 87-92.

TABLE V-4. Classification of Public Programs According to Economies of Scale, Benefit Spillouts, and Political Proximity

Program	Allocation Criterion			
	Economies of Scale	Benefit Spillouts	Political Proximity	Composite
Local Schools	+	+	O	=
Transportation	+	+	X	+
Public Welfare	O	+	O	=
Health and Hospitals	+	+	+	+
Police				
Basic Services	O	O	O	O
Special Services	+	+	O	+
Fire	O	O	O	O
Water Supply	+	+	+	+
Sewage Disposal	+	+	+	+
Refuse Collection	O	O	+	O
Refuse Disposal	+	+	+	+
Parks and Recreation	O	+	X	=
Public Housing	O	+	O	=
Urban Renewal	X	+	X	=
Libraries				
Basic	O	O	O	O
Special	+	+	+	+
Air and Water Pollution	+	+	+	+
Urban Planning	+	+	X	+

+   favors areawide control because economies of scale are important, or benefit spillouts are significant, or political proximity is unimportant
O   favors local control for the opposite reasons
=   favors joint control
X   indicates that the allocation criterion yields a debatable result

ize such programs as water supply, sewage disposal, public health services and hospitals.[20] Others may be found in Table V-4, which classifies the most important municipal services by the presence or absence of economies of scale.

Finally, mention should be made of one important factor that affects the operation of all programs, though in varying degrees. Large governments, other things being equal, are better able to hire top-quality technical and professional personnel than are small governments, and they should, therefore, be able to provide better public services at a given cost. This provides a strong argument either for consolidating small urban governments until they are large

[20] ACIR, *Performance of Urban Functions: Local and Areawide* (September 1963), pp. 154-55, 168, 200-03.

enough to be able to afford high quality officials or for making intergovernmental cooperative arrangements designed to attract the technical expertise needed for the more complex urban programs and to make it available to participating jurisdictions.

VARIETY OF CONSUMER CHOICE. Voters in federal elections frequently complain about the similarity of the economic programs offered by the two major parties. Too often, it has been said, they have "an echo not a choice." Consumers of metropolitan public services, however, are in a somewhat more favorable position. Different parts of the area are likely to offer different combinations of governmental services at different local tax rates, and the alert resident may seek out the specific package that is most appealing to him. Since individual tastes in this respect seem to be diverse, a city that offers a variety of local public programs should be a more attractive place to live than one that does not. One of the virtues of metropolitan decentralization, in other words, is the opportunity it gives for a better adaptation of public goods to the desires of different groups of residents.[21]

In the nature of things, however, these opportunities are strictly limited. The system will work only for programs with benefits that flow mainly to the residents of a given area and that are financed by taxes with a strong benefits-received orientation. Two difficulties are immediately apparent. As may be seen in Table V-4, many of the most important local programs generate benefits that spill over local boundaries, and some programs, public welfare being a prime example, cannot be financed by benefit levies at all. This means, for example, that local financing of welfare activities is likely to produce a flight of the affluent from above-average levels of public charity, either in the core city with its disadvantaged minorities or in residential suburbs with a high concentration of low-income residents. Though local financing of education by property taxation may produce a healthy competition among jurisdictions of approximately equal wealth per pupil, it also stimulates the use of zoning restrictions and other devices to create protected enclaves with relatively high tax capacities and low public service needs.

Vigorous competition among independent metropolitan govern-

[21] For a theoretical analysis of this question see Charles M. Tiebout, "A Pure Theory of Local Expenditures," *Journal of Political Economy*, Vol. 64 (October 1956), pp. 416-24.

ments, then, is likely to produce a mixture of good and bad effects. At its best it replaces sloth and inertia with an active search for better and more varied public services and for more efficient ways of providing them. At its worst, however, it enables some to enjoy high-quality services and low tax rates while others suffer from exactly the reverse. One of the most difficult problems facing the urban policy maker is how to achieve the former while avoiding the latter. To solve this he will need, among other things, to experiment with new kinds of intergovernmental relations.

POLITICAL PARTICIPATION. Essential though it is to effective democracy, active citizen participation in political decision-making is no guarantee of success in government. Under the right circumstances, it results in programs that are well adapted to voter wishes and that are operated without waste or graft. Under less favorable circumstances, however, it can produce divisive debate and stalemate instead of action or, as is sometimes worse, it can produce actions that exacerbate rather than solve the problems at hand. There is no need at this point to discuss the various organizational devices that can be used to increase the chances of good results.[22] People-to-government proximity is generally regarded as one of them and it is a quality that tends to flourish in small jurisdictions.[23] Participation that is not rewarded with tangible results, however, is not likely to continue long, and local governments can be too small to cope with many urban problems entirely on their own. Nor is the nearness of the voter to his government equally important for all local programs, and Table V-4 attempts to distinguish those, such as local libraries, that are likely to benefit most from a high degree of accessibility, from those, such as air and water pollution control, that are likely to benefit least.

[22] In the words of the ACIR these features include "the number and nature of elective officials, the manner of their election (by district or at large), their terms, the distribution of powers among them and the appointive personnel, provisions for notice and hearings on proposed policy changes, administrative provisions for receiving and acting on complaints, provisions for initiative and referendum, and recourse to the courts." *Alternative Approaches to Governmental Reorganization in Metropolitan Areas* (June 1962), p. 13.

[23] For a discussion of ways of strengthening neighborhood government in large urban areas see Luther H. Gulick, *The Metropolitan Problem and American Ideas* (Alfred A. Knopf, 1962), pp. 107-13. In Gulick's opinion one reason that broad metropolitan institutions have so far failed to achieve a high degree of acceptability in this country is that reformers have concentrated on areawide decision-making processes and have neglected ways of preserving legitimate local interests.

INTERPROGRAM EVALUATIONS. In principle, each use of public funds should be compared with every other use and only the most valuable ones chosen. Whereas in the private sector of the economy the impersonal forces of the money market are relied upon for this purpose, in the public sector it is the highly personal budgeting process that must produce the answers desired. Ideally, this means either that all urban programs should be managed by one multipurpose government,[24] or if separate governmental units are to exist for other reasons, that their activities should be subject to review at some higher level. In practice, however, the provision of areawide services often depends on the cooperative efforts of independent governmental units. In such cases, it is essential to have some reasonably objective basis for allocating costs to specific jurisdictions, and it is here that benefit-cost analysis, to be discussed later, has an important role to play.

It will be noted that the five criteria just discussed point, as criteria often do, in opposing directions. Whereas the first, second, and fifth all favor relatively large governmental units, the other two definitely throw their lots in with the small jurisdictions. How one makes the choice in practice, therefore, will depend on the importance he accords the different criteria. Diversity of opinion on this score is inevitable, but as a basis for further discussion, the tabulation below presents one considered choice, which has been guided particularly by the work of the Advisory Commission on Intergovernmental Relations(ACIR) and Werner Hirsch.[25] The tabulation shows the allocation of program responsibilities among metropolitan governments.

Primarily Local	*Joint*	*Primarily Areawide*
Fire	Elementary and Secondary	Planning
Basic Police Services	Schools	Health and Hospitals
Basic Libraries	Transportation	Water Supply
Local Parks	Public Housing	Sewage and Sanitation
Refuse Collection	Urban Renewal	Air and Water Pollution
	Public Welfare	Refuse Disposal
		Special Police Services
		Special Libraries
		Regional Parks

[24] For a discussion of the advantages and limitations of general government see *ibid.*, pp. 81-89.

[25] In addition to the studies already cited see Werner Z. Hirsch, "Local Versus Areawide Urban Government Services," *National Tax Journal,* Vol. 17 (December 1964), pp. 331-39.

If this classification is realistic, some solution intermediate between complete local control and complete metropolitan centralization is needed. In its simplest form it would be a two-level federal system, the base being formed by a number of independent municipalities dealing with all programs that generate purely local benefits and large enough to take advantage of most of the economies of scale inherent in such programs—50,000 to 100,000 people is a commonly suggested size. On the second level would be a single metropolitan government which, in addition to having jurisdiction over the areawide programs listed above, would assist the municipalities both by making grants to them for whatever external benefits their activities yield and by setting uniform revenue-raising rules, to be discussed later, designed to strengthen local taxing powers.

The present hodgepodge of metropolitan governments will not be converted overnight into some simple, functional system. The mere magnitude of the task is imposing enough, to say nothing of the distrust with which many people view big city governments,[26] or of the inertia and vested interests that always oppose basic reforms. In 1962, for example, the 212 SMSA's then recognized by the U.S. Census Bureau contained over 18,000 separate governmental units:[27]

Type	Number	Percent of National Total
Counties	310	10
Municipalities	4,144	23
Townships	2,573	15
School Districts	6,004	17
Special Districts	5,411	29
Total	18,442	20

[26] According to the ACIR, "distrust of the central city and its motives with respect to regional approaches is found in suburbia across the land." *Intergovernmental Responsibilities for Water Supply and Sewage Disposal in Metropolitan Areas* (October 1962), p. 50. See also ACIR, *Factors Affecting Voter Reactions to Governmental Reorganization in Metropolitan Areas* (May 1962).

[27] U.S. Bureau of the Census, *Census of Governments: 1962*, Vol. 5, *Local Government in Metropolitan Areas*, p. 2. Overlapping occurs mainly between counties and municipalities and between special districts and the other types of governmental units. School districts sometimes overlap other boundaries and sometimes are coterminous with counties, townships or municipalities.

The New York metropolitan region alone, as Robert Wood has so effectively publicized, spreads over parts of three states and contains more than 1,400 governments.[28] What rearrangements of these kaleidoscopes would contribute most to the solution of pressing metropolitan fiscal problems? The major possibilities are discussed briefly in the next section.

Reorganization of Metropolitan Governmental Systems

In its survey of eighteen major proposals for local government reorganization that were submitted to popular referendum in metropolitan areas between 1950 and 1961, the ACIR found that only one of the seven most sweeping reforms was adopted, compared to three out of six of intermediate scope and four of the five most limited proposals.[29] An overall batting average of only eight out of eighteen is hardly the most encouraging statistic one could present to the would-be metropolitan reformer. Nor, according to two recent studies of the problem, can he count on natural economic and social forces to simplify the task for him.[30] Nevertheless, the potential rewards are great, and as the ACIR's analysis makes clear, past failures were by no means unavoidable. State and federal assistance is becoming increasingly available, and cities certainly do not lack either for advice or for means of improving their environments.

INTERGOVERNMENTAL AGREEMENTS. Widely used in California, particularly in the Los Angeles region with its "Lakewood Plan," these are cooperative contractual arrangements under which one government sells services to another or several governments join to carry out a specific function.[31] Their basic purpose is to achieve greater economies of scale and to provide services of a more specialized nature than would otherwise be possible. Being voluntary,

[28] Robert C. Wood, *1400 Governments* (Harvard University Press, 1961).

[29] *Factors Affecting Voter Reactions to Governmental Reorganization in Metropolitan Areas,* p. 8.

[30] Curran, in *National Tax Journal;* and Charles S. Liebman, Harold Herman, Oliver P. Williams, and Thomas R. Dye, "Social Status, Tax Resources and Metropolitan Cooperation," *National Tax Journal,* Vol. 16 (March 1963), pp. 56-62.

[31] A 1961 study found 2,832 intergovernmental contracts in operation in California, their most common purposes being tax collection and property assessment, public health, library services, prisoner care, and election services. ACIR, *Alternative Approaches to Governmental Reorganization in Metropolitan Areas,* p. 27.

however, their creation is attractive only when both parties clearly stand to gain, and once contracts are established, disputes may arise over rates and the quality of service.[32] In addition, any extensive use of them is likely to damage local governmental operations by converting the recipients from active political units into passive purchasers of public services.

The role of intergovernmental agreements, then, is a limited but important one, and in its 1966 State Legislative Program the ACIR noted with approval a 1963 Georgia law that authorized special state grants-in-aid to support such joint urban development projects.[33]

METROPOLITAN COUNCILS AND PLANNING COMMISSIONS. These are voluntary associations of elected public officials which, with the help of a professional staff, survey metropolitan needs and resources, prepare and revise areawide plans, and attempt to coordinate local governmental activities that affect the economic well-being of the entire urban area.[34] Though their powers are only those of persuasion, they may promote informed discussion of regional problems, which gradually makes both elected officials and the general public aware of the costs of unintegrated metropolitan government and leads to the establishment of regional governments that do have suitable powers.[35]

[32] For some examples see ACIR, *Intergovernmental Responsibilities for Water Supply and Sewage Disposal in Metropolitan Areas*, p. 36. Particularly troublesome in this respect are contracts between the central city and a number of suburbs which give central city voters the sole right to vote on bond issues to finance suburban capital improvements. Favorable votes under these circumstances are likely to depend on the setting of profit-producing prices for the suburban services, and suburbanites, resentful of paying more than central city residents, may then seek to develop their own programs even though they are less efficient and produce more undesirable spillovers than the integrated contractual system.

[33] *1966 State Legislative Program of the Advisory Commission on Intergovernmental Relations* (October 1965), p. 357.

[34] For a more detailed statement of these functions see the ACIR's proposed statute "providing for the establishment of metropolitan area planning bodies." *Ibid.*, pp. 239ff.

[35] Among the notable activities of existing metropolitan councils have been the preparation by the New York Metropolitan Regional Council (a three-state intergovernmental body) of a plan to deal with air pollution; a study of regional park and open space facilities by the Association of Bay Area Governments in the San Francisco region; and the initiation of a coordinated six-year capital improvements program by local governments in the Salem, Oregon, metropolitan area. See ACIR, *Alternative Approaches to Governmental Reorganization in Metropolitan Areas*, pp. 34-37.

In addition, metropolitan planning bodies may serve as intermediaries to coordinate and supervise the flow of state and federal grants-in-aid to local governments in their areas.[36] There is, however, one important risk. Voluntary urban associations may appear to accomplish much more than they really do, and as a result they may retard, rather than accelerate, the solution of metropolitan problems.

THE URBAN COUNTY. The great attraction of this method of metropolitan reorganization is the relative ease with which functions can be transferred from small municipalities to an already existing, larger county unit. In this way areawide problems may be given their proper scope and focus without the birth pangs that usually accompany the creation of an entirely new governmental system.[37] For the method to work, however, the county in question must encompass the entire urban area, and this is now the case in only about two-thirds of the SMSA's in the country. Even in them, the gains from converting the county into a metropolitan government may, in time, bring about increased future difficulties when the city begins to expand beyond the county boundaries, since they have typically been more difficult to change than the boundaries of a municipality.[38] Legislative reapportionments, however, may help to mobilize greater support in the future for changes in urban county lines.

Any transference of power from municipal to county governments is likely to raise delicate questions of balance. Municipal planning and zoning activities are an example. On the one hand, there must be enough county control to prevent the formation of protected fiscal enclaves and to regulate those activities of any one municipality that may have undesirable effects on others. On the

---

[36] Federal and state grants-in-aid can also, of course, be used to stimulate the formation of metropolitan councils and planning commissions themselves, and the ACIR has for some time favored this type of intergovernmental program. See ACIR, *Governmental Structure, Organization, and Planning in Metropolitan Areas* (July 1961), pp. 35-51.

[37] Many California counties now have extensive urban functions, and Dade County, Florida, which was chartered in 1957, has responsibility for such areawide programs as transportation, water and sewerage systems, and building and zoning codes. See ACIR, *Alternative Approaches to Governmental Reorganization in Metropolitan Areas,* pp. 42-44.

[38] ". . . the difficulties of expanding boundaries in the future are heightened by the fact that constitutional restrictions on changing county boundaries are much greater, if not absolute, than statutory restrictions on moving boundaries of cities." *Ibid.,* p. 71.

other hand, sufficient local control must be preserved to permit each neighborhood to pursue its own individual tastes and, in the process, hopefully, to stimulate active competition among municipalities for ways of improving the quality of urban life. The problem, in other words, is to distinguish between those subfunctions that are primarily of local concern and those that generate effects more broadly. One approach would be to specify the latter as precisely as possible and to make those aspects of municipal planning and zoning subject to county review and approval throughout the entire urban area. Alternatively, one might vary the solution with the size of the community, as the ACIR did in their 1966 legislative program.[39] In general, they recommended that the county perform planning and zoning for the smallest communities, review and approve the extra-territorial aspects of the planning and zoning done by intermediate-sized municipalities, and leave the largest ones free to act independently, subject only to provisions designed to secure full discussion of any proposed land uses along community boundaries. A population of 30,000 was suggested as the minimum needed for such independence, both because it should result in a diversity of municipal interests sufficient to be representative of areawide needs and because it should provide an economic base large enough to finance the technical services required for effective planning and development.

THE SINGLE-PURPOSE SPECIAL DISTRICT. Of all the devices discussed in this section, special districts are undoubtedly the most flourishing. Between 1957 and 1962, 2,200 new ones were added, an increase of about 15 percent.[40] In 1962 over 5,400 were in metropolitan areas, most of them single-function districts providing fire protection, sewage disposal, water service, or the development of natural resources (Table V-5). The states varied greatly in their use of them—California, Pennsylvania, and Illinois leading with 894, 879, and 704,

[39] *1966 State Legislative Program of the Advisory Commission on Intergovernmental Relations,* pp. 250-62.

[40] This adjusts for a change in definition in 1962 which materially increased the number of governmental units classified as special districts. Without such adjustment the reported number increased from 14,424 in 1957 to 18,323 in 1962. U.S. Bureau of the Census, *Census of Governments: 1962,* Vol. 1, *Governmental Organization,* pp. 5 and 27. It should be noted that school districts are not included in the class of governments discussed in this section.

TABLE V-5. Number of Special Districts in 1962, by Location and Function

Function	Within SMSA's	Outside SMSA's
Single-Function Districts	5,233	12,780
Natural Resources	946	5,212
Fire Protection	1,174	2,055
Housing and Urban Renewal	391	708
Sewage	570	367
Water Supply	764	738
Other Single Functions	1,388	3,700
Multi-Function Districts	178	132
Total	5,411	12,912

Source: U. S. Bureau of the Census, *Census of Governments: 1962*, Vol. 1, *Governmental Organization*, p. 68.

respectively, in their metropolitan areas, compared to only one in Delaware and two in Mississippi and South Dakota.[41]

So popular an institution is bound to have numerous reasons for its rapid growth. Unfortunately, most of them are essentially negative in character. The comprehensive list given by the ACIR includes the following:

—To avoid tax and debt limitations imposed on local governments

—to circumvent other limitations on the powers of local governments such as their authority to contract with each other for services or to operate joint public enterprises

—to provide services requiring an area that overlaps the boundaries of existing general-purpose governments

—to avoid civil service restrictions on the hiring of people with specialized (and hence expensive) talents

—to avoid the controversy and long delays that often characterize attempts at more fundamental organizational reforms

—to escape the budgetary controls to which ordinary governmental programs are subject.[42] The one positive function of special districts, and it is an important one whenever governmental services are provided to a clearly identified group of people, has

[41] ACIR, *The Problems of Special Districts in American Government* (May 1964), p. 29.

[42] *Ibid.*, pp. 53-63.

been to serve as self-supporting public enterprises financed by user charges.

The main criticism of single-purpose special districts is that they are likely to accentuate, rather than to solve, the fragmentation problem that prevents the effective operation of many metropolitan systems of government.[43] Frequently too small to function efficiently, they all too often have enough power to operate quite independently, subject neither to the checks of the private market nor to the budgetary controls of the public sector.[44] In addition, voter participation in special district elections is often very low. In Oregon, for example, it has been reported to be only 10 percent of those eligible, compared to 50 to 80 percent for other types of elections.[45]

Special districts, then, tend to occupy a favored position in the political family. As a result, the relatively unambitious among them are likely to stagnate in a backwater of inertia and inefficiency, while the more energetic pursue their own ends regardless of their effects on others or of the availability of superior public investment opportunities elsewhere. To combat these dangers the ACIR has proposed a three-point program involving control, consolidation or cancellation, and contraception.[46]

By way of controls on existing special districts, they suggest improved accounting procedures and an expansion in the provision of information to interested parties; a review of district-imposed user charges by some general government agency, either state or local; approval of all district purchases of land by the unit of general government with jurisdiction over the area in question; and the right of all interested governmental agencies to comment on special district plans for capital improvements. The last proposal seems unduly liberal. Special districts exist either because their programs generate important social benefits or costs or because, though all district ser-

---

[43] For some examples of the inefficiencies of fragmentation see ACIR, *Intergovernmental Responsibilities for Water Supply and Sewage Disposal in Metropolitan Areas*, p. 23.

[44] On this point see Wood, *op. cit.*, pp. 114-72.

[45] ACIR, *The Problems of Special Districts in American Government*, p. 67. As a result, one encounters such bizarre cases as a $100,000 bond issue that was approved by a vote of 8 to 2, or a new tax base that was rejected by 32 to 31.

[46] *Ibid.*, pp. 73-84.

vices are private (that is, allocable to specific individuals), their provision requires the exercise of such basic governmental powers as the right of eminent domain or the control of monopoly pricing. In either case, the public nature of special districts seems important enough to justify the exercise by the appropriate unit (or units) of general government of budgetary controls over district capital expenditures.[47]

Given the large number of special districts already in existence, consolidation and cancellation are likely to pay rich dividends in many areas, and metropolitan councils and planning commissions could help in this regard by making periodic reviews of all special district operations in their areas.[48] Cancellation would be particularly desirable whenever the legislative or constitutional restrictions that the districts were set up in the first place to circumvent have been eliminated. Though a transfer of their functions to the appropriate unit of general government would help solve the fragmentation problem discussed above, it might encounter considerable opposition unless arrangements were made to ease the transition problems of district employees and to distribute whatever assets there are equitably. Even then progress is likely to be slow unless state governments encourage the reform movement with financial assistance.

The third, and final, part of the ACIR's reform program deals with the creation of new special districts. This should be possible, in their view, only after a metropolitan council, or some other public agency representing the area within which the district is to operate, has evaluated the proposal both as to the need for the services to be rendered and as to the inability and unwillingness of existing gov-

[47] Exactly the same arguments may be used in criticism of the widespread practice of earmarking gasoline-tax and automobile registration revenues for the support of streets and highways, and then freeing expenditures from ordinary budgetary controls. Even if none of the external costs and benefits to be discussed below existed, highway construction could not be left to petroleum companies and automobile manufacturers, and hence to the test of the private market, because the right of eminent domain is indispensable.

[48] SMSA's vary greatly in the number of special districts within their borders. Whereas the San Bernardino-Riverside-Ontario SMSA, with a 1960 population of 810,000, had 123 special districts in 1962, Miami, Florida, with a 1960 population of 935,000, had only three. See U.S. Bureau of the Census, *Census of Governments: 1962*, Vol. 1, *Governmental Organization*, Table 15.

ernments to perform them. Only if both tests are met would approval for a new special district be given.[49]

Single-purpose special districts, it seems clear, are now in excess supply in many parts of the country. Much of their popularity is attributable to the ease with which they can be created, but they represent only an *n-th* best solution to metropolitan fiscal problems, and not the least of their drawbacks is the impediment that they are likely to present to the undertaking of more fundamental and more effective organizational reforms.

MULTIPURPOSE SPECIAL DISTRICTS. One of the most promising of these reforms is the metropolitan service corporation. The first example in this country was the Municipality of Metropolitan Seattle. Founded in 1958, it now has two areawide functions (sewage disposal and water pollution control) and is empowered to add others (transportation, water supply, garbage disposal, and planning) if and when the localities concerned wish it to do so.[50] This ability to begin with a few areawide programs and gradually to expand until all of the important ones are included is one of the most attractive features of the multipurpose district. Established early enough in an SMSA's development it could forestall the formation of a large number of uncoordinated, independent, single-purpose districts with the weaknesses already noted.

The metropolitan service corporation, then, is a highly flexible governmental unit capable of operating some or all areawide public services and of supervising such joint local-regional programs as urban renewal and elementary and secondary schools. Its creation would, however, deprive existing governmental units of some of their functions, and their natural reluctance to see this happen presents one of the major obstacles to be overcome. How serious the opposition turns out to be in practice will depend, among other things, on the skill with which the case for metropolitan ser-

---

[49] The ACIR has also recommended that the federal government design its aid programs so as to favor general-purpose units of local government rather than special districts. *Impact of Federal Urban Development Programs on Local Government Organization and Planning*, prepared in cooperation with the Senate Committee on Government Operations, 88 Cong. 2 sess. (1964), Committee Print, p. 23.

[50] For further details see ACIR, *Alternative Approaches to Governmental Reorganization in Metropolitan Areas*, p. 54.

vice corporations is presented to the people[51] and on the extent of the consensus required for positive action. If majority approval is required within each participating local government, as it was in the case of the Seattle district, special interests will be able to block the reorganization much more readily than if only a simple majority of the entire metropolitan region is needed. The latter voting procedure has been recommended by the ACIR both for the establishment of multipurpose districts and for the addition of new functions to them.[52] In order to ensure continuing political control over these functions the ACIR has also recommended that the governing body of the corporation be composed of elected officials or their representatives.[53]

FEDERATION. Developed to its fullest extent either the urban county, provided it were large enough to cover the entire metropolitan area, or the multipurpose special district would produce a two-tier federated system of urban government, the upper level dealing with areawide, and the lower level with local, public functions. At the moment, however, this evolutionary process seems to be proceeding at an exceedingly slow pace; therefore, critics may advocate immediate federation of metropolitan governments instead. To date such a radical plunge into reorganization has promised too cold a shock to attract any U. S. cities. North of the border, on the other hand, either because the people there are more accustomed to cold waves and their invigorating aftereffects, or because action was taken by the provincial governments rather than by local referendum, two major urban areas have adopted the federation plan. In 1954 the Municipality of Metropolitan Toronto, covering the central city and twelve suburbs, began operations with wide jurisdiction over

---

[51] From its study of eighteen 1950-61 proposals for metropolitan governmental reorganization, the ACIR concluded: "One condition for success in metropolitan reorganization is an intensive and deliberate effort to develop a broad consensus on the best attainable alternative to the status quo;" and "Enlistment of popular support for governmental change in a metropolitan area calls for the use of a variety of promotional methods, suited to the diverse composition of the electorate." *Factors Affecting Voter Reactions to Governmental Reorganization in Metropolitan Areas,* pp. 29 and 31, respectively.

[52] *1966 State Legislative Program,* pp. 127 and 132-34.

[53] Specifically, the governing body would include: a member of the board of commissioners of each component county, the mayor of the central city, the mayor or one city councilor from each of the three next largest cities, and representatives of the mayors of all other cities in the area. *Ibid.,* pp. 139-40.

nonlocal public functions,[54] and in 1960 the Metropolitan Corporation of Greater Winnipeg was established with a smaller initial roster of functions but with the prospect of acquiring more in the future.[55] In Toronto, schools remain under local control, but a Metropolitan School Board has been set up to distribute basic financial aids, to plan for future needs, and to review local school borrowing. It is also worth noting that the assessment of property for tax purposes has been transferred to the metropolitan government.

Federation seems the logical ultimate goal for any large city that wishes to deal effectively with areawide problems while maintaining the freedom of its local governments to handle their own affairs in their own ways and to offer the discriminating resident a variety of public services from which to choose. As experience with the Toronto and Winnipeg plans is gained, the way may be paved for similar reorganizations in this country, either directly by federation or indirectly by the expansion of urban counties and metropolitan service corporations.

ANNEXATION AND CONSOLIDATION. For best results federations should combine only municipalities that are themselves large enough to take full advantage of the several kinds of scale economies discussed earlier. For suboptimal communities the obvious solutions are either to annex adjacent unincorporated areas or to consolidate operations with one or more other municipalities. Up to a population of 50,000 to 100,000 the effects of such reorganizations would appear to be largely beneficial. Beyond that point, it would be a matter of balancing the increased control over externalities that annexation or consolidation would bring against the potential losses of active political participation and of variety in local programs. Of particular significance here is the Goldenberg Report on Metropolitan Toronto which was released in June 1965 and which recommended both further consolidation of existing municipalities

---

[54] These included water supply, sewage disposal, housing, education, arterial highways, metropolitan parks, air pollution control, certain welfare services, and area planning. ACIR, *Alternative Approaches to Governmental Reorganization in Metropolitan Areas*, p. 77.

[55] *Ibid.*, pp. 78-79.

and greater centralization of primary and secondary education.[56] Nevertheless, complete amalgamation was rejected on the argument that a federal system would provide for greater flexibility and better adaptation to changing economic and social conditions.

EXTRATERRITORIAL PLANNING AND ZONING. The uncontrolled development of unincorporated urban fringes may result in ugly neighborhoods, unsanitary conditions, and inefficient business locations that seriously impede efforts toward metropolitan reform. Whenever the county does not exercise authority over such areas, an alternative solution to the problem is to grant existing municipalities extraterritorial planning and zoning powers so that they, together with the residents of the unincorporated areas, may work out mutually agreeable lines of urban development for the whole area.[57] Such action may, of course, stimulate defensive incorporations designed to protect local interests, but undesirable developments of this sort may be prevented either by strengthening state control of new incorporations or by giving counties, as suggested above, authority over the planning and zoning activities of small municipalities.

INTERSTATE METROPOLITAN AREAS. The problems of metropolitan cooperation are difficult enough when all of the area lies within a single state. In 1963, however, over one-fifth of the nation's population lived in 32 SMSA's that overlapped state boundaries,[58] and here the difficulties are compounded. Areawide operations would require either the enactment of similar legislative authority in each of the states involved or the establishment of interstate compacts such as the Port of New York Authority. Here is an area where federal financial and technical assistance, designed to encourage program coordination and integration, is likely to yield especially rich dividends.

[56] Canadian Tax Foundation, "Goldenberg Report—The Royal Commission on Metropolitan Toronto," *Local Finance*, 18 (July 1965). The Commission recommended that thirteen municipalities, ranging in population from 9,000 to 650,000, be amalgamated into four regional cities and that the public schools be financed by a uniform areawide tax.

[57] Legislation to this effect was included in the ACIR's *1966 State Legislative Program*, pp. 119-25.

[58] See Table V-6.

TABLE V-6. Interstate Metropolitan Areas in 1963

(Population in thousands)

Metropolitan Area	States	1960 Population
New York, Northeastern New Jersey[a]	New York, New Jersey	14,759
Chicago, Northwestern Indiana[b]	Illinois, Indiana	6,794
Philadelphia	Pennsylvania, New Jersey	4,343
St. Louis	Missouri, Illinois	2,060
Washington	District of Columbia, Maryland, Virginia	2,002
Cincinnati	Ohio, Kentucky, Indiana	1,268
Kansas City	Missouri, Kansas	1,039
Portland	Oregon, Washington	822
Providence, Pawtucket	Rhode Island, Massachusetts	816
Louisville	Kentucky, Indiana	725
Memphis	Tennessee, Arkansas	675
Springfield, Chicopee, Holyoke	Massachusetts, Connecticut	494
Toledo	Ohio, Michigan	631
Allentown, Bethlehem, Easton	Pennsylvania, New Jersey	492
Omaha	Nebraska, Iowa	458
Wilmington	Delaware, New Jersey, Maryland	415
Binghamton	New York, Pennsylvania	284
Chattanooga	Tennessee, Georgia	283
Duluth, Superior	Minnesota, Wisconsin	277
Davenport, Rock Island, Moline	Iowa, Illinois	270
Huntington, Ashland	West Virginia, Kentucky, Ohio	255
Columbus	Georgia, Alabama	218
Augusta	Georgia, South Carolina	217
Evansville	Indiana, Kentucky	199
Wheeling	West Virginia, Ohio	190
Lawrence, Haverhill	Massachusetts, New Hampshire	188
Steubenville, Weirton	Ohio, West Virginia	168
Fall River	Massachusetts, Rhode Island	138
Fort Smith	Arkansas, Oklahoma	135
Sioux City	Iowa, Nebraska	120
Fargo, Moorhead	North Dakota, Minnesota	106
Texarkana	Texas, Arkansas	92

Source: ACIR, *Metropolitan Social and Economic Disparities: Implications for Intergovernmental Relations in Central Cities and Suburbs,* p. 45.
[a] A "standard consolidated area" consisting of four SMSA's (New York, Newark, Jersey City, and Paterson-Clifton-Passaic) plus Middlesex and Somerset Counties, N. J.
[b] A "standard consolidated area" consisting of two SMSA's (Chicago and Gary-Hammond-East Chicago).

Systems Analysis and Program Evaluation

After immersing oneself for some time in the intricacies of organization theory, one often emerges wondering whether it was all worthwhile. For good organization merely sets the proper stage—it does not guarantee that the play will be a success. For that, much more is required. The successful city official must first know what public services are needed and why, and he must then be able to provide them, which means, among other things, that sufficient revenues must be at hand or readily obtainable. These two metropolitan fiscal problems are discussed in the rest of the chapter.

Systems analysis, it must be admitted at the outset, is not without its critics. One group, which regards government as a negative component of the total economic system, relies only on the simple proposition that the less of it there is the better. While such an attitude might make some sense in a town that had saddled itself with a corrupt government and was too lazy, or inept, to enact the required reforms, it is not a realistic approach to modern urban living with its many problems that cannot be solved by individuals, or groups of individuals, acting independently.

The second line of criticism comes from the opposite side, those who feel that the economy suffers from a great lack of public programs. Noting that many of the benefits of these programs are intangible, they argue that to compare only tangible benefits and costs, which is all that quantitative program analysis can do, is to run grave risks of underestimating the importance of the intangible benefits and hence of undersupporting governmental activities. The answer to this criticism is that people *are* capable of rational decision-making, and for that process the more one knows the better. Given a private project yielding 10 percent per annum and a public project with important intangible benefits, the right choice between them is more likely to be made if it is known that the public project also has tangible benefits of 6 percent a year than if the value of these benefits remains unquantified. Moreover, the 6 percent and 10 percent figures are themselves intangible to a high degree since they are both based on uncertain future benefits. Choosing between investment projects, be they private or public, is a difficult task for which one needs all the help he can get. Systems analysis, provided it is handled with appropriate attention to its limitations, can be an important ally.

The potential accomplishments of benefit-cost analysis can best be seen by applying it to specific urban problems, and one of the most challenging of these concerns the kinds of new transportation

TABLE V-7. Transportation to Work Used by Workers in 190 Largest SMSA's, 1960

Means of Transportation	Percent of Workers Using
Private Automobiles	64
Bus or Streetcar	12
Railway or Subway	6
Walked Only	8
Worked at Home	3
Other Means	2
Not reported	5
Total	100

Source: Committee for Economic Development, *Developing Metropolitan Transportation Policies: A Guide for Local Leadership* (April 1965), p. 25.

facilities that should be constructed in large cities. Should these be mainly freeways, so that the already dominant position of the private automobile is further strengthened (see Table V-7), or should greater attention be given to rapid rail and bus transit systems, which at the moment play an important role only in densely populated cities with highly concentrated business districts? (This may be seen by comparing the first five cities in Table V-8 with the last

TABLE V-8. Population Density and Use of Common Carriers by Workers in Ten SMSA's, 1960

SMSA	Population per Square Mile 1960	Percent of Workers Using Common Carrier Transportation to Work in 1960
New York[a]	4,977	55
Chicago	1,657	32
Philadelphia	1,224	28
Boston	2,672	25
San Francisco, Oakland	840	18
Houston	727	11
Denver	254	10
Providence, Pawtucket	1,287	9
Los Angeles, Long Beach	1,393	8
San Bernardino, Riverside[b]	30	2

Source: Committee for Economic Development, *Developing Metropolitan Transportation Policies: A Guide for Local Leadership*, p. 26.
[a] Has the highest percentage of workers using public transportation.
[b] Has the lowest percentage of workers using public transportation among the 30 largest SMSA's listed by the Committee for Economic Development.

five.) In determining its own transportation policy each city will, of course, have to deal with a number of factors more or less unique to itself. Nevertheless, there are many important common considerations. A brief discussion in the next section will serve to bring out the strengths and weaknesses of systems analysis.

City Transportation Systems

Determining the best future means of intra-urban transportation means involvement in all of the difficulties to which benefit-cost analyses typically are prone, and then some. There are complex quality variables to be considered, intangibles to be weighted, externalities to be included, technological improvements and other uncertain future benefits to be accurately forecast, and important redistributional effects to be evaluated. Anyone who looks for a neat, precise solution, therefore, is bound to be disappointed. Nevertheless, as the following discussion of these five problems makes clear, a combination of quantitative program analysis with qualitative discussions of intangible values offers much more hope for the future of urban transportation than does ad hoc decision-making based on unorganized, and frequently inadequate, data.

USER BENEFITS. Urban transportation services have become, sad to say, almost entirely intermediate rather than final consumer goods. How often does the modern city dweller go out in his car for the pure pleasure of moving along attractive and uncrowded streets and highways? On Sundays perhaps, but virtually never on weekdays. The transportation qualities in which he is interested, therefore, are speed, convenience, and safety, as well as cost and comfort. The difficulty is that no one means of transport has a monopoly on all of these under all conditions. Rapid rail transit, for example, can move large numbers of people quickly and comfortably, but unless population is highly concentrated along its routes, passengers will be faced with time-consuming transfers that may make their trip both tedious and unpleasant.[59] Rapid bus transit, in contrast, can reduce the transfer problem by using the same vehicle both for the

[59] Estimates indicate that railways can move up to 40,000 people per track per hour, compared to 30,000 by express buses and only 3,000 per lane per hour by private automobile. Costs per passenger mile to and from the central business district have been placed at 3 cents a mile for rail and bus systems and from 6 to 10 cents for automobiles. See Donald S. Berry and others, *The Technology of Urban Transportation* (Northwestern University Press, 1963), p. 115.

express part of the trip on freeways and for nonexpress feeder
routes at either end. Passenger comfort, however, is likely to be less
than can be provided on modern, efficient trains, and unless special
lanes are set aside, freeway congestion may make buses much slower as well.

The great advantage of the automobile is its flexibility in moving people between widely scattered origins and destinations. Under
uncrowded conditions it is a pleasant means of transit for both driv-
er and passengers, and even though congested freeway driving has
its strains and frustrations, many people may find this segment of
their working day the only time when they can be alone and able to
enjoy results that are clearly attributable to their own individual
efforts. In an increasingly automated world, such moments are to be
cherished, and mass transit planners who ignore these values are
likely to do so at their own peril. On the other hand, not everyone
can cope with the dangers of fast freeway driving. Heavy reliance
on the automobile for commuting, therefore, may place the elderly
at an even greater disadvantage in the working world than they already face, and interchanges may soon become so complicated that
out-of-town drivers will have to take on pilots before entering the
system. Moreover, as will be seen below, the automobile imposes
important external costs that must be taken into account.

These considerations all emphasize the need for the broadest
kind of systems analysis—one that includes all types of transit and
all possible combinations of them. The advantages of rapid-rail
commuting, for example, can be increased by combining it with
well-designed feeder bus lines or with parking facilities at suburban
stations. Commuters alone, however, are typically not enough to
support urban rail operations at sufficiently profitable levels. In
such cases, improved delivery services, either on the part of down-
town businesses or by the railway itself, might induce shoppers to
use the rail system during off-commuting hours, and though trains
have been conspicuously unsuccessful in attracting theater-goers
and other seekers of evening entertainment in the central city, the
addition of lounge and bar cars might overcome even this traditional disadvantage. Important gains might also be achieved by converting rail and bus stations from the drab, littered facilities
through which patrons now hurry as rapidly as possible into attractive concourses that encourage more relaxed attitudes. In its new

airports at Toronto, Montreal, and Winnipeg, for example, Canada has achieved an impressive combination of modern art and design with utilitarian transportation services.

Whether these, and other, changes in rapid transit systems will greatly reduce the reliance of city dwellers on the automobile remains to be seen. Unless they are seriously considered and tried out whenever they do appear to have a significant comparative advantage, however,[60] some of the oldest cities may stagnate or decline, and some of the newer ones may become so spread out that they will miss many of the real advantages of urban life. Few cities can be proud of the results produced in the past by a combination of free market forces and unintegrated governmental planning. There is an obvious need for better and more comprehensive programming, and there are great advantages in having it done, not by the government alone, but by the joint efforts of public officials and representatives of a broad range of private groups. Businesses can lend the services of their technical experts and improve their own future planning in the process; labor unions can participate in the development of programs for displaced workers so that new transportation systems can benefit from both the latest forms of automation and good labor relations; and commuters and shoppers can help by making known the service values for which they are willing to pay. Cities such as Philadelphia have already shown the way toward cooperation of this sort, and there are good prospects of similar successes elsewhere. Modern systems analysts have much sharper tools to work with than in the past, and being free of the many tasks that can now be done by machines, they can devote most of their time to the really difficult problems of urban transportation.

RELOCATION PROBLEMS. Among the most important costs imposed by the construction of new transportation facilities in crowded urban areas are the readjustment losses, some tangible and some intangible, suffered by those who must move to new locations. Poor families may find few equally attractive dwelling units within their means, nonwhites may be trapped by restrictive practices, elderly people may be reluctant to leave their familiar neighborhoods, and

[60] See, for example, the interesting comparison of the transit problems of a high density city (Chicago), a low density city (Los Angeles), and a city with no rapid rail facilities (Washington, D.C.) in Berry and others, *ibid.*, pp. 118-21.

small businessmen with well-established local clienteles may find it very difficult to begin again in a different part of the city.[61]

The role of systems analysis here is to quantify as many of these costs as possible, so that they may be dealt with realistically in the evaluation of alternative transit systems. The services of such federal programs as low-cost housing, civil rights enforcement, and the technical aid and credit departments of the Small Business Administration, for example, may be made available to displaced groups, and the costs of doing so then allocated to the new transportation programs. Even such intangibles as the loss of familiar and much-preferred surroundings may be dealt with by estimating, before there has been any indication that new transit facilities are to be built in the area, the minimum sums that would persuade a random sample of residents to move elsewhere voluntarily. While in some cases these amounts would differ little from the fair market values currently determined in property condemnation proceedings or from the displacement allowances now available under federal urban renewal and highway programs,[62] in others they could be substantially greater. This would appear to be the case in the neighborhoods through which the Lower Manhattan Expressway is to be constructed.[63] Had estimates of these intangible costs been made early in the planning of the expressway, they might well have exceeded the additional costs of placing the freeway underground or of providing alternative means of transport.

Urban transit systems differ greatly in the extent to which they are likely to impose significant relocation costs in congested areas. Rapid-rail transport requires the least amount of land for routes and terminals to deliver large numbers of passengers to and from

[61] For a detailed analysis of the problems of these, and other, groups of people see ACIR, *Relocation: Unequal Treatment of People and Businesses Displaced by Governments* (January 1965).

[62] The ACIR has pointed out, however, that there is great diversity in the displacement aids now offered under different programs and by different levels of government. *Ibid,,* p. 104.

[63] As Samuel Kaplan reported: "People gathered in clusters along the cobblestone streets to talk about the decision [to begin construction on the expressway]. Some cursed the Mayor, the city, and the automobile. Some cried. Mr. Wagner has promised liberal relocation stipends to the businesses and new low-cost housing for the residents, but these offers were viewed yesterday as little compensation for the loss of the neighborhood." *New York Times*, May 27, 1965.

the central business district.[64] The automobile, in contrast, has very high land requirements, and one of the reasons that the modern city has been experiencing severe fiscal problems is that rapid construction of freeways has removed much valuable property from the tax roll.

Since relocation costs are among the items that enthusiastic transit planners are prone to underestimate, top city officials should insist on systems analysis that employ the talents of specialists in all types of transportation. In this way, strong advocates of one kind of transit can be brought to concentrate on the weaknesses of the others, and with all of the relevant evidence thus set before them, the electorate and their representatives will, or at least should, be in a position to make the best final choice.

ENVIRONMENTAL EFFECTS. Other intangible effects, which are also likely to be externalities from the point of view of transit planning authorities, are the changes in living and working conditions that occur when transportation facilities are constructed in the immediate vicinity. Residence along railway lines has never been an attractive prospect, and much the same can be said about many modern freeways. The banks of the Charles River in Boston and Cambridge provide a favorite site for the construction of luxury apartment houses, but the presence of expressways on both sides of the river necessitates careful sound-proofing if the noise level is to be reduced to acceptable levels. It is doubtful, however, that the costs of such special construction were allocated to the freeways when their development was being compared with alternative means of achieving the same movement of people within the urban area. In addition, some consideration should have been given to purely aesthetic considerations. How much more, it might have been asked, could Charles River apartment dwellers be expected to pay for a quiet, pastoral outlook from buildings serviced by underground rapid transit than they would pay to contemplate, in their leisure hours, the restless, continuous motion of the modern freeway? Though such questions are difficult to answer, simply to include them in the analysis is to place the final evaluation on a more realistic basis.

Undoubtedly the most discussed environmental effect of the automobile and bus in urban areas is air pollution. Smog problems have long since ceased to be a monopoly of the Los Angeles basin,

[64] Berry and others, *op. cit.,* p. 124.

and even in such an unlikely spot as Athens, Greece, a short walk along Akademias Street provides a dramatic illustration of what cohorts of diesel buses, struggling uphill, can do to the atmosphere. Other cases, fortunately or unfortunately, are less obvious, so city residents become more or less accustomed to living in unclean air. Nevertheless, a federal grant-in-aid program to deal with the problem was established in 1963 by PL 88-206, smog control devices for automobiles are under development, and when the two-car family becomes the rule in affluent America, the electric town car may do much to solve the air pollution problem.

Clearly there are no simple and easy ways of dealing with the environmental effects of urban transit systems. The best that program analysts can do is to make as accurate estimates as possible of all external benefits and costs so that city officials and their constituents, utilizing some of the areawide forms of government discussed earlier in the chapter, can make realistic appraisals of the available alternatives. The way may be a difficult one, but it is likely to produce far fewer unpleasant surprises than uncoordinated decision-making on the part of independent highway, rail, and bus authorities.

UNCERTAIN FUTURE BENEFITS. Since urban transit systems have to be built to last for many years, it is important that due consideration be given to all technological improvements that appear to be reasonably imminent. The electric car has already been mentioned, though it is likely to be some time before it becomes a practicable form of city transportation. Already feasible, on the other hand, are some highly promising applications of automation to rapid-rail transit systems. Fully automatic fare collection, for example, can be achieved by providing regular commuters with magnetically coded credit cards to be used at entrance and exit turnstiles,[65] and by having cash clients purchase machine-issued, nonreusable cards for trips of preselected lengths.[66] With the right equipment and "with automatic fail-safe speed control, maximum train speeds of 70 or 80 miles per hour are attainable, even under 90-second headways."[67] Electronic controls and computer systems can also be used to im-

[65] The records made by such use could then be processed on a central computer and monthly bills sent to all card holders.
[66] Berry and others, *op. cit.*, p. 94.
[67] *Ibid.*, p. 93.

prove traffic flows on freeways and to reduce the incidence of accidents.[68]

These few examples of impending technological improvements are included to emphasize the importance, in urban transportation planning as in other benefit-cost studies, of including more than one projection of future net benefit flows. In addition, as has been much discussed in the literature, these flows should be converted into present values by means of several different discount rates, in order to show the sensitivity of different systems and subsystems to changes in the rates at which their net proceeds will be able to be invested in the future.[69]

REDISTRIBUTIONAL EFFECTS. Though quantitative-minded economists tend to regard redistributional effects as too imprecise to be included in their analyses, city officials and their economic advisers typically find them very difficult, if not impossible, to ignore. A new freeway from the central city to a given suburban area, for example, should raise land values in the suburb and lower them in any area that loses either residents or business because of the freeway. Not only will the importance of these changes be communicated to city officials by their constituents, but tax departments will also be concerned because of their heavy reliance on property tax revenues. How much influence these prospective capital gains and losses have on governmental programming will depend, among other things, upon the type of voting system used for the approval or disapproval of urban improvements. Localized income redistributions, for example, are given much more weight when district vetoes are allowed than when only an areawide majority is required. If the first alternative is thought to be the more equitable but is regarded as too great an impediment to the adoption of new metropolitan programs, separate district approval could be combined with a tax-subsidy program that compensated losers at the expense of gainers. When the number of serious losers is reduced in this way, local vetoes should pose less of a threat to new developments.

[68] Though not discussed in the text, the costs of accidents and injuries, to say nothing of deaths, should be important considerations not only in the choice among different designs of the same transportation system, but also in the evaluation of different transportation systems themselves.

[69] See, for example, Roland N. McKean, *Efficiency in Government Through Systems Analysis* (Wiley, 1958), Chapters 5 and 7.

Redistributional effects of a much more subtle nature occur because primary reliance on the automobile favors low density land
uses, while extensive use of rapid transit systems encourages the opposite. By choosing between the two alternatives, then, planners can
have a fundamental impact on the future development of their cities
—encouraging certain kinds of businesses and discouraging others.
The resulting effects on prices and incomes are complex and debatable, and their welfare implications, consequently, remain largely
unspecified.[70] The one bright spot is that by developing in different
ways, as appears likely to be the case, different American cities will
steadily provide the empirical evidence needed to identify more and
more of the effects in question.

It may be helpful at this point to summarize the conclusions to
which the preceding discussion leads:
1. Even in such a complex area of public policy making as
urban transportation planning, systems analysis has a very important role to play. It cannot deal with all of the relevant factors, but it can quantify enough of them to provide a core of objective evidence without which realistic program evaluations
would not be possible.
2. Objective evidence is particularly needed for areawide metropolitan programs, since the enactment of these typically requires agreement among several independent municipal governments as to who receives what benefits and hence who should
pay what portion of the total program costs.
3. To be at all realistic, urban transportation planning must
cover an entire metropolitan area, must deal with all means of
transit as part of a single, integrated system, and must be coordinated with such other governmental programs as land-use planning, low-cost housing development, and the design of local tax
systems.
4. These considerations all favor grant assistance from higher
levels of government designed to deal with externalities and to
encourage coordinated action on an areawide, systemswide basis.
Though in the past federal grants have tended to lack such

[70] On this point see Herbert Mohring, "Urban Highway Investments," in Robert
Dorfman (ed.), *Measuring Benefits of Government Investments* (Brookings Institution, 1965), p. 291.

breadth,[71] definite progress in that direction has been made in recent years. Urban planning assistance grants, initiated in 1954, reached an annual level of $15 million in 1964-66, and two new programs for the support of mass transportation projects[72] provide at least some balance to the federal government's heavy investment in highways. Thanks to the stimulus of such groups as the Advisory Commission on Intergovernmental Relations, there is an increasing awareness at all levels of government of the gains to be obtained from coordinated and integrated metropolitan planning.

Metropolitan Revenue Development

A good case can be made, at least in principle, for the proposition that many metropolitan fiscal problems could be solved by a systematic reform of metropolitan revenue systems. Whether cities could break the chains of political fragmentation sufficiently to accomplish this entirely on their own, unfortunately, is extremely doubtful. With the right kind of assistance from federal and state governments, however, the prospects would be much brighter. This section considers what could be done by these means, first with the property tax—which is still very much the mainstay of metropolitan governments and second, with the fast-growing group of nonproperty taxes, and finally with the often neglected set of user charges and public service prices. As will be seen, metropolitan revenue reform is a highly promising means of placing urbanized areas in a position to deal effectively with their own internal fiscal problems.

The Property Tax

For some years now the early decline and fall of the property tax has been widely prophesied. Oblivious of its much discussed weaknesses, however, the tax grew at an average rate of 11½ per-

[71] For a criticism of federal grants from this point of view see ACIR, *Impact of Federal Urban Development Programs on Local Government Organization and Planning,* Senate Committee on Government Operations, 88 Cong. 2 sess. (1964), Chapter III.
[72] Grants paying up to two-thirds of the cost of mass transportation demonstration projects were established in 1961 [42 USCA 1453(b)], and in July 1964 similar support was authorized for the construction and improvement of mass transit facilities (PL 88-365).

TABLE V-9. Distribution of States[a] by Effective Property Tax Rates,[b] 1960 and 1962

Property Tax Rate (Percent)	Number of States	
	All Taxable Property, 1960	Locally Assessed Real Property, 1962
0.5–0.9	16	14
1.0–1.4	21	19
1.5–1.9	9	8
2.0–2.5	5	5
2.6 and 2.7	0	4

Source: Dick Netzer, *Economics of the Property Tax* (Brookings Institution, 1966), pp. 102–03.
[a] Includes D. C. Alaska not available in 1962.
[b] Estimated state-local property tax revenue divided by estimated market value of property.

cent between 1953 and 1963, and in 1963-64 yielded local governments $20.5 billion, or some 87 percent of their total tax receipts. Effective tax rates (see Table V-9) vary widely over the country—from little more than .5 percent in some southern states to 2.5 percent and more in Maine, Massachusetts, New York, and New Jersey. If property taxation has already been pushed to its limits, as many believe, it is in the northeastern section of the country that the strains should be greatest.

There is no need at this point to go into great detail concerning the sources of these strains. In general they arise from faulty administration and from the highly uneven incidence of property tax burdens. On the first score, Netzer has estimated that property can be efficiently assessed by local tax officials only in communities with over 40,000 to 50,000 people, a test that is met by fewer than 500 counties and cities in the country.[73] In many areas, consequently, effective administrative reforms, which are discussed briefly later, will require positive actions either by state governments or by some of the areawide metropolitan organizations discussed earlier in the chapter.

It would not be difficult to assemble a long and detailed list of property tax inequities. Unwarranted burden differentials frequently exist among firms operating in different industries, among owners of different kinds of taxable property, and among families living in different areas or in houses with different market values. Two re-

[73] Dick Netzer, *Economics of the Property Tax* (Brookings Institution, 1966), p. 176.

TABLE V-10. Ratio of Property Tax Payments to Value Added in Manufacturing Industries and Public Utilities, 1957

Industry	Property Taxes as a Percentage of Value Added
All Manufacturing	.98
Food and Kindred Products	1.07
Tobacco Manufactures	.80
Textile Mill Products	.76
Apparel and Related Products	.32
Lumber and Wood Products	1.53
Furniture and Fixtures	.85
Pulp, Paper, and Products	1.30
Printing and Publishing	.60
Chemicals and Products	.96
Petroleum and Coal Products	2.56
Rubber Products	1.04
Leather and Leather Goods	.38
Stone, Clay, and Glass Products	1.00
Primary Metal Industries	1.29
Fabricated Metal Products	1.05
Machinery, Except Electrical	1.00
Electrical Machinery	.67
Transportation Equipment	.96
Instruments and Related Products	.69
Miscellaneous Manufactures	.65
Public Utilities:	
Electric and Gas	11.6
Pipelines	7.0
Telephone and Telegraph	5.8
Railways	4.9
Airlines	0.04

Source: Dick Netzer, *Economics of the Property Tax* (Brookings Institution, 1966), pp. 26–27.

cent empirical studies will illustrate the range of variations that can occur. Relating 1957 property tax payments to national income originating in different sectors of the economy, Netzer found ratios that varied from 1 percent in manufacturing to 8 percent in agriculture and 24 percent on owners of nonfarm houses.[74] Table V-10 shows the wide variations found in the ratios within the manufacturing sector and for different public utilities. Netzer has also made a comprehensive analysis of the incidence of the tax on different income groups. Derived from 1957 data, the results show the nonresidential component to be regressive up to a family income level of $15,000 a year and progressive thereafter, whereas the residen-

[74] *Ibid.*, pp. 24-29.

tial component was regressive up to $5,000, progressive from there to $15,000 and regressive again thereafter.[75] By itself, then, the property tax fails to meet the usual tests of vertical equity, but as Netzer points out, its revenues do tend to finance programs whose benefits flow primarily to middle- and low-income groups. Though these families would be better off under some alternative forms of taxation, they do tend to be net beneficiaries of local government fiscal operations.[76]

The second empirical study, by Oliver Oldman and Henry Aaron, used data for 13,769 properties that were sold between January 1, 1960, and March 31, 1964, within the property tax jurisdiction of the city of Boston.[77] Dividing assessed values by sales prices, the authors found significant differences among the resulting ratios for different types of property, for the same kind of property in different price classes, and for properties located in different parts of the metropolitan area. The following tabulations illustrate the first two types of differentials:

Type of Property	1962 Assessment-Sales Percentages
Single Family Residences	34
Two Family Residences	41
Three to Five Family Residences	52
Six or More Family Residences	58
Mixed Commercial and Residential	64
Commercial	79[78]

Single-Family Homes by Price Class	
0- $4,999	60
$5,000- $9,999	44
$10,000-$19,999	31
$20,000-$34,999	32
$35,000-$49,999	34
$50,000-$99,999	37[79]

[75] Both of these patterns take into account the effects of the deductibility of property taxes under the federal income tax. *Ibid.*, pp. 45 and 55.

[76] Netzer's computations for 1957, based on admittedly rough assumptions as to tax and expenditure incidence, show families below $7,000 a year to be net gainers and families above $10,000 to be net losers when property tax burdens and expenditure benefits are combined.

[77] "Assessment-Sales Ratios Under the Boston Property Tax," *National Tax Journal*, Vol. 18 (March 1965), pp. 36-49.

[78] *Ibid.*, p. 40.

[79] *Ibid.*, p. 44.

Regional assessment-sales ratios, after being adjusted for differences in the type of property located in different districts, ranged from a high of 68 percent in congested Roxbury to a low of 41 percent in affluent West Roxbury, Boston itself showing a relatively high ratio of 53 percent.[80] Since these results are by no means unique to the Boston area, it is clear that the property tax is far from being a uniform, proportional levy on all types of property. As Oldman and Aaron point out, however, some of the observed nonuniformities may result from deliberate attempts of assessors, perhaps with the support of local voters, to adjust tax burdens for differential abilities of property owners to shift the tax or for differential flows to them of local governmental benefits as indicated, say, by different population densities per dollar of property value. These possibilities, which need more study than they have yet received, indicate that large assessment nonuniformities need not imply poor assessment administration.

It seems clear, then, that U.S. property taxes do have serious defects, though these may be less fundamental and less widespread than some critics have maintained. Against its defects, moreover, the property tax does have one very important virtue to offer. It is, particularly when confined to residential property, the only highly productive tax that can readily be levied and collected by local governments on their own; and their fiscal independence, therefore, depends very much on the maintenance of its position in the total tax structure. For this goal to be achieved various reforms will be required in different areas, and the remainder of this section, therefore, deals with the major possibilities.

ASSESSMENT REFORM. It has long been recognized that property valuation is a highly technical process requiring the services of a large professional staff, yet many states still use assessment districts that are too small and personnel that are inadequately trained. Rapid elimination of these weaknesses is likely to require cooperative action on the part of both state and local governments. Indeed, the ACIR has recommended that states give serious consideration to the complete centralization of property assessment, the valuations thus obtained being certified to local officials as the base to which they can then apply their own tax rates.[81] Hawaii has already adopt-

[80] *Ibid.*, p. 42.
[81] *The Role of the States in Strengthening the Property Tax,* Vol. 1 (June 1963),

TABLE V-11. Distribution of States by Average Ratios of Assessed Values to Sales Prices of Nonfarm Residential Properties Sold in Metropolitan Areas, 1961

Average Assessment—Sales Ratio in SMSA Portion of State	Number of States[a]
Less than 15%	6
15–19.9	7
20–24.9	6
25–29.9	6
30–34.9	4
35–39.9	5
40–49.9	8
50 and over	5

Source: U. S. Bureau of the Census, Census of Governments, 1962, Vol. 2, Taxable Property Values, Table 8 (Revised, August 1964).

[a] Includes the District of Columbia and excludes the four states that have no SMSA's (Alaska, Idaho, Vermont, and Wyoming).

ed this system, together with state assistance with some of the other aspects of property tax administration. As data processing systems are developed, the advantages of such operations are likely to increase, and they can be adopted without compromising the freedom of local governments to set their own tax rates.

Additional needs for reform arise from the widespread practice of under-assessing property holdings (Table V-11). In 1961, for example, nonfarm residential properties sold in metropolitan areas were assessed, on the average, at only 33 percent of full market value, the statewide range being from a low of 6 percent in South Carolina to a high of 66 percent in Rhode Island.[82] Since nonuniformities in property valuations tend to increase at low assessment ratios, reform should aim at raising these to as high a level as possible. Full value assessment, however, is probably not attainable on any large scale in the near future. Until it is, state supervisory agencies should make annual determinations of average assessment ratios in all of their taxing districts, publish the information as a basis for taxpayer appeals against over-assessments, and use it in

p. 14. For a detailed discussion of assessment administration see Part III of the same volume.

[82] U.S. Bureau of the Census, Census of Governments, 1962, Vol. 2, Taxable Property Values, Table 8 (Revised, August 1964).

both the distribution of equalizing grants-in-aid and in the certification of state-assessed property to local tax rolls.[83]

EXEMPTIONS. In her classic 1953 study of the problem Mabel Newcomer concluded that since 1900 property tax exemptions had grown more rapidly than had taxable property,[84] and five years later M. Slade Kendrick reported that the same trends had continued to operate.[85] Though comprehensive current data on exemptions are lacking, it is doubtful that the erosion of the property tax has slackened materially since 1958. As noted in Chapter I, state and local governments are actively competing against one another for new business, and in recent years property tax exemptions for the elderly have exhibited a growing political appeal. The result, of course, is that the property tax now reaches only a small portion of the nation's total wealth.[86]

The exemptions that have produced this situation are a mixed lot. Some, like those granted to religious and educational institutions, assist worthy causes with a minimum of political pressure and interference. Others, however, either serve no public purpose at all or do so in a highly inefficient way. What is needed, as the ACIR has recommended, is the institution of regular assessments for all tax-exempt property and the publication of summary totals by type of exemption for each taxing district.[87] Only with this information in hand can the public evaluate the subsidies that they are extending under the property tax, and it is to be expected that many exemptions would fail to survive the light of publicity. If so, local governments would be provided with some badly needed revenues for which they would be beholden to no other level of government. In addition, knowledge of the uneven incidence of certain exemp-

---

[83] For a detailed discussion of these matters, see ACIR, *The Role of the States in Strengthening the Property Tax*, Vol. 1. Their discussion of the appropriate functions of the state supervisory agency (pp. 18-21) is particularly informative.

[84] "The Growth of Property Tax Exemptions," *National Tax Journal*, Vol. 6 (June 1953), pp. 116-28.

[85] "Property Tax Exemptions and Exemption Policies," *Proceedings of the Fifty-First Annual Conference on Taxation*, National Tax Association (1958), pp. 84-98.

[86] Netzer, for example, has estimated that some 40 percent of the country's total personal property was legally exempt in 1956-58, and that less than 20 percent of the remainder showed up in tangible personal assessments. *Op. cit.*, p. 146.

[87] *The Role of the States in Strengthening the Property Tax*, Vol. 1, p. 11.

tions from one local district to another would help to identify those cases in which in lieu payments from the state would be justified. In judging such needs, one should, of course, attempt to estimate the extent to which the exemption of a given parcel of property does in fact lower the assessable wealth available to the local government. Federal and state parks or state and private universities, for example, may so raise the value of nearby properties that there is little or no need for in lieu payments from a higher level of government.

BUSINESS PROPERTY. If all municipalities knew the cost of the instrumental services, such as fire and police protection, or water supply and waste disposal, that they render to business firms and based their property taxes on this figure, there would be little opportunity for fiscal distortions of locational decisions. Lacking such information, however, local communities are free to compete aggressively for new enterprises and, in the process, to divert businesses from their optimal economic locations. These inefficiencies could be avoided by assessing and taxing business property on a uniform basis throughout each metropolitan area and returning the proceeds to local jurisdictions on the basis of some mutually agreeable tax-sharing formula.

A second problem with business property taxes concerns the extent to which they should be levied by school districts. A benefits-received justification for such use is questionable because in many labor markets wage rates are likely to be pushed up, either by competitive forces or by union activity, to marginal-value product levels, and when they are, businesses receive no nonpriced benefits from public education. Moreover, whatever benefits are generated by any one school district are likely to be enjoyed equally by business firms located in that district and in other parts of the same metropolitan area. Benefits-received considerations, then, suggest either that school taxes should not be levied on business property at all, or if they are, that tax rates on it should be uniform throughout the metropolitan area.

The alternative procedure is to treat primary and secondary education as a public good and to seek to finance it according to ability-to-pay principles. Business property taxes, however, leave much to be desired on this score. To the extent that they are shifted forward, they burden spenders in a haphazard and inequitable fashion; and to the extent that they are not shifted, they impose burdens that are not closely related to businessmen's own abilities to pay. For the most part this is due to the fact that the tax is imposed on gross property values rather than on net wealth; but inequities also result whenever, as seems often to be the case, different types of business property are assessed at different ratios to full market value.

Regardless of the point of view, therefore, one reaches the same conclusion concerning school district taxes on business property— their role should be minimized as much as possible and if they are used, it should only be on a uniform basis throughout the metropolitan area.

HOUSEHOLD PERSONAL PROPERTY. Consumer durables and household holdings of corporate stocks, bonds, and other intangibles have long been considered too elusive to be successfully brought under the full scope of the property tax. In 1962 household personal property was completely exempted in sixteen states, intangibles were exempted in fifteen, and in many others both types of property were treated more favorably than was real estate.[88] Netzer has estimated, for example, that in 1961 all intangible property in the country had a market value of approximately $1,100 billion, whereas only $2.4 billion was assessed for property tax purposes in that year.[89]

Three major problems would have to be solved before intangibles could be successfully taxed at the local level. The first, which is much less formidable than it once was, is the administrative problem of inducing taxpayers to report accurately their holdings of stocks, bonds, and mortgages to the appropriate tax authorities. Many taxpayers have long been doing so under the federal income tax, and others have recently begun to do so with the initiation of reporting at the source by corporations and banks. As the use of data processing becomes more widespread, it should be a relatively simple matter to extend this system of information returns to cover stock on which no dividends are paid and demand deposits in banks. Since mortgage interest paid is deductible for income tax purposes, all mortgagees who file tax returns could easily be in-

[88] U.S. Bureau of the Census, *1962 Census of Governments*, Vol. 2, *Taxable Property Values*, pp. 5-6.
[89] Netzer, *op. cit.*, p. 142.

duced to report the name and address of the mortgagor and the amount of the principal still due. It would appear, therefore, that a local tax on intangible wealth is now, or soon will be, within the realm of administrative feasibility.

Instead of reporting his holdings of intangibles, the reluctant taxpayer may simply move to a nearby locality that does not include them in its tax base. Only if such options are not widely available can a tax on intangibles be a productive part of local revenue systems. Several solutions to this second problem seem possible:

1. Intangibles could be taxed only on a uniform statewide basis, the proceeds being shared with local governments either according to the residence of the taxpayer or on one of the other bases discussed in Chapter IV. States with heavy concentrations of population along their borders would probably have to act in unison with their neighbors.

2. A state could abolish the so-called general property tax and replace it with a truly general tax on net wealth (discussed more fully below) which all local governments would be authorized to use provided they did so on a uniform basis—by imposing the same tax rate on all types of wealth. Under the circumstances, it is to be expected that all local governments would choose to exercise this option. Tax rates could still differ from one locality to another, but if the revenues from the wealth tax were used solely, or even mainly, to finance local benefits, there should be little danger of tax-induced migration. The tax could be expected to work well, in other words, only if intergovernmental functional grants-in-aid did a good job of financing the external benefits of locally-administered public programs. Once again states with overlapping SMSA's would probably have to act in concert.

3. Unconditional intergovernmental grants could be authorized at either the state or the federal level, and made contingent on the recipient's adopting a general tax on net wealth. The argument here would be that unrestricted aid should be given only to local governments that make sufficient effort to pay their own way, and sufficient effort might be construed to involve the use of a net wealth tax, or at least a property tax that included intangibles in its base.

The third problem with a local tax on intangibles is the avoidance of double taxation of the same wealth in two different forms.

This would mean, for example, the elimination of all taxes on corporate real and personal property as soon as corporate stock was made fully taxable to the shareholder. Similarly, the taxation of home mortgages in the hands of the mortgagor would be combined with their deduction by the mortgagee from the gross taxable value of his house. What should result, as already suggested, is the conversion of the property tax into a tax on all wealth holders, levied annually on the market value of their equity interest in assets of all kinds.

A local net wealth tax, it must be admitted, is not an imminent fiscal phenomenon in this country. To develop it would require much hard work, as well as close cooperation among all state and local governments. The potential gains, however, are also great. A net wealth tax is widely regarded as an equitable and highly productive levy that would add much to any ability-to-pay tax system. To state and local governments, therefore, it represents an important means of diversifying their revenue systems and hence of strengthening their closely guarded fiscal independence. Expanded use of more familiar taxes—on individual incomes or retail sales— undoubtedly constitutes a superior short-run solution to metropolitan fiscal problems, but these methods have a limited scope. A systematic study of ways and means of enacting a local net wealth tax might pay rich dividends to those who are uneasy about the escalating role of the federal government in metropolitan fiscal affairs.[90]

In the meantime, less sweeping changes, such as more comprehensive taxation of intangibles, might well be enacted. If this were done at relatively low rates, the double taxation problem should not be unduly formidable, and Blackburn's estimates indicate that even rates as low as 1 to 3 mills (0.1 to 0.3 percent) could add as much as $3 billion a year to state-local property tax receipts.[91]

[90] Much foreign experience, in such countries as Norway and Sweden, could be drawn on with profit. See, for example, Harvard Law School, International Program in Taxation, World Tax Series, *Taxation in Sweden* (Little, Brown, 1959), pp. 617-52.

[91] John O. Blackburn, "Intangibles Taxes: a Neglected Revenue Source for States," *National Tax Journal*, Vol. 18 (June 1965), pp. 214-18. The estimates given were based on household holdings of intangibles of $1,208 billion at the end of 1963, the most important single category being corporate stock at $514 billion.

Blackburn minimizes the importance of the double taxation argument by pointing out that many local property taxes currently finance the provision of inter-

Whether consumer durables should also be added to the property tax base is more doubtful. While automobiles and boats can readily be taxed because they must be registered for regulatory purposes, other consumer goods could be reached only by regular (every five years, for example) inventory-taking by governmental officials, which is likely to be objectionable to many property owners, or by taxpayer self-assessments, which are likely to be costly to administer equitably. In addition, correlations between home values and furnishings may be so high that taxation of only the home does not involve substantial inequities among taxpayers.

During the postwar period the general property tax has responded well to economic growth and to the most pressing needs of local governments for additional revenue. Whether it will continue to do so in the future, however, is open to serious question. As noted earlier, the tax has many faults, and unless these are remedied, it is likely to prove a weak support for the aspirations of city dwellers for more and better public services. On the other hand, reforms are under way in different parts of the country,[92] and there is evidence that the tax can be made into an efficient, equitable, and productive part of the tax system. When it is, cities will be in a much better position to deal in their own way with their own fiscal problems.

Nonproperty Taxes

Between 1934, when they first came to national notice with the adoption of a retail sales tax by New York City, and 1963-64, local nonproperty tax revenues rose from $130 to $3,023 million, or from 3 percent of local tax collections to 13 percent. Most of the revenue is received by cities, and as Table V-12 shows, large cities in 1962 tended to rely more heavily on nonproperty taxes than did small cities. Eight of the nation's largest cities obtained more than

---

mediate governmental services to property owners. In principle, however, this situation calls for a replacement of property taxes with user charges that are more closely related to family and business usage of the public services in question. If this were done generally, property taxes would appear more clearly in their proper role—namely, as an ability-to-pay levy used to finance unallocable government output—and the double taxation argument would retain its validity.

[92] For further details see ACIR, *The Role of the States in Strengthening the Property Tax*, Vol. 2 (June 1963).

TABLE V-12. City Tax Collections, by Major Type of Tax and City Size, 1962

Tax	All Cities	Cities with 1960 Populations of						
		1,000,000 and over	500,000 to 999,999	300,000 to 499,999	200,000 to 299,999	100,000 to 199,999	50,000 to 99,999	Less than 50,000
Total Collections ($ millions)	7,646	2,466	1,118	536	305	666	829	1,726
Property (% of total)	73	63	73	73	76	84	82	79
Nonproperty (% of total)	27	37	27	27	24	16	18	21
General Sales	11	24	5	5	6	5	5	5
Selective Sales	6	5	8	9	10	4	4	6
Other Taxes and Licenses	10	9	14	13	9	6	8	10

Source: ACIR, *Tax Overlapping in the United States* (1964), p. 49.

half of their total 1962 tax revenue from nonproperty sources, but there were also some, such as Detroit, Cleveland, and Boston, that still relied almost exclusively on the property tax (Table V-13).

Of the local nonproperty taxes now being used, the most promising as sources of additional city revenues appear to be those on retail sales or on individual and corporate incomes. As indicated in Chapter II, such coordinating devices as tax supplements and tax sharing can reduce the administrative and compliance costs of municipal sales and income taxes to low levels. Sharing was used by

TABLE V-13. Nonproperty Taxes in the Nation's Fifty-one Largest Cities as a Percentage of Total Tax Collections, 1962

Under 10%	10–19%	20–29%	30–39%	40–49%	50% and over
Detroit	Baltimore	Atlanta	New York	Los Angeles	Philadelphia
Cleveland	Houston	Oklahoma City	Chicago	Seattle	Washington, D. C.
Milwaukee	San Francisco	Omaha	Pittsburgh	Cincinnati	St. Louis
Boston	Dallas	Tulsa	San Diego	Denver	New Orleans
San Antonio	Newark		Honolulu	Long Beach	Kansas City
Buffalo	Portland, Ore.		Memphis	Birmingham	Columbus
Minneapolis	El Paso		Phoenix	Tampa	Louisville
Indianapolis	Wichita		Oakland	Dayton	Toledo
Fort Worth			Norfolk		
Rochester			Miami		
St. Paul					
Akron					
Jersey City					

Source: ACIR, *Tax Overlapping in the United States* (1964), p. 50.

thirteen states in 1962,[93] but supplements are well developed only for local sales taxes.[94] Municipal income taxes, much influenced by Philadelphia's pioneering levy of 1939, have typically used their own special definitions of the tax base, but in mid-1964 Michigan took an important step forward by authorizing its cities to impose an income tax on a uniform base that was closely related to the federal definition of adjusted gross income.[95] Administration will be at the local level, but in an income tax state these costs could be considerably reduced by authorizing only municipal taxes that used the state income tax base and were collected by the state for subsequent return to the jurisdictions of origin. If the state tax also used the federal base, the result should be a highly efficient three-tier system of income taxation.[96] In large metropolitan areas similar results could presumably be achieved with a set of uniform municipal levies that were centrally administered by some areawide unit of government.

Local taxes of either the sales or income variety face troublesome jurisdictional problems. For example, should a sale be allocated for tax purposes to the district in which the order is processed, the district from which the goods are shipped, or the district in which they are received? The choice of any one of these would be arbitrary, and multijurisdictional companies might react to it by rearranging their transactions so as to concentrate their taxable sales in districts where they owned large amounts of taxable proper-

[93] Alabama, Arizona, Florida, Hawaii, Kansas, Michigan, North Dakota, and Ohio all shared portions of their state general sales taxes; Maryland, New Hampshire, South Carolina, and Wisconsin shared part of their individual income tax collections, and Tennessee did both. ACIR, *Tax Overlapping in the United States* (1964), pp. 112-38.

[94] In 1962 supplements were authorized in California, Illinois, Mississippi, New Mexico, Tennessee, and Utah. *Ibid.*, pp. 107-08. For a discussion of the administrative experience with some of these supplements see John F. Due, *State Sales Tax Administration* (Public Administration Service, 1963), pp. 240-43.

[95] See Michigan's City Income Tax Act enacted June 12, 1964. For a discussion of some of the background to that statute see Leonard D. Bronder, "Michigan's First Local Income Tax," *National Tax Journal*, Vol. 15 (December 1962), pp. 423-31.

[96] Though less efficient, independently managed local income taxes can apparently achieve ". . . levels of compliance and enforcement [that] satisfy the collective conscience of the taxpaying public." Milton C. Taylor, "Local Income Taxes after Twenty-One Years," *National Tax Journal*, Vol. 15 (June 1962), p. 118. As Taylor notes, withholding at the source is an essential feature of such taxes.

ty, hoping thereby to keep down property tax rates. One solution, used in California, is to place all multijurisdictional sales in a common "pot" from which the tax proceeds are allocated according to the distribution of all the other taxable sales with an objectively identifiable location. Similar problems occur whenever sales taxes are levied in an area that has several overlapping units of local government. Some mutually agreeable allocation of the proceeds will then have to be determined, presumably on the basis of the relative needs and resources of the jurisdictions involved.

The problems involved in dividing local income tax revenues between the jurisdictions of residence and origin have already been discussed in Chapter II. Since each local government can make a strong case for taxing both the total income of their residents and any income that is earned or produced within its borders, some administratively simple compromise solution that precludes overtaxation is essential. One possibility, recently adopted in Michigan, is to enact a broad-based income tax and to give residents a credit for taxes paid to any other local government. This arrangement, if adopted universally, would allocate wages, salaries, and profits to jurisdictions of origin and interest and dividends to jurisdictions of residence. Should this favor the jurisdiction of origin unduly, perhaps because business property yields a larger share of total metropolitan property tax receipts than does residential property, an alternative solution would be to allocate business and labor income equally between the governments of origin and residence. This could be accomplished by each giving its taxpayers a 50 percent credit for taxes owed to the other, or by each dividing, say, a 1 percent income tax into a ½ percent tax on the total income of residents plus a ½ percent tax on any income earned or produced in its own area. Finally, still greater precedence could be given to bedroom communities by restricting tax credits to nonresidents, thus tending to shift all income to jurisdictions of residence. Which of these three solutions is the most desirable is likely to vary from one urban area to another, depending on the intra-metropolitan distribution of needs for public services and of abilities to finance them from existing revenue sources.

In summary, then, sales and income taxes do give rise to troublesome administrative and jurisdictional problems whenever they are levied by local governments on an independent basis. Intergovernmental cooperation can help greatly in metropolitan areas, and if the state imposes sales or income taxes, its local governments can be authorized to impose tax supplements, a system which can reduce their administrative and compliance costs materially. Jurisdictional problems will remain, but even these can be avoided if the local taxing authorities are able to agree on an arbitrary, but simple, rule for handling questionable transactions when the state apportions the tax proceeds among the different claimants.

Recognizing these possibilities, however, may not lead to increased local use of sales and income levies. Each municipality, particularly when it is only one part of a large metropolitan area, may hesitate to push its tax rates very high for fear of losing business and residents to its less aggressive neighbors. Such fears would be well founded if the higher taxes were needed to finance programs that spread their benefits broadly over the whole metropolitan area, but if the benefits in question were primarily local, the high-tax community might well attract, rather than repel, residents. The best way to strengthen local taxing powers, in short, is to finance all areawide programs by areawide taxes and to use functional grants from higher levels of government to pay for the external benefits of programs that also generate an important flow of local services.[97] Such a solution to metropolitan fiscal problems seems well worth working for.

User Charges and Miscellaneous Fees

In 1962 metropolitan governments raised nearly 15 percent of their general revenues from a diverse group of current charges levied on the recipients of public services.[98] Partly because of this diversity and partly because they are administered by many different agencies, user charges often receive little attention from top govern-

[97] For a program such as education, which spreads its benefits broadly over the whole country, these optimizing grants should come to the local school district, partly from the federal government, partly from the state government, and partly from an areawide metropolitan government.

[98] Current charges in 1962 in SMSA's were $23.48 per capita, compared to tax revenue of $130.19 and total general revenue from own sources of $163.52 per capita. Corresponding figures for local governments outside SMSA's were $19.18, $82.04, and $108.10, respectively. U.S. Bureau of the Census, *Census of Governments: 1962*, Vol. V, *Local Government in Metropolitan Areas*, p. 184.

mental officials. In California, for example, the first known comprehensive compilation of financial information on fees and licenses was made in 1964 by Alice J. Vandermeulen for the Assembly Interim Committee on Revenue and Taxation.[99] From her analysis of the data came not only specific recommendations for reform in California but also "a dozen clues for making a fee structure more lucrative" that will be of great interest to many financially pressed state and local officials.[100]

One important group of fees includes all those imposed to finance the highly diverse regulatory activities of local governments that are designed to protect consumers and workers against unethical business practices, to enforce professional standards, and to exclude undesirable persons and groups from certain occupations.[101] Several economic guidelines can be suggested as a basis for the rationalization of such fees. The first is that they should cover the full costs of regulation, including any nonpriced services which the regulatory agencies receive from other governmental departments. Charges that simply pay for the clerical costs of collecting them, for example, should either be increased in amount or eliminated.

A second principle is that fees should vary from one licensee to another only to the extent that regulatory costs vary. It is always tempting to charge a big business more than a small one, but ability-to-pay financing is best left to the tax authorities who can design their levies so as to treat equally all persons with the same income or wealth. Graduated fees, on the other hand, would reach only those whose activities require public regulation.

A third rule is that fees should be reexamined at regular intervals to determine whether they should be raised or lowered because agency costs per unit of output have gone up or down.

Finally, whenever licensing so restricts supply in a given line of activity as to create intangible rights of considerable value, as is often the case with the retail sale of alcoholic beverages, there is no

[99] *Fees and Licenses: a Major Tax Study*, Pt. 2 (California Legislature, July 1964).

[100] Alice John Vandermeulen, "Reform of a State Fee Structure: Principles, Pitfalls, and Proposals for Increasing Revenue," *National Tax Journal*, Vol. 17 (December 1964), p. 402.

[101] For the many examples of these fees in California see Vandermeulen, *Fees and Licenses: a Major Tax Study*, pp. 14-54.

reason why the state should not secure for itself the monopoly profits that its own actions create.[102] This could be done by charging market prices for nontransferrable licenses— that is, by auctioning new ones to the highest qualified bidders and by using a set of positive and negative renewal fees that reflect the capital gains or losses accruing on existing licenses as economic conditions change.

A second major group of fees includes those that are in effect charges for beneficial services rendered by the government to specific groups of people. These, too, are a highly diverse lot, including such examples as the prices at which official documents and records are sold, admission fees for state and local recreational facilities, and the charges levied for sewerage and water services. Though each case requires its own individual analysis, there are three general problems that recur sufficiently to justify a brief discussion of them here.

The first has to do with sunk costs. Economists have long argued, with only a limited degree of success, that while both fixed and variable costs must be taken into account when a new facility is being planned, only the latter are relevant to the rational pricing of its services once the facility is in existence. Failure to observe this principle results in such anomalies as a new highway bridge that is greatly underutilized because full-cost pricing dictates a high toll, or an old bridge that is badly overcrowded because its toll was removed as soon as the construction bonds had been repaid. Though the information is not always easy to obtain, efficient pricing requires close attention both to the sensitivity of consumers to price changes and to the impact of a given alteration in government output on the society's total use of resources.

A second problem arises whenever a government program generates both private and social benefits and has to do with the relative importance of these two types of economic gain. In principle, public prices should be based only on the former, but the intangibility of the latter makes implementation of the principle exceedingly difficult. Underpricing may exist, for example, partly because the users of any public facility have an obvious incentive to overempha-

---

[102] This assumes, of course, that some restriction on supply is desirable because of the social benefits it creates. If these are negligible, the appropriate solution is either to issue licenses without limit at a price sufficient to cover administrative costs or to eliminate public regulation altogether.

size the value of its social benefits, and partly because people often think that simply because the government provides a given service it should be made available at zero or purely nominal prices. Take the usual argument that state and local recreational services should be priced below cost because this makes for a healthier and happier society to the joint benefit of everyone. This argument has merit only if it can be shown that the demand for the recreational services that are in question is in fact highly price elastic; otherwise low prices fail to fulfill their stated objective. Worse still, they may result in an overuse of the facilities that forces the diversion of resources from superior alternative uses, and there may even be cases, as Mrs. Vandermeulen has documented,[103] where nominal fees fail to cover the costs of collecting them and result in an actual loss of government revenues. Failure to evaluate social benefits correctly may, of course, also result in overpricing, but its significance depends very much on the price elasticity of user demand for the public services in question. If that elasticity is low, no great loss of public goods, and hence of their social benefits, results; and if there are undesirable distributional effects, they may be neutralized by suitable changes in existing tax-transfer programs. When the price elasticity of demand for private-public goods is great, however, high prices will restrict their output considerably and important social benefits may be sacrificed.

The last, and most difficult, problem is how to combine efficient public pricing with suitable attention to the needs of the poor. To set prices low simply because many of the customers to be serviced have low incomes is a common practice but one that may result in serious inefficiencies and inequities. A single low price for a given public service, for example, means that less is collected per unit from middle- and high-income clients than economic conditions justify, and this wastage of public funds may mean that the poor receive less support than they should. One solution, of course, would be to restrict the use of subsidized prices to low-income groups, but the administrative and compliance costs of operating such a dual, or multiple, price structure may be high enough to make it unattractive. Here one notes immediately the advantage of having a centralized storehouse of quantitative information about all low-in-

[103] *Fees and Licenses: a Major Tax Study*, p. 54.

come individuals and families, such as would result from the adoption of a comprehensive, federal negative income tax and from which public officials dealing with the poor could obtain confidential "economic needs" reports similar to those now obtained by businessmen on the credit standing of more affluent families.

Even when price discrimination is administratively feasible, or when it is not needed because most of the potential customers are poor, price subsidies are not necessarily the best means of raising below-minimum family living standards to acceptable levels. If the price elasticity of demand is low, such subsidies are objectionable because they add free funds to the budgets of people with certain tastes and not to those of others at equally low income levels; and if the price elasticity of demand is high, they may divert consumer demand from superior alternatives. Were the government to give to the poor as unconditional income supplements the amount of money that it spends on its price subsidies, in other words, the poor might be able to reach a higher level of economic welfare than the price subsidies permit them to achieve. Whether they can or not, of course, is a debatable question, but in a democracy it seems appropriate to begin with the presumption that people, including the poor, do know what is best for them and to place the burden of proof on anyone who would argue otherwise. When that proof is forthcoming for certain public goods—technical and professional education may well be an example—they should then be sold at lower prices than otherwise would be desirable; when it is not, however, public pricing should be based on the first two sets of factors considered above, and income subsidies should be used to improve the economic lot of the poor.

In principle, then, fees and user charges should be set only after full account has been taken of their impact on governmental use of resources, on the composition of consumption, on the location of business activity, and on the flow of social benefits and costs. Though quantitative information on these matters is not as complete or as reliable as one would like, it is being expanded steadily; and enough is already available to permit many state and local governments to improve their fee and price structures greatly and to realize increased general revenues in many cases. Some years ago

J. A. Stockfisch estimated that Los Angeles could increase its revenues by approximately 40 percent in this way.[104]

Summary

It is doubtful that any city has yet come very close to the limit of its ability to finance its own public services. Property taxes could be improved in many ways, local sales and income taxes could be used more effectively and intensively than they now are, and a revamping of municipal service charges could convert them into a more equitable and productive source of general revenue. Action on one or more of these fronts would not only make a direct contribution to metropolitan fiscal problems but would also increase the willingness of higher levels of government to extend grants-in-aid in the volume needed to optimize the operation of metropolitan programs with external benefits and to raise the fiscal capacities of the poorest cities to acceptable levels.

[104] "Fees and Service Charges as a Source of City Revenues: a Case Study of Los Angeles," *National Tax Journal,* Vol. 13 (June 1960), pp. 97-121. The computations were for fiscal 1957 when Los Angeles had total revenues of $175 million.

CHAPTER VI

Summary of Conference Discussion

A TWO-DAY CONFERENCE on intergovernmental fiscal relations in the United States not only provides a forum for the discussion of that many-faceted problem but also serves as a laboratory experiment in the sociology of interdisciplinary coordination. Happily, this conference produced some worthwhile analysis of different aspects of a number of promising fiscal reforms and also showed that economists, political scientists, and other fiscal experts can focus jointly on a problem and even air fundamental disagreements in a purposeful and cordial atmosphere. It gives hope that cooperation on a widespread scale may in the years to come produce fruitful results in an area of increasing importance to our national well-being.

In their search for solutions fiscal policy-makers face a wealth of difficulties, but they also possess a rich source of ways and means. Conference discussion made clear the fact that there is no one grand reform that would solve all problems. It also made apparent, however, the existence of a large number of useful policy tools, each capable of adding its own contribution and hence of filling some of the gaps left by other policy measures. What is needed, then, is a skillful integration of selected policies, each blend

224

being adapted to the specific circumstances of the locality where it will be applied. The general tone of the conference seemed to be one of cautious but definite optimism, evincing an expectation that the outstanding problems of intergovernmental fiscal relations will be resolved in such a way as to ensure a salient role for all three levels of government.

State-Local Fiscal Prospects for 1970

The conference began with a review of the 1970 projections of state-local expenditures and receipts that have been worked out over a two-and-a-half year period on behalf of the Inter-Agency Committee on Economic Growth and are being published by the Council of State Governments (CSG) in a series of research memoranda.[1] When aggregated for all of the states, these projections yield the following broad totals:

Category	*Amounts* *(Billions of dollars)*
General expenditures	108.3
General revenues	106.0—108.1
From own sources[2]	84.3— 86.4
From federal sources	21.7
Total fund requirements[3]	121.8
Total funds available[4]	107.9

Discussion of these figures centered around two closely related features, both of which elicited some sharp reactions from several of the conference participants. The first was the projection of growth of general expenditures at a rate below their rate of growth in the past five or in the past ten years.[5] In large part this conclusion

[1] In addition to those cited in Chapter I, see Selma J. Mushkin and Eugene P. McLoone, *Local School Expenditures: 1970 Projections* (Council of State Governments, November 1965).

[2] The higher figure assumes constant effective tax rates; the lower figure assumes that nominal property tax rates remain constant and that there is some slippage of assessed values behind the market values of existing property. See the discussion of this point in Chapter I.

[3] Includes amounts needed for debt redemption, for contributions to government retirement funds and for working cash funds.

[4] These fall short of general revenues because of projected negative net utility revenues.

[5] As noted in Chapter I, a continuation of trends of the recent past would produce 1970 state-local general expenditures of $120 billion.

was drawn from the expectations that primary and secondary school enrollments will grow at significantly slower rates, that the federal social insurance and Medicare programs will take some of the load off state and local welfare and public hospital expenditures, that highway construction will fall short of its recent rapid rate of growth, and that a slowing down of internal population migration will mean fewer people moving into relatively high-cost local governmental jurisdictions. While the projections also take full account of some rapidly growing state-local programs, such as higher education, regional economic development, and poverty eradication, it is not expected that these will take up all of the slack left by the first set of programs. The second controversial feature of these projections is the relatively optimistic fiscal picture they paint of the country as a whole in 1970. Even with no further increases in tax rates, general revenues, it is estimated, will come within $2 billion of general expenditures, and total fund requirements will be only $13.9 billion greater than total funds available, a gap that is likely to be well within the borrowing capacity of state and local governments in 1970. In fiscal 1964, for example, those governments issued new long-term debt of $11.2 billion.

Considerable doubt was expressed by some conference members about the realism and usefulness of these projections. As one participant put it, "I don't know of a single individual in any responsible position who is willing to say 'I shall not need any further tax increases from now on to 1970.'" In the view of another ". . . to suggest any substantial decline in the rate of growth of expenditures is to be more sanguine than for the good of society we ought to be." Others, however, minimized the danger that optimistic fiscal projections would induce state and local legislators or administrators to moderate their efforts to expand spending levels. These officials, they reasoned, are much more likely to react by throwing up their hands in disbelief than by sitting on them complacently.

Extended discussion of the many difficulties involved in making long-term fiscal projections emphasized the importance of three sets of factors: (1) unpredictable effects of new economic and political developments and of technological and scientific advance in particular; (2) the impact of federal grants-in-aid on state-local spending levels; (3) the complex interactions and feedbacks that undoubtedly exist between one side of the government budget and the other—that is, between state-local expenditure and revenue programs.

On the first point it was noted that ". . . scientific advances continually bring into being new functions of government that we can't forecast five or ten years ahead." In the political sphere legislative reapportionment was seen as a factor making long-term predictions especially difficult at this time. If federal expenditures on research and development are continued at their current high levels, they may well, it was argued, produce important technological breakthroughs in such areas as the control of air and water pollution that will stimulate new bursts of spending by state and local governments. In general, there seemed to be a widespread feeling that it is all too easy to underestimate the stimulus that scientific research is likely to give to public expenditures.

Federal grants-in-aid, it was noted, are particularly troublesome to the fiscal forecaster because they enter his calculations both as a source of funds for state and local governments and as one of the important factors making for higher levels of state-local spending. In neither case is their future importance easy to predict. As noted in Chapter I, a linear projection of the 1952-62 trend in the ratio of grants to GNP yields federal grants of $17 billion in 1970, and this figure does not even fall within the range of the CSG projections, which extend from a low of $18.5 billion (no further expansion of existing programs) to a high of $24 billion (some enactment of new programs). Uncertainty is compounded when one turns from these figures to their potential significance for state-local spending levels in 1970. The few empirical studies that have been made of the relationships between federal grants and state spending have failed for various reasons to produce satisfactory results. Though the issue was not directly debated at the conference, one expert did state that in his opinion:

. . . federal aid has exercised a multiplier effect on state and local government activity. The entry of the federal government into a new functional field quite often has triggered state and local expenditures in that field for matching purposes, and then the state and local governments have gone on and on and on—way beyond the original federal stimulation.

Other conferees, however, felt that these expansionary effects, which have occurred in vocational education and public health, tended to be the exception rather than the rule.

For present purposes the most important fiscal feedback mechanism is that between rising revenues and new expenditure programs. Will the former typically pull the latter up with them so that projected budgetary surpluses are eliminated by expenditure levels higher than originally expected, or will rapidly rising revenues simply lead to a reduction in tax rates? Opinion on this question was divided. While some did anticipate falling tax rates, especially on property, in the surplus states, others argued that expenditures "will simply in the ordinary normal course of events expand to eat up the anticipated surplus." Two very disparate pictures of state and local finance in the 1970's can be drawn, depending upon which of these alternatives is accepted.

Suppose, to take a highly simplified example, that a 1970 surplus of $100 million is projected for one group of states and that a deficit of $100 million is projected for another. If there is no feedback from expected surpluses to expenditure levels, fiscal pressures and rising tax rates in one area will be offset by fiscal ease and falling tax rates in the other, so that for the nation as a whole average tax rates may remain virtually unchanged. In that sense there would be no aggregate fiscal gap in 1970, though no one would minimize the difficulties faced by public officials in the states with projected deficits. On the other hand, if spending levels do react to rising revenues in the surplus states, projected expenditures for them will in fact be too low by $100 million, and the fiscal gap of $100 million in the deficit states will be the total gap for the nation as a whole. To fill it, program service levels will either have to be cut back or tax rates increased.

Neither of these two extreme cases is likely to materialize. Presumably in some areas public attention is focused on high tax rates rather than on low public service levels, and there autonomously generated surpluses will be used to reduce tax burdens. Wherever additional public benefits are thought to outweigh additional private ones, however, such surpluses are likely to provide the occasion for expenditure increases. To some unknown extent, then, the CSG 1970 projections, which take no account of the surplus-expenditure feedback mechanism, underestimate total state-local spending levels and hence the size of the nationwide fiscal gap in that year.

In discussing the rapidly rising state-local spending levels, which everyone thought were inevitable, participants raised questions about the size of the tax rate increases necessary to deal with them, but to some the more important problem concerned the kinds of tax increases that are in prospect. In the words of one participant:

. . . the real issue, therefore, is not the exact number, but how to have a mix of grants-in-aid, property taxes, sales taxes, income taxes, to meet this [the pressure for higher expenditures] that would be better than simply letting things grow through pressure and through no planning at all.

One of the paradoxes of state and local governmental finance is that where the need for revenue reform is greatest—namely, where expenditures regularly outstrip the built-in growth of revenues—the means for achieving it are likely to be in shortest supply. Ad hoc policy-making is not good enough, and one of the important contributions that the 1970 CSG projections have made is to give governments that face a potential financial problem in that year an opportunity to engage in effective fiscal planning. Indeed, stimulus of such planning has been the main objective of Project '70, and much of the work of its staff has been directed to that end.

Tax Coordination

Since it ordinarily involves shifting revenues from one governmental unit to another, tax coordination has always provoked considerable controversy among state and local officials, and its explosive qualities were duly demonstrated by conference reaction to some of its complex issues. These issues included the adoption of credits against an individual's federal income tax liability for part or all of any state or local income tax he pays, the search for an optimal set of state income taxes on multistate corporations, and the devising of workable solutions to the problems created by the application of state sales and use taxes to interstate transactions.

Tax Credits

To its supporters a federal credit for some fraction of a person's state or local income tax liability is attractive as a means of inducing states to raise more money by their own tax efforts and to do so by relying on a revenue source that is equitable and highly responsive to economic growth. It was pointed out that interstate tax competition, though not demonstrably important in terms of statistics, is uppermost in the minds of many state and local officials and therefore plays a very important role in the decision-making process. As an antidote to those pressures, tax deductibility, as currently allowed under federal law, seemed inadequate to some because: "it is not very visible. You can always argue, but it is awfully hard to get people to pay attention to it when I talk to them about it. The credit is a lot more visible." In the eyes of several participants, fractional federal tax credits appeared as highly useful levers that, by raising the political palatability of state income taxes, would permit substantial increases in their rates.

Opposition to this tax coordination device came from widely different quarters. To some, both deductibility and credits represented unjustifiable interferences with state-local fiscal freedoms. As one put it, "I would like each state to decide it is going to have this tax or that tax entirely on its own and not because the federal government will pay a third or half or some percentage of it." In rebuttal it was pointed out that "everything the federal government does interferes with state tax policies." In particular, state freedoms to adopt or to expand income taxes are very much limited by federal preemption of that field. Admittedly, the federal government, whenever the appropriate circumstances arose, could simply reduce its own income tax rates, but there was considerable doubt about the extent to which states would in fact take up much of the slack.

In part the problem stems from a basic fact of political life. On the one hand, had Congress publicized the 1964 and 1965 tax reductions as policies to encourage increases in state and local tax rates, the states would probably now be in a better position to expand their revenues and expenditures than they in fact are. On the other hand, much support for the 1964 and 1965 Revenue Acts came simply because they did reduce nationwide tax rates. As one close observer of the Congressional scene stated:

. . . in the '65 act whenever the argument was brought up should the federal government get out of this revenue source or should we have a reduction in order to make it possible for the states to take this over, the reaction was almost always negative in this respect. They were less inclined to give it up as a federal revenue source if they thought the states were going to take it over than they would otherwise. . . .

This suggests, of course, that federal tax credits may not be as appealing to Congress as some might hope. Nevertheless, they can, at least to voters in the income-tax states, be sold by Congressmen as tax reduction measures and be bought at the same time by state and local officials as means of lowering the political price of tax increases.

A quite different attack on federal income tax credits was based primarily on equity considerations. It was pointed out that the richest states stood to gain the most, since tax credits, unlike grants-in-aid, have inconsequential redistributional effects. They are of no help, in other words, to areas whose fiscal resources are inadequate in the first place. It was also noted that a federal tax credit, particularly one covering a high percentage of each taxpayer's state income tax liability, would in effect confer a substantial windfall gain on those states that do not now use income taxes, and the desirability of doing this was seriously questioned.

Opinion on federal income tax credits, then, was sharply divided, some supporting the Advisory Commission on Intergovernmental Relations' recent recommendation that Congress enact a tax credit covering some substantial percentage of income tax payments to state and local governments before it considers the need for other general forms of federal financial aid, while others argued exactly the reverse.

Allowances for state-local income taxes are not, of course, the only kind of credit against federal individual income taxes that Congress could adopt. Of the other leading contenders, only a credit for state sales taxes attracted much attention, and, in general, it received less support than an income tax credit. For some critics this opinion rested on the proposition that the inhibiting effects of interstate competition tend to be considerably greater for income taxes than for sales taxes. Others stressed the regressive burden structure of most state sales taxes and the consequent undesirability of stimulating their use by means of fractional federal tax credits. Questions were also raised about the whole logical basis for sales tax credits—namely, as offsets to burdens supposedly placed on consumers by the sales tax states. If these burdens are in fact negligible, as some believe, a sales tax credit must be viewed as a straight consumer subsidy, justifiable to the extent that society wants to stimulate consumption but not otherwise. On the other side of the question two points were made. The first was that interstate competition may well be as important for sales as for income taxes—witness the closeness of the numbers of states now using each—and the second was that if a one hundred percent tax credit were to be adopted by Congress, its distributional effects would be more progressive if it were granted against state sales taxes rather than income taxes.

While support for sales tax credits at the federal level was distinctly lukewarm, it was recognized that the device may be a useful one at the state level. Thus a state with both an income tax and a sales tax that exempted consumer necessities, such as food, might wish to broaden the base of the sales tax in order to raise revenues and reduce administrative and compliance costs, but might be deterred from doing so by popular opposition to the taxation of necessities. In such a case a well-designed credit against state income tax, varying directly with family size and perhaps also inversely with income, would offset the objectionable regressive burdens of the broader sales tax while sacrificing only a part of the additional revenues that it would yield.

Finally, the potential role of state credits for local property taxes (presumably against state individual or corporate income taxes) was discussed briefly. Not only could these credits be used either to relieve high property tax burdens or to mitigate the effects of interlocal tax competition, but their availability might be made dependent upon the adoption by local governments of some of the badly needed property tax reforms noted in Chapter V.

Interstate Corporate Income

Interest in reform of existing uncoordinated state taxes on the profits of multistate corporations has been stimulated by the recent work of the House Committee on the Judiciary which has so far resulted in three volumes of data and analysis, one volume of recommendations,[6] and two bills for the consideration of Congress. Discussion of this problem at the conference centered on two questions: whether corporate income provides a suitable base for state taxation in the first place; and if interstate corporations are to be taxed on their profits, how these should be allocated among the potential claimants. Since theoretical considerations failed to provide a definite answer in either case, the pragmatists, who stressed the importance of an early solution even though it fell short of many people's ideal, had the final word.

It was readily agreed that retention versus elimination of the corporate income tax was largely an academic question because of the great appeal the levy has to legislators almost everywhere.[7] Corporate profits are a highly visible source of ability to pay taxes, and many voters would oppose any tax on individual incomes unless corporate income was reached as well. There seems little doubt, therefore, that state corporation income taxes are here to stay unless Congress should decide either to outlaw them completely, a move that would have little or no political appeal, or to pay the states to eliminate them, a policy that would likely be a costly one. As one participant put it:

. . . to buy the fifty states out you would have to buy them out on terms that are acceptable to the three [that make the greatest use of the tax] and it would therefore become so costly that we are obliged to put up with a tax which I think for the good of the federal system and the operation of the national economy should never have been used at the state level.

Given the proposition that state corporation income taxes will continue to exist, there is much that can be done by way of tax coordination to improve their operation. All conferees agreed on the

[6] *State Taxation of Interstate Commerce,* H. Rept. 1480, 88 Cong. 2 sess., Vols. 1 and 2 (June 15, 1964); H. Rept. 565, 89 Cong. 1 sess., Vol. 3 (June 30, 1965); and H. Rept. 952, 89 Cong. 1 sess., Vol. 4 (Sept. 2, 1965).

[7] Nor is there any one answer to that academic question, as the following exchange makes clear:

". . . I think I can find a rationale for a business value added tax at the state level. But I find it extremely difficult to rationalize the state corporate net income tax, although under certain circumstances I think I can make a case for a federal corporate net income tax."

"I would say the opposite. I could make a good case for a state rather than a federal one."

virtues of uniformity—that is, on the desirability of having all states use the same jurisdictional tests, the same income-apportionment formula, and the same definitions of the factors used in that formula. Discussion here centered on apportionment formulas, the two leading contenders being a two-factor formula based on property and payroll and a three-factor formula using property, payroll, and sales allocated on a destination basis.

Each formula has an impressive amount of support, though from diverse sources. Tax specialists have praised the two-factor formula for its comparative simplicity; fiscal economists have favored it because of its logical consistency with the benefits-received principle of taxation,[8] and the House Judiciary Committee picked it from among all candidates as the formula to be used as a uniform standard for the state taxation of interstate corporations. In 1963, however, only Hawaii made use of it, and then only for corporations whose principal activity in Hawaii was producing or manufacturing rather than selling.[9] Twenty-six states, in contrast, used a three-factor formula based on property, payroll, and sales; four used sales only, and none of the others omitted sales from consideration.[10] Though considerable variety characterized the geographical assignment of sales, a destination standard was significantly more popular than any other,[11] and a number of conferees strongly supported the argument that simply by providing a

[8] The argument here is that businesses enjoy the services of a specific government only to the extent that they carry out economic activities within its jurisdiction, that economic activity is measured by value added, that value added results from the use of land, labor, and capital, and that these are fully reflected in an apportionment formula based only on property and payroll. In the words of two of the participants:

"The activities of corporations that impose costs on states are where the corporation is making the stuff, not where it is sold."

"The basic issue, it seems to me, is 'Do the importing states have a claim to taxation created through the sale?' My own view is that they have a claim only to the extent that there is value added through the activities of sales forces within the purchasing state."

[9] State Taxation of Interstate Commerce, H. Rept. 1480, Committee on the Judiciary, 88 Cong. 2 sess. (1964), Vol. 2, p. A271.

[10] Ibid., Vol. 1, p. 119.

[11] In late 1963, for example, twenty-four states used a single sales standard, sixteen of them being based on destination, and among all sales factors (53) used, the three most popular were destination (24), location of sales office (12), and origin (7). Ibid., p. 122.

market for corporate output the state of destination acquires a right to tax some portion of the profits earned on the manufacture and sale of that output.

It would appear, therefore, that a three-factor, destination-sales, income-apportionment formula would attract more support at the state level than any other potential uniform standard, and there is much to be said, under a federal system, for letting the states work out their own tax systems, free of all federal interference not needed to protect interstate commerce. Widespread adoption of a three-factor formula, however, would not be without its problems. Critics particularly stressed the high administrative and compliance costs that might accompany the multistate splitting of a large corporation's total income tax liability. Others argued, however, that these costs could be kept within reasonable bounds by rules that would restrict taxing jurisdiction to states that either had some property or payroll of the corporation or attracted some above-minimum amount of its annual sales. Increased uniformity, both in the definition of taxable income and in procedures for allocating it among the different states, would also help. Even if these difficulties could be solved, however, some specialists would remain unhappy with a destination-sales apportionment formula. As was pointed out, its widespread use by the states creates, in effect, a set of export subsidies and import duties whose effects may not cancel each other out in the aggregate and which, if imposed directly, would be unconstitutional. In addition, those who opposed state corporation income taxes in principle tended to favor the two-factor, property and payroll, formula on the argument that its use as a uniform standard would inhibit the adoption of new state corporate taxes more than would the destination-sales formula.

Nevertheless, as one participant put it: "I was never very happy with the sales destination principle, but I think it has gained so much political acceptance that it is going to be almost a prerequisite to embrace it in order to get what we all think is the important principle—namely, uniformity."

In sum, then, there exist a number of income apportionment formulas which most people would regard as reasonable, if not as ideal, and the important thing, it was agreed, is to secure as soon as possible the adoption of one of them as a uniform standard for state taxation of corporate income.

Interstate Aspects of State Sales and Use Taxes

Though sales taxes in this country are predominantly levied on intrastate sales, there is an important fringe of interstate tax transactions which give rise to three major problems. The first is the undertaxation of interstate sales that results from state inabilities to reach either the out-of-state seller or the in-state purchaser and user. The second is the imposition on interstate vendors of excessive compliance costs because of the diversity in state rules and regulations concerning the taxability of different kinds of sales. Opinions differ, however, on the importance of these burdens. The Judiciary Subcommittee study featured them prominently in its criticism of existing sales tax inequities, but one conference participant stated:

I feel that the subcommittee report tremendously exaggerates this, and it is in part because of the nature of the sample of firms that they have. They are taking the extreme examples to make their point, and I think they are greatly overmaking their point. But there is a certain amount, I think, of unnecessary nuisance in some instances.

The third problem, finally, is the double taxation of interstate sales that results from the failure of some states to allow credits for sales taxes paid to other states.

Having considered these problems at length, the Judiciary Subcommittee concluded that the states, by insisting that interstate businesses take a national view of their collection responsibilities[12] while staunchly maintaining their own right to have their individual sets of sales tax rules, were in fact pursuing two inconsistent goals. As a result, the philosophy behind the subcommittee's proposed reforms, as was noted at the conference, was that:

. . . what is sauce for the goose is sauce for the gander. If the states want businesses all over the country to collect their sales taxes for them, then they ought to make the system easier for that work to be done. However,

[12] That is, by collecting taxes for states in which they sell goods but carry on little or no business activities. How far the states will be able to go in this respect is a debatable question. Up to the present time, the U.S. Supreme Court has sustained the enforcement of this collection responsibility only in situations where the seller's representatives are actually present in the state, soliciting orders or conducting other business activities.

if they are willing to let the interstate seller off, then there is no reason why they should not maintain their own individual systems.

In line with this view, the reforms, as included in House Report 952[13] and in House Report 11798, present the states with two alternatives:

1. They can adopt a uniform model sales tax law under which the federal government would enforce payment of taxes by interstate sellers directly to the states of destination.[14]

2. They can continue to operate their own independent taxes but with authority to require sellers to collect sales or use taxes for them only if the seller owns or leases realty in the state, has an employee performing services there, or delivers goods to private homes in the state.

Conference discussion made clear, however, that what the subcommittee sees as two desirable alternatives may appear to the states as a choice between two evils. On the one hand, by continuing with their existing laws they face the loss of some of their enforcement powers over out-of-state sellers and hence the sacrifice of valuable revenue; and on the other, by going over to the model sales tax law they would have to modify their current tax policies, drastically in some cases, and integrate their administration of intrastate sales with the federal government's administration of interstate sales. Less drastic reforms than these, the critics argued, would solve most or all of the existing problems. One suggestion was to restrict the application of a model sales tax base to those interstate sellers that the states now have greatest difficulty in reaching. Mail-order sellers, some of whom now advertise the tax-free status of their sales, could, for example, be given the option either of paying the tax due to each state into which they ship goods or of paying a uniform tax on their interstate sales to the federal government, which would then remit the proceeds to the states of destination.

Concern was also expressed about the subcommittee's proposed solution to the double taxation problem—namely that sales be

[13] 89 Cong. 1 sess. (1965), pp. 1136-37.

[14] Each state would be free to set its own tax rate, and all interstate sellers would be reached except those offering only prepaid mail order services and having no contacts with the state other than the dissemination of advertising.

made taxable by the state in which the buyer first takes physical delivery of the goods and that states imposing a use tax be required to
give a credit for any sales taxes paid in the state of delivery. Would
this not, it was asked, induce the automobile-producing states to
levy a sales tax on the delivery of new cars to out-of-state purchasers, thereby reducing significantly the use taxes that the states of
destination are now able to collect when the new cars are registered
in their jurisdictions? The problem here seems to be mainly one of
resolving the conflicting interests of the states involved without imposing discriminatory tax burdens on interstate businesses, since for
any consumer good that has to be registered taxation by either the
state of delivery or the state of use is practicable. For other products, however, taxation by the state of destination requires some
arrangement whereby the amounts due can be collected from out-
of-state sellers. While these complexities could be reduced by giving
precedence to taxation by the state of origin, such a solution would
be regarded by many as an undesirable departure from the "taxation of consumption" philosophy of sales and use taxes. The latter
school of thought holds that any firm that undertakes interstate selling should, if it regards sales taxation as a desirable basic source of
state revenues, accept the responsibility of collecting the sales tax
for all states into which it ships goods. Moreover, conference proponents of this viewpoint were optimistic about the ability of the
states to reach most out-of-state sellers if Congress would
specifically authorize them to do so and if the states would work out
among themselves cooperative arrangements such as are now being
used in parts of the Midwest—in Illinois, Indiana, Kentucky, Iowa,
and Missouri.

Less controversial problems of intergovernmental tax coordination were also discussed at the conference. Income tax simplification through the use by the states of the federal tax base, for
example, received wide support—partly for the increased efficiency
it was expected to bring to the tax system and partly because it
might make it easier for more states to add the income tax to their
fiscal structures. Even here, however, there was disagreement about
how strong an incentive such arrangements would provide to the
states without income taxes, and it was also noted that some states,
regarding the federal tax base as less than ideally defined, prefer to

have their own tax laws. In any case, it is already clear that the work of the House Special Subcommittee on State Taxation of Interstate Commerce has stimulated an increased interest in the long-continued search for greater horizontal intergovernmental tax coordination. At a special meeting in January 1966, for example, the National Association of Tax Administrators adopted a policy statement that both urged Congress to delay action on H.R. 11798 pending state attempts to reform their own tax systems and provided the states with ten general guidelines for this purpose. Hopefully, these efforts, combined with the excellent work of the Advisory Commission on Intergovernmental Relations, will produce some long-overdue solutions to both vertical and horizontal tax coordination problems.

Functional Grants-in-Aid

Functional grants-in-aid are, in the opinion of a number of the conferees, an overdeveloped and underanalyzed federal expenditure program. As a result, serious distortions and inequities exist, many of which could be eliminated if only there were a precise, quantitative rationale for these grants. While the basic justification for them stressed earlier in Chapter III—namely, the existence of state and local expenditure programs that generate significant benefit spillovers—was accepted as a useful general principle, its limitations in practice clearly troubled everyone. Two participants made these comments:

It is quite impossible to develop a complete measurement of this phenomenon [benefit spillouts] in the case of particular grants and for all units of the country.

. . . I have never been able to find an exact statement which would help us decide which particular programs ought to be financed by federal functional grants and which should be financed either by state-local activities or general grants.

The same complaint recurred in the discussion of what, if anything, could be done to simplify existing federal grant programs by reducing the large number of different matching formulas now used in them:

One of the reasons that it is hard for people who are trying to bring sense in this area to make progress against all these pressures is that we were unable to discover any good clearcut basis for deciding whether in a given program the grant should be 50, 60, 70, or 90 percent, and it is very hard to fight irrationality if you don't have a good sound rationale to put up against all the pressures and everything. . . .

Participants also stressed that benefit spillovers are not the only explanation of the existence of intergovernmental grant programs. To a considerable extent public spending in this country responds to the activities of pressure groups that seek to achieve their goals at all levels of government simultaneously. Unless they have a singular degree of success in promoting the local governmental programs they want at the local level, they are likely to promote the use of grants-in-aid for the same purposes at the state and federal levels. Grants may also have much political appeal because ". . . a local taxpayer will often make the decision that he would rather pay a certain kind of state or federal tax in order to perform a local function than the tax that is available to him at the local level." This being the case, political and fiscal reforms at the local level, making governments there more sensitive to voter tastes for public services and giving them a more flexible and varied tax system, should moderate future demands for intergovernmental grants and perhaps permit the cutback of programs that were adopted in the past largely because there was no other way of acquiring the public services they supported.

One of the important policy implications of the discussion of benefit spillouts in Chapter III was that the role of open-ended functional grants should be expanded. Considerable doubt was expressed at the conference whether the time had yet arrived for such actions, at least at the federal level. It was pointed out that, to begin with, very little is known about the impact of grants on the amount and kinds of expenditures made by the recipient:

. . .that is where a good deal of economic research could be devoted; and very little has been done, it seems to me, to attempt to find out what the effects are of these various formulas and then to appraise these results in terms of whatever it is that they are trying to accomplish.

Knowledge about the price elasticity of state-local governmental demands for public services is obviously especially important in the case of open-ended grants since they involve a commitment on the part of the grantor to support whatever levels of spending the recipients decide upon. Such grants, therefore are not likely to become widespread until federal and state legislators can predict with some confiden e the costs that their enactment will entail.

A· ' .her criticism of open-ended federal grants was that they are not well adapted to the achievement of national minimum standards for basic public services. The conclusion to which the spillout thesis leads, as one participant noted, is that:

. . . because of out-migration from Mississippi, Mississippi will not spend sufficiently to take care of the benefits that flow out. Therefore, the federal government finances the spillovers and Mississippi decides what its optimal level of expenditures will be in Mississippi for the non-spillout benefits. But Mississippi's spillouts come to New York City, and New York City's optimal level of expenditure is very different from the optimal level of decision-making in Mississippi.

For an agricultural economy you need one kind of education; for a highly complex industrial structure you need another. Given this, you can't have a grant going to Mississippi to let Mississippi decide what the optimal level of expenditures should be for the spillouts, even if they are all federally financed. It implies national standards, and once there is an implication of national standards you can't have an open-ended grant.[15]

A final question, which gave rise to some sharp disagreements, concerns the extent to which federal grants designed to assist local governmental programs should be made directly to the municipalities and counties concerned rather than being channeled through their state governments. Proponents of the former procedure, as would be expected, stressed the past inadequacies of many states:

[15] As stated, this argument confuses Mississippi's right to set the level of program operations (which it would have) with its freedom to determine the program's content and quality (which it would not have). It is an essential part of the optimizing grant theory that all supported programs would be operated to the joint satisfaction of the grantor and the grantee.

. . . what really disturbs me is the bland way the states have been fed into this. For years they sit and ignore city problems, are totally unresponsive to the demands of the cities, until the cities finally build up enough political power to get some response from the federal government. As soon as the money starts to flow to the cities, the states have somehow gotten interested—and what is their interest? They want to get hold of that money before it gets to the cities. What for? To be as unresponsive as they were in the past and use the money for their own purposes.

Others, however, argued that some states, at least, are very much aware of urban needs and that others, under the stimulus of legislative reapportionments, can be expected to become so unless their vitalities are sapped by the continued expansion of direct federal-local grants.

Two positive arguments were made in support of the use of state governments as intermediaries in the flow of federal aid to local governments. The first rests on the virtues of geographical decentralization when the problems to be dealt with vary greatly from one area to another. "It is difficult for me to see," one participant stated, "how the federal government, when dealing directly with local governments, can adapt itself and its policies properly to the vast variety of circumstances existing in the different states." The individual state, on the other hand, faces a much less bewildering variety of local problems and is therefore, it was argued, in a much better position to deal with them effectively. Moreover, and to some this was an even more important point, the states have something the federal government lacks—namely, the legal power to change the structure of local government whenever such actions would assist in the solution of local problems. Some participants felt strongly that such structural changes are badly needed in many of the large urban areas of the country.

The second argument in favor of state participation in the extension of federal aid to local public services was that the states would stress the broad needs of a whole region or urban area rather than the special, and often conflicting, interests of the separate local jurisdictions that compose it, and they would be able to deal with those needs more expeditiously than the local governments acting on their own. Not only, it was argued, could the federal government accomplish more by channeling its funds through the states, but it could also save itself much frustration. As one person put it:

. . . dealing with a multiplicity of government units in a metropolitan area is going to confront the federal agency with a very unwelcome chore of trying to pick and choose and so get into the midst of the interjurisdictional rivalry. So I think a lot of things are operating here that will strengthen the state's role in the federal activities regarding metropolitan areas.

This forecast, however, was not allowed to stand without dispute. Was not the new Department of Housing and Urban Development (HUD), one participant asked, set up to do the opposite—to circumvent the states and bring more and more federal money directly to the urban areas? In response to this question it was noted that more than half of the state governors had testified in favor of the establishment of HUD, and that in any case the states have the legal power to regulate the relations between their own local governments and Washington. In the words of one discussant:

. . . if any given state wants its local units of government to deal through it in connection with HUD matters, all that they have to do is pass a law to that effect, and the federal agency has no choice except to follow the channel laid down by the state.

Though there was clear disagreement about the future importance of direct federal-local functional grants, a broad consensus did develop as to how those grants could best be designed in order to minimize their unfavorable effects. Three goals were stressed here: flexibility, the coordination of governmental activities throughout broad geographical regions, and the integration of separate, but related, local governmental functions. What HUD officials need, it was argued, is the freedom to choose among a number of different ways of implementing their programs—to be able, as one person put it, ". . . to shift their focus as soon as they get some responsiveness from the states, and I do not think the cities will object to that if they have a state government that is responsive to them." Though administrative flexibility is not something that is granted lightly by Congress, several participants felt that incorporation of a high degree of it in federal urban grant programs is fully justified by the rapidity with which metropolitan economic, social, and political problems are changing.

There is no need to stress at this point the importance of achieving a close coordination of all local public programs that affect a whole region or urban area. Several conferees deplored the tendency of federal grants in the past to have just the opposite effect. As one put it:

. . . one of the great problems generated by the conditional grant—the specific functional grant—is the fragmentation of local government and of state government increasingly, so that the Kestnbaum report could speak of the great functional autocracies responsive to each other, but not to the political officers at the political level.

Others noted, however, that in recent years grants have been used to encourage areawide urban planning and that the federal government is attempting to administer more and more of its programs on a regional basis.[16] Finally, the operations of the Office of Economic Opportunity were cited as an example of the progress that is being made in integrating and coordinating governmental services as they relate to people and families, and thus in breaking down some of the orthodox functional lines that in the past often have resulted in frustration and missed opportunities for many people.

Unconditional Grants-in-Aid

Not unexpectedly, discussion of the 1964 Presidential Task Force plan for unrestricted federal grants to the states brought forth a well-balanced blend of sympathy and skepticism. Supporters of the proposal stressed the capacity of state and local governments for imaginative programming and the extent to which this could be

[16] Further evidence in support of these trends was provided in two special messages that President Johnson sent to Congress on successive days in January 1966, the first proposing the creation of community development districts that would involve a number of cities, towns, or counties in a cooperative program for economic development, and the second recommending a six-year $2.3 billion city improvement program that would seek both to coordinate the activities of independent local governments and to assist them in making integrated use of the whole array of federal urban grants and aids. See *New York Times*, Jan. 26, 1966, p. 1; Jan. 27, 1966, p. 20.

strengthened by giving them additional funds without strings attached. Others felt that because the federal government tends to experiment more successfully than the states, grant funds should always be extended for specific purposes and with appropriate controls attached. One interchange illustrates the extent of the disagreement. An opponent said:

As I watch the growth of the bureaucracy and its behavior at all levels of government, I realize that the tendency is to solve problems by doing more of what they are doing. If you give more money to the states and cities unconditionally and you have a crime problem, they hire more police. This doesn't seem to have much impact on the crime problem. In fact, it may complicate it because then you have to watch crime in the police force, too. . . . If you give it to the welfare workers they will want more intensive welfare programs of the kind they are already familiar with, and so on down the line.

A supporter stated:

. . . I think it is a strange doctrine to think that the federal government is superior as an experimenter to the state governments. I think most of the political history would argue otherwise, that you had in the states essentially laboratories for all kinds of economic and social experiments, and more often than not the federal government has been the follower rather than the leader in this.

The past, of course, is not necessarily an accurate guide to the future, and several experts stressed the ability of federal block grants to bring forth new and better programs at the state and local levels and to increase the administrative effectiveness of those governments:

. . . One of the major reasons for the federal grants is to stimulate innovation in the programs and processes within the country. Those of you who follow the researches in the area of grants will remember the studies made by Paul Mort in the educational field. He demonstrated (taking the grant system of Pennsylvania over a considerable period of time in relation to school programs and state aid) that the factor which seemed to be most important in the process of innovation in the school system was fiscal elbow room on the part of the local school board and the school superintendent.

Now we can all say well, of course, we all knew that. But it was a very useful thing to have the statistical elements examined with care and the elements of quality priced out with reference to the achievement of the educational system because they gave tests—standardized tests in different school systems—and demonstrated that there was introduction of new processes, and that these new processes paid off with reference to defined goals, and that this took place where there was fiscal elbow room.

Stressing both the additional funds and the new responsibilities that unconditional grants would confer on the states, another argued:

. . . just the existence of this money is going to provide a lot of encouragement to all of the pressure groups which in states like New York and California we have. And this is what adds to the administrative effectiveness, and I think that the quickest way to improve the administrative effectiveness of a state is to increase the complexity of its programs and the responsibility of its officials, and hopefully, there will be talent—a shortage of talent at first in some cases obviously, but this is not really very important, and hopefully the salary levels, etc., of officials will have to go up with increasing responsibility.

In order to maximize the chances of securing these administrative advantages some participants argued for a twin program of unconditional block grants and technical assistance to the recipients by the new federal Department of Housing and Urban Development. The importance of having this combination from the very beginning was stressed:

. . . The time when innovation can be built in is the first three years after the receipt of the un-earmarked block grant, because at the end of that period it will be completely absorbed into a pattern of habit and nothing will be changed. Therefore, during this period of the initial receipt there must be techniques of technical assistance which will lead the states to desire to make workable plans, which after public discussion will be acted on by the newly modified legislative bodies that will have a better recognition of urban requirements.

In this way you would introduce rationalization and measurement of needs so that the unconditional block grant would come to the localities, to the states first and then to localities, on the basis of a public exposure of the opportunity, and with technical assistance in the development of those plans and programs.

While the theoretical economist typically insists that a new governmental program be judged by comparing it with all alternative uses of the relevant resources, the political economist will often direct his attention to a more restricted set of alternatives that he regards as politically feasible. At the conference it soon became clear that there was no agreement as to whether federal block grants would be substitutes for, or complements to, other federal aids to state and local governments, and that the answer given to this question would influence individual attitudes to the proposed fiscal innovation. In the view of one participant, Presidential support of the special task force report in the fall of 1964 would have precluded adoption of the aid to education bill as well as some of the other new grant programs enacted in the first session of the 89th Congress. Another, however, argued that the forces supporting functional grants are so great that block grants would in no way substitute for them.

Since one of the main purposes of unconditional grants is to give substantial financial support to the poorer states, enactment by the federal government of a negative income tax, a long-standing proposal that seems to be receiving increasing attention of late, must be regarded as a major alternative. Though its merits and weaknesses received only cursory attention, the negative income tax proposal clearly appeared to some to have a prior claim on federal financial resources which, when exercised, might well eliminate any need for federal block grants. Others, however, reacted in exactly the opposite way, thus providing, if nothing else, a strong incentive to economic researchers to try to resolve some of these differences by means of quantitative analyses of the two proposals.

One of the more difficult questions for such research to answer would be the extent to which unconditional federal grants would be used to lower state-local tax rates rather than to expand expenditures. Uncertainty on this score clearly makes the block-grant plan less attractive in the eyes of some, while others, as the following remark indicates, regard it with equanimity:

I think the major point has to be made in terms of the fact that this plan is viewed as an alternative to a further federal tax cut, and I favor this plan even if it doesn't add a nickel to state-local expenditures and even if it doesn't add one point to the intelligence quotient or ability quotient of state-local administrators, because if it doesn't do either of those things then what it must do by definition is to reduce the extent to which state and local governments will depend upon taxes on beer and cigarettes and property and general consumption, and even some of their peculiar income taxes; and if it achieves that latter objective, and only that latter objective, I am all for it because of the improve- ments that I can see forthcoming in terms of resource allocation, and certainly in terms of distributional effects of the overall federal-state- local tax system.

A second uncertainty, of perhaps even greater importance, con- cerns the extent to which unconditional grants would be passed on by the states in some reasonable fashion to local governments, particularly those in urban areas. Those optimistic about the plan stressed the increased powers the cities are likely to derive from leg- islative reapportionments and cited as hopeful evidence such fiscal reforms as those under serious consideration in Maryland.[17] The skeptics, however, remained unconvinced, tending to feel that solu- tions to the nation's metropolitan fiscal problems would have to be sought elsewhere.

Metropolitan Fiscal Problems

That large urbanized areas exist and that they have complex fiscal problems are fully recognized facts of modern life. Whether the governmental unit known as "the city" has become an anachro- nism, or whether it continues to serve some distinctive, definable purposes amid these conditions, are matters of opinion. Conference discussion of these points proved only that a wide diversity of opin- ion does exist.

Does the concentrated central city characteristic of the north- east contribute something unique and important to the national welfare that cannot be supplied by the pattern of sprawling metrop- olises growing up in the west and southwest? Should the power vested in municipalities be strengthened, or should it be increasing- ly turned over to larger jurisdictions responsible for entire metro-

[17] The proposal, which at the time of the conference had been approved by two independent commissions, involved tax reforms designed to raise an addi- tional $59 million to be distributed to local governments. Thirty-eight percent was to go to Baltimore, which has only 27 percent of the state's population. (The pro- posal was voted down subsequently by the legislature due to opposition from the wealthier counties.)

politan areas or even for groups of metropolitan areas? Answers to these questions cannot be settled upon unless preliminary agreement has been reached on the specific values that local governmental units should be responsible for preserving and developing. That such agreement is far from possible at the present time was amply demonstrated by the discussion. As one participant put it:

So this neat theory that the activities of government, be they in education or health or international relations, can be split up into neat packages on the basis of logic has no logical foundation.

Despite the lack of clarity as to what is being accomplished or why, however, a further fact of modern life is that metropolitan councils are being formed and that large sums of money are being channeled into them. One discussant described these councils as "always starting out with a wonderful Young People's Christian Association beginning and then ending up in futility," while another spoke of them as having "a vested interest in not trying to do anything for fear they will collapse." Other conferees were less pessimistic about their promise, or perhaps simply more resigned to making the best of their inevitability:

I would point out to everybody that you may look down your noses at these councils, but there is one thing for sure—you are going to have a lot more of them and they are going to have more power, because the Housing Act of 1965 contains a little amendment, subsection (g) to 701, which will start underwriting on a permanent basis two-thirds of the administrative costs of these councils from this time on—two-thirds of their budget will be funded by the Department of Housing and Urban Development, provided they meet the specifications of plans and move in the way that HUD wants them to go. Well, they are going to be given more and more power in terms of reviewing applications for federal grants.

There was considerable support for using the county as the basic unit of metropolitan government, whenever it is big enough, within the foreseeable future, to encompass the urban area. Unlike metropolitan councils, counties have well-established powers and responsibilities,[18] and to shift functions to them from smaller mu-

[18] It should be noted, however, that three states—Alaska, Connecticut, and Rhode Island—do not have counties as part of their local governmental structure.

nicipalities would, it was argued, moderate some of the destructive interlocal tax competition that now exists, spread the costs of metropolitan services more equitably by combining rich suburbs and industrial enclaves with the poorer parts of the urban area, and permit full utilization of available economies of scale, especially those derived from the ability to attract top quality personnel. In the words of one participant:

. . . as you move from ten to twenty thousand population and the resulting budget to one that covers a population of fifty, a hundred thousand, or a little bit more, you go up the scale in the quality of men that you can attract, and this has a tremendous impact on the behavior of the government.

It was also stressed that too often in the past divided responsibilities in urban areas have precluded a positive and dynamic response to emerging social and economic problems, even after they have matured into fullblown crises, as in Watts, California, in the summer of 1965:

. . . Sargent Shriver sent a team out to study Watts, to determine what the Poverty Program could do there. The Department of Health, Education, and Welfare sent a group, the State of California sent a group, the county of Los Angeles sent a group, the city of Los Angeles sent a group, and then they invited some private agency people and they worked around the clock for several days.

They got what the federal people thought were commitments on who was going to do what, and the federal people made some commitments on their own of what they would do. And as of two weeks ago, I am told, not one thing has been done by anybody, except one little minor program dealing with vocational training.

Others, however, were skeptical of the importance of the contributions that better governmental organization was capable of making to problems of the Watts variety. In the view of one, "If anybody really wanted to do anything about Watts it could be done now," and another remarked:

One of the great arguments against the creation of metropolitan areas . . . is that to the Negroes they look precisely like a measure to keep the metropolitan areas in white hands. Just at the time that the Negroes are really getting hold in the cities you enlarge the boundaries of the cities by including lily-white suburbs into which they can't get, and say now we are going to govern over this larger area. Watts would not have been prevented by a metropolitan government—it might have been intensified by it.

These observations brought forth a discussion of two opposite, but not necessarily conflicting, trends that seem to be developing in metropolitan areas. On the one hand, there is a move to reduce the number, and increase the size, of decision-making units in the hope of achieving more rapid and more efficient solutions to urban problems. On the other hand, there is a move, particularly by minority groups who lack political power at higher levels of government, to make the local neighborhood the sovereign unit of control over a number of important public programs.

What this suggests, of course, is a highly decentralized kind of metropolitan federalism, and the conference discussed at some length the problems involved in establishing such a system. Few seemed optimistic about the ability of cities and municipalities to achieve the reforms on their own. What limited success there has been in this respect in the past, it was noted, is mainly attributable either to the dedicated work of lone individuals—New York City was cited as an example—or to purposeful action on the part of higher levels of government, as in Winnipeg, or to both, as in Toronto. On the latter score it was recommended that federal functional grants, particularly those administered by the Department of Housing and Urban Development, be used more and more to encourage the development of metropolitan political institutions. An even more important role, however, could be played by the states, either individually or in association with their neighbors where interstate metropolitan areas are involved. The Tennessee Valley Authority was cited as a valuable guideline for these purposes:

I would like to call your attention to the remarkable experience we have had in TVA. TVA was a national institution which was geographically located in a given area and spanned a number of states and succeeded in managing itself with a very high sensitivity to the political structures and underlying functional requirements of that area.

This argues that the states might be able to do the same thing in their metropolitan areas, to establish metropolitan authorities which are state authorities, which in the initial stage would be purely dependent politically on the state, but which in time might add other representatives and eventually might have a legislative body that was completely elected from the metropolitan region. But in the initial stage they might be branches of the state, so that you don't raise the issues of local home rule, and so forth; and then you give this body, this state body, control over the allocation of those federal funds that go to the structures of the metropolitan nexus—transportation, federally supported highways, state supported highways, water pollution control, air pollution control, etc.

With help from above and continued pressure from below, city governments, it was generally felt, have a reasonable chance of improving their structure and hence of getting on with the important tasks that face them. The major guidelines provided to them by the conference discussion were well summarized by one participant:

Well, then, we take the county as the basic governmental unit for the bulk of urban areas, and we experiment with various things, including councils, in the other metropolitan areas that are not covered by the county, and then we counsel patience and fanatic work on the part of all.

List of Conference Participants

Harvey E. Brazer
University of Michigan

George F. Break
University of California
(Berkeley)

John E. Burton
Cornell University

Robert D. Calkins
The Brookings Institution

William Capron
The Brookings Institution

Hale Champion
Department of Finance
State of California

Samuel B. Chase, Jr.
The Brookings Institution

William G. Colman
Advisory Commission on Intergovernmental Relations

Charles F. Conlon
Federation of Tax Administrators

Murray Drabkin
Office of the Mayor
New York City

John F. Due
University of Illinois

L. Laszlo Ecker-Racz
Advisory Commission on Intergovernmental Relations

Kermit Gordon
The Brookings Institution

Harold M. Groves
University of Wisconsin

Luther Gulick
Institute for Public
Administration

Robert Herman
Bureau of the Budget
State of New York

Herbert Kaufman
Yale University

Lawrence Kegan
Committee for Economic
Development

Wilfred Lewis, Jr.
Council of Economic Advisers

Allen D. Manvel
U.S. Bureau of the Census

Frederick C. Mosher
University of California
(Berkeley)

253

Conference Participants *(Continued)*

Selma Mushkin
   Council of State Governments

Joseph A. Pechman
   The Brookings Institution

Alice M. Rivlin
   U.S. Department of Health,
   Education, and Welfare

Earl R. Rolph
   University of California
   (Berkeley)

Stanley S. Surrey
   U.S. Treasury Department

Ronald Welch
   California State Board of
   Equalization

Anita Wells
   U.S. Treasury Department

Louis Winnick
   The Ford Foundation

Laurence N. Woodworth
   U.S. Congress, Joint Committee
   on Internal Revenue Taxation

APPENDIX A

General Tables

TABLE A-1. Basic Time Series Used in Defining Unconditional Grant Allocators[a]

States[b]	Federal Individual Income Tax Collections, 1962 (In millions) (1)	Per Capita Personal Income, 1963 (In dollars) (2)	Population July 1, 1963 (In thousands) (3)
District of Columbia	$ 285	$3,398	798
Nevada	125	3,372	368
Delaware	183	3,250	476
Connecticut	947	3,160	2,666
New York	5,779	3,000	17,708
California	5,281	2,980	17,590
Illinois	3,306	2,945	10,182
New Jersey	2,028	2,900	6,470
Massachusetts	1,493	2,850	5,218
Alaska	60	2,819	248
Maryland	967	2,778	3,289
Michigan	2,107	2,528	8,116
Oregon	418	2,515	1,826
Missouri	980	2,508	4,328
Washington	781	2,505	3,050
Ohio	2,558	2,483	10,173
Hawaii	167	2,476	694
Indiana	1,111	2,475	4,694
Pennsylvania	2,776	2,444	11,424
Wyoming	74	2,427	337
Rhode Island	215	2,398	885
Colorado	456	2,386	1,961
Wisconsin	896	2,380	4,061
Minnesota	707	2,332	3,500
New Hampshire	141	2,303	627
Nebraska	291	2,293	1,460
Iowa	508	2,274	2,780
Montana	119	2,239	707
Kansas	450	2,231	2,225
Utah	182	2,129	983
Arizona	299	2,115	1,559
Florida	1,002	2,111	5,652
Vermont	62	2,092	390
Virginia	813	2,066	4,331
Texas	1,973	2,046	10,323
North Dakota	89	2,030	634
Maine	167	2,008	982
Oklahoma	407	1,953	2,487
Idaho	108	1,934	713
South Dakota	96	1,932	737
New Mexico	164	1,887	1,018
West Virginia	273	1,872	1,778
Georgia	616	1,865	4,140
North Carolina	642	1,813	4,760
Kentucky	451	1,789	3,095
Tennessee	613	1,776	3,694
Louisiana	502	1,768	3,418
Alabama	436	1,656	3,347
Arkansas	215	1,598	1,858
South Carolina	292	1,584	2,483
Mississippi	189	1,379	2,290
United States	44,798	2,443	188,533

Sources: Column 1, U. S. Treasury Department, Internal Revenue Service, *Statistics of Income, 1962: Preliminary Individual Income Tax Returns for 1962* (1964), p. 23. The combined figure for Maryland and the District of Columbia was allocated between the two on the basis of 1961 income tax collections.

Column 2, U. S. Office of Business Economics, *Survey of Current Business* (April 1964), p. 21.

Column 3, U. S. Bureau of the Census, *Current Population Reports*, Series P-25, No. 273 (Oct. 4, 1963).

[a] For the tax effort series used as an allocator see Column 1 of Table A-6.

[b] Arrayed in order of 1963 per capita personal income.

TABLE A-2. Distribution of $1 Billion Among the States by Six Alternative Allocators

(In millions of dollars)

Quintile	States[a]	Federal Income Taxes (1)	State Personal Income (2)	Population (3)	Population and Personal Income (4)	Population, Personal Income and Tax Effort (5)	Hill-Burton Formula (6)
				Allocator			
I	District of Columbia	6.3	5.9	4.2	2.9	2.3	4.0
	Nevada	2.8	2.7	2.0	1.4	1.5	4.0
	Delaware	4.0	3.4	2.5	1.8	1.3	4.0
	Connecticut	20.8	18.3	14.1	10.5	8.6	6.0
	New York	127.1	115.4	93.8	73.5	83.1	50.0
	California	116.2	113.9	93.2	73.5	83.8	52.0
	Illinois	72.7	65.1	54.0	43.1	36.6	32.5
	New Jersey	44.6	40.7	34.3	27.8	23.6	20.1
	Massachusetts	32.8	32.3	27.7	22.8	23.5	20.6
	Alaska	1.3	1.5	1.3	1.1	0.8	4.0
	Maryland	21.3	19.8	17.4	14.8	13.6	13.9
II	Michigan	46.4	44.6	43.0	40.0	41.6	36.6
	Oregon	9.2	10.0	9.7	9.0	10.2	9.8
	Missouri	21.6	23.6	22.9	21.5	16.1	24.3
	Washington	17.2	16.6	16.2	15.2	17.2	13.6
	Ohio	56.3	54.8	53.9	51.0	44.9	42.6
	Hawaii	3.7	3.6	3.7	3.5	4.3	4.0
	Indiana	24.4	25.2	24.9	23.6	21.7	25.7
	Pennsylvania	61.1	60.6	60.6	58.2	49.5	55.3
	Wyoming	1.6	1.8	1.8	1.7	2.0	4.0
	Rhode Island	4.7	4.6	4.7	4.6	4.4	4.6
III	Colorado	10.0	10.2	10.4	10.2	11.6	9.9
	Wisconsin	19.7	21.0	21.5	21.3	23.0	22.2
	Minnesota	15.6	17.7	18.6	18.7	22.3	21.1
	New Hampshire	3.1	3.1	3.3	3.4	3.4	4.0
	Nebraska	6.4	7.3	7.7	7.9	7.4	8.6
	Iowa	11.2	13.7	14.7	15.2	17.2	17.4
	Montana	2.6	3.4	3.8	3.9	4.7	4.0
	Kansas	9.9	10.8	11.8	12.4	14.4	13.5
	Utah	4.0	4.5	5.2	5.8	6.8	6.2
	Arizona	6.6	7.2	8.3	9.2	11.1	8.2
IV	Florida	22.0	25.9	30.0	33.4	34.4	31.2
	Vermont	1.4	1.8	2.1	2.3	3.0	4.0
	Virginia	17.9	19.4	23.0	26.1	21.4	28.3
	Texas	43.4	45.9	54.7	62.9	57.9	62.5
	North Dakota	2.0	2.8	3.4	3.9	5.3	5.3
	Maine	3.7	4.3	5.2	6.1	7.3	7.2
	Oklahoma	9.0	10.5	13.2	15.9	16.7	17.2
	Idaho	2.4	3.0	3.8	4.6	5.3	4.9
	South Dakota	2.1	3.1	3.9	4.8	6.7	5.6
	New Mexico	3.6	4.2	5.4	6.7	7.0	6.9
V	West Virginia	6.0	7.2	9.4	11.8	11.4	14.9
	Georgia	13.6	16.8	21.9	27.7	26.9	34.8
	North Carolina	14.1	18.7	25.2	32.7	32.4	42.7
	Kentucky	9.9	12.0	16.4	21.6	17.9	27.2
	Tennessee	13.5	14.2	19.6	25.9	24.6	32.4
	Louisiana	11.0	13.1	18.1	24.1	30.4	27.4
	Alabama	9.6	12.0	17.7	25.2	22.9	31.5
	Arkansas	4.7	6.4	9.8	14.5	14.5	19.1
	South Carolina	6.4	8.5	13.2	19.5	20.1	24.7
	Mississippi	4.2	6.9	12.1	20.8	25.0	25.6
	United States	1,000.0	1,000.0	1,000.0	1,000.0	1,000.0	1,000.0

Sources: Columns 1, 2, and 3—Table A-1; columns 4 and 5—computed as described in Chapter IV from data given in Tables A-1 and A-6; column 6—I. M. Labovitz, Federal Grants to States: Comparison of Selected Hypothetical Distribution Formulas and Matching Requirements (Library of Congress, Legislative Reference Service: March 29, 1961), Table 2.
[a] Arrayed in order of 1963 per capita personal income.

TABLE A-3. Hypothetical Unconditional Grants, $1 Billion Program, as a Percentage of 1963 State Per Capita Income

Quintile	States[a]	Grant Allocator			
		Federal Income Taxes	Population	Population and Personal Income	Population, Personal Income, and Tax Effort
I	District of Columbia	.233	.156	.107	.085
	Nevada	.233	.167	.117	.125
	Delaware	.267	.167	.120	.087
	Connecticut	.248	.168	.125	.102
	New York	.239	.177	.138	.156
	California	.222	.178	.140	.160
	Illinois	.242	.180	.144	.122
	New Jersey	.237	.182	.148	.126
	Massachusetts	.220	.186	.153	.158
	Maryland	.234	.191	.163	.149
	Average	.2375	.1756	.1355	.1270
II	Michigan	.226	.210	.195	.203
	Oregon	.200	.211	.196	.222
	Missouri	.198	.210	.197	.148
	Washington	.226	.213	.200	.226
	Ohio	.222	.213	.202	.177
	Hawaii	.218	.218	.206	.253
	Indiana	.210	.215	.203	.187
	Pennsylvania	.219	.217	.209	.177
	Wyoming	.200	.225	.212	.250
	Rhode Island	.224	.224	.219	.210
	Average	.2143	.2152	.2039	.2053
III	Colorado	.213	.221	.217	.247
	Wisconsin	.203	.222	.220	.237
	Minnesota	.190	.227	.228	.272
	New Hampshire	.221	.236	.243	.243
	Nebraska	.194	.233	.239	.224
	Iowa	.178	.233	.241	.273
	Montana	.162	.238	.244	.294
	Kansas	.198	.236	.248	.288
	Utah	.190	.248	.276	.324
	Arizona	.200	.252	.279	.336
	Average	.1949	.2366	.2445	.2738
IV	Florida	.185	.252	.281	.289
	Vermont	.175	.262	.288	.375
	Virginia	.201	.258	.293	.240
	Texas	.206	.259	.298	.274
	North Dakota	.154	.262	.300	.408
	Maine	.185	.260	.305	.365
	Oklahoma	.184	.269	.324	.341
	Idaho	.171	.271	.329	.379
	South Dakota	.150	.279	.343	.479
	New Mexico	.190	.284	.353	.368
	Average	.1801	.2656	.3114	.3518
V	West Virginia	.182	.285	.358	.436
	Georgia	.177	.284	.360	.349
	North Carolina	.164	.293	.380	.377
	Kentucky	.180	.298	.393	.325
	Tennessee	.204	.297	.392	.373
	Louisiana	.183	.302	.402	.507
	Alabama	.174	.322	.458	.416
	Arkansas	.157	.327	.483	.483
	South Carolina	.164	.338	.500	.515
	Mississippi	.131	.378	.650	.781
	Average	.1714	.3124	.4376	.4552
	Alaska	.186	.186	.157	.114

Sources: Tables A-1 and A-2.
[a] Arrayed in order of 1963 per capita personal income.

TABLE A-4. Hypothetical Unconditional Grants, $1 Billion Program, as a Percentage of Total State-Local Tax Collections

Quintile	States[a]	Federal Income Taxes	Population	Population and Personal Income	Population, Personal Income, and Tax Effort
				Grant Allocator	
I	District of Columbia	3.04	2.03	1.40	1.11
	Nevada	2.44	1.74	1.22	1.31
	Delaware	3.26	2.04	1.47	1.06
	Connecticut	2.90	1.97	1.47	1.20
	New York	2.19	1.62	1.27	1.43
	California	2.08	1.66	1.31	1.50
	Illinois	2.84	2.11	1.68	1.43
	New Jersey	2.80	2.15	1.74	1.48
	Massachusetts	2.30	1.94	1.60	1.64
	Maryland	2.76	2.26	1.92	1.76
	Average	2.661	1.952	1.508	1.392
II	Michigan	2.21	2.04	1.90	1.98
	Oregon	2.05	2.16	2.00	2.27
	Missouri	2.54	2.70	2.53	1.90
	Washington	2.14	2.02	1.89	2.14
	Ohio	2.71	2.60	2.46	2.16
	Hawaii	2.08	2.08	1.97	2.42
	Indiana	2.43	2.48	2.35	2.16
	Pennsylvania	2.56	2.54	2.44	2.08
	Wyoming	1.86	2.09	1.97	2.32
	Rhode Island	2.28	2.28	2.24	2.14
	Average	2.286	2.299	2.175	2.157
III	Colorado	2.01	2.09	2.05	2.33
	Wisconsin	1.69	1.84	1.82	1.97
	Minnesota	1.66	1.98	1.99	2.38
	New Hampshire	2.38	2.53	2.61	2.61
	Nebraska	2.20	2.65	2.72	2.55
	Iowa	1.66	2.18	2.25	2.55
	Montana	1.54	2.24	2.30	2.78
	Kansas	1.79	2.13	2.24	2.60
	Utah	1.86	2.42	2.69	3.16
	Arizona	1.77	2.23	2.57	2.98
	Average	1.856	2.229	2.324	2.591
IV	Florida	1.96	2.67	2.98	3.06
	Vermont	1.49	2.24	2.45	3.20
	Virginia	2.56	3.29	3.74	3.06
	Texas	2.22	2.80	3.22	2.97
	North Dakota	1.43	2.44	2.80	3.80
	Maine	1.84	2.58	3.03	3.62
	Oklahoma	1.88	2.75	3.32	3.48
	Idaho	1.67	2.65	3.21	3.70
	South Dakota	1.32	2.46	3.03	4.22
	New Mexico	1.76	2.64	3.28	3.42
	Average	1.813	2.652	3.106	3.453
V	West Virginia	1.86	2.91	3.66	3.53
	Georgia	1.99	3.21	4.06	3.94
	North Carolina	1.78	3.17	4.12	4.08
	Kentucky	2.01	3.33	4.39	3.64
	Tennessee	2.39	3.46	4.58	4.35
	Louisiana	1.59	2.62	3.49	4.41
	Alabama	2.03	3.74	5.32	4.84
	Arkansas	1.70	3.56	5.26	5.26
	South Carolina	2.54	3.75	5.54	5.71
	Mississippi	1.24	3.58	6.16	7.40
	Average	1.913	3.333	4.658	4.716
	Alaska	2.32	2.32	1.96	1.43

Sources: Tables A-2 and A-7.
[a] Quintiles based on 1963 per capita personal income.

TABLE A-5. Hypothetical Unconditional Grants, $1 Billion Program, as a Percentage of State-Local "Own" Expenditures[a]

Quintile	States[b]	Grant Allocator			
		Federal Income Taxes	Population	Population and Personal Income	Population, Personal Income, and Tax Effort
I	District of Columbia	2.32	1.55	1.07	.85
	Nevada	1.76	1.26	.88	.94
	Delaware	2.51	1.57	1.13	.82
	Connecticut	2.33	1.58	1.18	.96
	New York	1.80	1.32	1.04	1.17
	California	1.66	1.33	1.05	1.20
	Illinois	2.46	1.82	1.46	1.24
	New Jersey	2.42	1.87	1.51	1.99
	Massachusetts	1.93	1.63	1.34	1.38
	Maryland	2.14	1.75	1.49	1.37
	Average	2.133	1.568	1.215	1.192
II	Michigan	1.78	1.65	1.53	1.60
	Oregon	1.51	1.59	1.48	1.67
	Missouri	2.00	2.12	1.99	1.49
	Washington	1.57	1.48	1.39	1.57
	Ohio	2.13	2.04	1.93	1.70
	Hawaii	1.46	1.46	1.38	1.69
	Indiana	1.91	1.95	1.85	1.70
	Pennsylvania	1.96	1.94	1.87	1.59
	Wyoming	1.48	1.66	1.57	1.85
	Rhode Island	1.98	1.98	1.94	1.86
	Average	1.778	1.787	1.693	1.670
III	Colorado	1.56	1.62	1.59	1.80
	Wisconsin	1.39	1.52	1.51	1.63
	Minnesota	1.36	1.62	1.63	1.94
	New Hampshire	1.73	1.84	1.90	1.90
	Nebraska	1.65	1.99	2.04	1.91
	Iowa	1.35	1.77	1.83	2.07
	Montana	1.20	1.75	1.80	2.16
	Kansas	1.45	1.73	1.82	2.12
	Utah	1.39	1.81	2.01	2.36
	Arizona	1.40	1.75	1.94	2.35
	Average	1.448	1.740	1.807	2.024
IV	Florida	1.38	1.88	2.09	2.15
	Vermont	1.22	1.82	2.00	2.61
	Virginia	1.78	2.28	2.59	2.12
	Texas	1.77	2.23	2.56	2.36
	North Dakota	.99	1.68	1.93	2.62
	Maine	1.47	2.07	2.43	2.90
	Oklahoma	1.36	2.00	2.40	2.52
	Idaho	1.28	2.02	2.45	2.82
	South Dakota	1.05	1.96	2.41	3.36
	New Mexico	1.29	1.94	2.41	2.52
	Average	1.359	1.988	2.327	2.598
V	West Virginia	1.62	2.54	3.18	3.08
	Georgia	1.42	2.29	2.90	2.81
	North Carolina	1.49	2.67	3.46	3.43
	Kentucky	1.31	2.17	2.86	2.37
	Tennessee	1.77	2.57	3.40	3.23
	Louisiana	1.12	1.85	2.46	3.11
	Alabama	1.45	2.68	3.81	3.46
	Arkansas	1.33	2.77	4.09	4.09
	South Carolina	1.46	3.01	4.44	4.58
	Mississippi	.91	2.63	4.53	5.44
	Average	1.388	2.518	3.513	3.560
	Alaska	1.16	1.16	.98	.72

Sources: Tables A-2 and A-7.
[a] Direct general expenditures for all functions minus intergovernmental revenue from the federal government.
[b] Quintiles based on 1963 per capita personal income.

TABLE A-6. Tax Effort Indexes of States, Based on 1960 Tax Collections

State[a]	1960 Tax Collections Related to		
	Personal Income (1)	Income Produced (2)	Yield of ACIR Representative Tax System (3)
U. S. Average	100	100	100
District of Columbia	79	67	85
Nevada	109	97	93
Delaware	73	103	87
Connecticut	82	93	94
New York	113	112	136
California	114	116	109
Illinois	85	81	88
New Jersey	85	93	97
Massachusetts	103	111	121
Alaska	71	71	116
Maryland	92	105	106
Michigan	104	108	110
Oregon	113	123	113
Missouri	75	73	76
Washington	113	116	114
Ohio	88	88	91
Hawaii	124	125	155
Indiana	92	88	87
Pennsylvania	85	89	96
Wyoming	115	111	73
Rhode Island	96	109	112
Colorado	114	115	100
Wisconsin	108	112	110
Minnesota	119	112	105
New Hampshire	101	112	95
Nebraska	94	87	72
Iowa	113	108	91
Montana	121	116	86
Kansas	116	124	96
Utah	117	104	98
Arizona	121	112	104
Florida	103	113	90
Vermont	132	141	130
Virginia	82	81	84
Texas	92	84	67
North Dakota	136	124	91
Maine	119	139	126
Oklahoma	105	99	94
Idaho	116	115	89
South Dakota	140	121	92
New Mexico	104	96	84
West Virginia	97	91	101
Georgia	97	95	102
North Carolina	99	91	96
Kentucky	83	80	80
Tennessee	95	96	93
Louisiana	126	116	106
Alabama	91	92	91
Arkansas	100	112	90
South Carolina	103	107	106
Mississippi	120	133	113

Source: Advisory Commission on Intergovernmental Relations, *Measures of State and Local Fiscal Capacity and Tax Effort* (October 1962), pp. 75–76.
[a] Arrayed in order of 1963 per capita personal income.

TABLE A-7. State and Local Tax Revenue and "Own" Expenditures, by States, 1963

(In millions of dollars)

State[a]	Tax Revenue	Own Expenditures[b]
District of Columbia	207	271
Nevada	115	159
Delaware	122	159
Connecticut	717	892
New York	5,794	7,079
California	5,594	7,012
Illinois	2,559	2,960
New Jersey	1,595	1,841
Massachusetts	1,428	1,699
Alaska	56	112
Maryland	771	994
Michigan	2,102	2,607
Oregon	449	609
Missouri	849	1,082
Washington	803	1,094
Ohio	2,074	2,640
Hawaii	178	254
Indiana	1,004	1,274
Pennsylvania	2,384	3,115
Wyoming	86	108
Rhode Island	206	237
Colorado	498	642
Wisconsin	1,167	1,414
Minnesota	938	1,148
New Hampshire	130	179
Nebraska	290	388
Iowa	674	831
Montana	169	217
Kansas	553	681
Utah	215	288
Arizona	373	473
Florida	1,122	1,597
Vermont	94	115
Virginia	698	1,008
Texas	1,952	2,454
North Dakota	140	202
Maine	202	251
Oklahoma	480	662
Idaho	143	188
South Dakota	159	199
New Mexico	204	278
West Virginia	323	371
Georgia	683	956
North Carolina	794	944
Kentucky	492	754
Tennessee	566	762
Louisiana	690	978
Alabama	473	662
Arkansas	276	354
South Carolina	352	439
Mississippi	338	459
Total	44,281	56,095

Source: U. S. Bureau of the Census, *Governmental Finances in 1963* (November 1964), pp. 31–39.

[a] Arrayed in order of 1963 per capita personal income.

[b] Direct general expenditures for all functions minus intergovernmental revenue from the federal government.

Index*

Aaron, Henry, 206, 207
ACIR. *See* Advisory Commission on Intergovernmental Relations
Adams, Robert F., 74n
Administration, tax: centralization and coordination of, 32-33, 45-50, 109. *See also* Tax coordination
Administrative costs: of grants, 84; of tax collection, 29, 31-34, 37, 56, 61, 98-99, 152, 215, 221-22, 232
Admissions tax, 31
Advisory Commission on Intergovernmental Relations (ACIR): re grants, 80, *81*, 82, 85n, *105*, 120n, *122*, 123n, 125n, 126n, *127*, 129, 160n; re metropolitan areas, 167n, 175n, 176n, 178n, 179, 180n, 183n, 184n, 185n, 186-88, 189, 190, 191n, *192*, *198*, *203*, 207-08, 209, 214n, *215*, 216n; representative state and local tax system of, 116-17; 1966 state legislative program of, 33; re state-local fiscal characteristics, 17, *18*, 20, *21*, *27*, 48n, *114*, 115, *119*, 133; re tax coordination, 7, 32n, 34n, 35n, 38, 42n, 43n, 45-47, *49*, 52n, 231, 239; re transportation, 70
Agriculture, 89, 111n, 117
Ainsworth, Kenneth G., 105n
Air pollution, 1-2, 26, *69*, 92-93, *176*, 179, 182n, 199-200, 227
Airports, *69*, *105*
Alabama, *27*, *49*, 112-13, 216n; fiscal capacity of, *113*, *114*, *263*; grant allocators for, *133*, *257-61*; tax effort of, 134, *135*, *262*
Alaska, 126n, 130n, 249n; fiscal capacity of, *113*, *114*, *119*, *263*; grant allocators for, *257-61*; tax effort of,

135, *262*; taxes in, 34n, 35, 38, 39, *49*, 59n
Alcoholic beverage tax, *18*, 29, 102, 151n, 219-20, 248
Altman, George T., 56n
Amusement tax, 29, 32n
Area Redevelopment Administration, 145
Arizona, 23n, *49*, 216n; fiscal capacity of, *113*, *114*, *263*; grant allocators for, *257-61*; tax effort of, *262*
Arkansas, 23n, *49*, *104*, *262*; fiscal capacity of, *113*, *114*, *119*, *263*; grant allocators for, *257-61*; tax effort of, 134, *135*, *262*
Atlanta, 171
Automobiles. *See* Gasoline tax; Highways; Transportation

Barber, Arthur B., 56n, 57n
Benefit taxes, 40-42, 151n, 177
Benefits, external and internal: as criteria for grants, 77, 85, 86, 104-06, 138, 142, 153-55, 239-41; of public programs, 44, 62, 69-70, 92, 98-99, 108, 157, 158, 163, 169, 174-77, 180, 186-87, 193-97, 218, 220-21, 223; and state-local fiscal effort, 52, 63-70, 71-77, 175, 228
Benefits-received theory of taxation, 51, 237
Benson, Charles S., 174n
Benson, George C. S., 157n
Berry, Donald S., 195n, 197n, 199n, 200n
Birkhead, Guthrie S., 169n
Bishop, George A., 101n, 102
Blackburn, John O., 213-14n
Bonds, 34, 182
Boston, 199, 206, 207, 215

* References to tables are in italics.

265

Missouri, 66, *81*; fiscal characteristics of, 27, 36, 49, 113, *114*, *139*, 238, *262*, *263*; grant allocators for, *257-61*
Mobility, 15, 66; of labor, 137, 144-48; of taxpayers, 50-52. *See also* Migration
Mohring, Herbert, 202*n*
Montana, 34*n*, 35, *49*, 59*n*, *113*, *114*, *119*, *262*, *263*; grant allocators for, *257-61*
Montreal, 197
Monypenny, Phillip, 105*n*
Mort, Paul, 245
Mosher, Frederick C., *3*, *4*, *5*, *6*, 253
Motor fuel tax. *See* Gasoline tax
Motor vehicle and operators' fees and charges, 7, *8*, 16, *18*, *19*, *20*, *29*, 32*n*, *171*, 187*n*
Mushkin, Selma J., 10*n*, 11, *12*, *14*, 17*n*, 85*n*, 160*n*, 225*n*, 254

National Association of Tax Administrators, 239
Natural resources, 3-4, *18*, 94, *138*, 145, *171*, 184, *185*
Nebraska, *113*, *114*, *257-61*, *262*, *263*
Neenan, William B., 40*n*
Negative income tax, 161-62, 247
Negroes, 112-13, 161*n*, 250-51
Net wealth tax, 26, 212, 213
Netzer, Dick, 9*n*, 11*n*, 102, 204, 205, 206, 209*n*, 211*n*
Nevada, 118; fiscal characteristics of, 23*n*, 45, *113*, *114*, 116*n*, *119*, *135*, *262*, *263*; grant allocators for, *257-61*
Newcomer, Mabel, 209
New England: fiscal characteristics of, *110*, *111*, *112*, 116, 117; school study in, 101-02
New Hampshire, 103, 104, *113*, *114*, 216n, *262*, *263*; grant allocators for, *257-61*
New Jersey, 80, *81*, 113; fiscal capacity of, *27*, *113*, *114*, *119*, *139*; grant allocators for, 132-33, *257-61;* tax policy in, 34*n*, 35*n*, 42, *49*, 102, 134, *135*, 204, *262*
New Mexico, 118; fiscal characteristics of, 34*n*, 35, 37, *49*, 103, 104, *113*, *114*, *119*, 216*n*, *262*, *263*; grant al-

locators for, *257-61*
New York, 102, *104*; fiscal capacity of, *27*, *113*, *114*, *119*, *139*, *263*; grants for, 79, *81*, 82, 132-33, 246 *257-61*; tax effort of, 134, *135*, *262*; tax policy of, 34, 35, *49*, 57, 59*n*
New York City, 57, 168-69, 171-72, 181, 182*n*, 191, 241, 251
North Carolina, 112; fiscal characteristics of, 46*n*, 48, *49*, *113*, *114*, 116*n*, *135*, *161*, *162*; grant allocators for, *257-61*
North Dakota, 34*n*, *49*, *113*, *114*, *119*, 216, *262*, *263*; grant allocators for, *257-61*

Office of Economic Opportunity, 148, 244
Ohio, 113; fiscal characteristics of, 29, 36, 42, *113*, *114*, 216, *262*, *263*; grant allocators for, *257-61*
Oklahoma, 23*n*, *113*, *114*, *257-61*, *262*, *263*
Old-age assistance, 80, *81*, 91, 118
Oldman, Oliver, 206, 207
Oregon: fiscal characteristics of, *27*, 46*n*, *49*, 59*n*, *113*, *114*, 116, *139*, *262*, *263*; grants for, *81*, 82, 132-33, *257-61*

Parks. *See* Recreation
Pechman, Joseph A., *25*, 35, 38*n*, 39*n*, 107*n*, 136, 142, 254
Pennsylvania, *104*, 184, 245; fiscal capacity of, *113*, *114*, *119*, *263*; grant allocators for, *257-61*; taxes in, 29, 42, *49*, 59*n*, *262*
Personnel problems, 140, 176-77, 185, 207, 246
Phelps, Charlotte De Monte, 149
Philadelphia, 36, 168, 197, 216
Plains states, *110*, *111*, *112*, 116, 117
Planning, 106, 140, 148; for metropolitan areas, *176*, 179, 183-84, 187, 191. *See also* Systems analysis
Poland, Orville F., *3*, *4*, *5*, *6*
Police protection, 66, 68, *69*, 74, 118*n*, *138*; in metropolitan areas, 170, *171*, 175, *176*, 179, 210, 245
Political constraints, on fiscal policy,